# The Pullman Strike



This book examines the 1894 Pullman Strike, one of the most consequential clashes between labor and capital that paralyzed America's railroad system.

The Gilded Age saw rapid economic growth, expansion of industrialization, and real wage growth. Yet between 1800 and 1900 there were nearly 37,000 strikes, and the Pullman Strike reflected the broad dissatisfaction and unrest among American workers. The book consists of an engaging narrative, analysis of existing scholarship, sidebars, and primary source documents which collectively answer why the Pullman Strike is so critical to the American experience: it exposed the limits of paternalistic capitalism, revealed the extraordinary power of big business, introduced the use of injunctions to stop strikes, and launched the career of the iconic labor leader Eugene Debs. Overall, it reveals what struggles workers encountered when forming unions, the changing role of government regarding the economy, and the threat that unchecked big business posed to democracy.

*The Pullman Strike* is useful for all undergraduate students who study the Gilded Age, industrial relations, and labor, urban, and economic history in the United States.

**Edward T. O'Donnell** is an associate professor of history in the history department at the College of the Holy Cross in Worcester, MA, USA. He is the author of several books including *Henry George and the Crisis of Inequality: Progress and Poverty in the Gilded Age* (2015) and *Ship Ablaze: The Tragedy of the Steamboat General Slocum* (2003), and is co-author of *Visions of America: A History of the United States* (3rd ed. 2016). His scholarly articles have appeared in *The Public Historian*, *Journal of Urban History*, and the *Journal of the Gilded Age and Progressive Era*.

## Critical Moments in American History

*Edited by William Thomas Allison, Georgia Southern University*

**America Enters the Cold War**
The Road to Global Commitment, 1945–1950
*Kevin Grimm*

**Title IX**
The Transformation of Sex Discrimination in Education
*Elizabeth Kaufer Busch & William E. Thro*

**The "Silent Majority" Speech**
Richard Nixon, the Vietnam War, and the Origins of the New Right
*Scott Laderman*

**When Women Won the Vote**
The Final Decade, 1910–1920
*Sandra Opdycke*

**The Gulf of Tonkin**
The United States and the Escalation in the Vietnam War
*Tal Tovy*

**The Advent of the All-Volunteer Force**
Protecting Free Society
*William A. Taylor*

**From Desert One to Desert Storm**
Operation Eagle Claw as a Critical Movement
*Tal Tovy*

**The Pullman Strike**
A Gilded Age Clash between Labor, Capital, and Government
*Edward T. O'Donnell*

# The Pullman Strike

## A Gilded Age Clash between Labor, Capital, and Government

*Edward T. O'Donnell*

Routledge
Taylor & Francis Group
NEW YORK AND LONDON

Designed cover image: 1894 Pullman Strike National Guardsmen fire into a mob of strikers © Pictorial Press Ltd/Alamy Stock Photo

First published 2025
by Routledge
605 Third Avenue, New York, NY 10158

and by Routledge
4 Park Square, Milton Park, Abingdon, Oxon, OX14 4RN

*Routledge is an imprint of the Taylor & Francis Group, an informa business*



*Library of Congress Cataloging-in-Publication Data*
Names: O'Donnell, Edward T., 1963– author.
Title: The Pullman Strike : a Gilded Age clash between labor, capital, and government / Edward T. O'Donnell.
Description: Abingdon, Oxon ; New York, NY : Routledge, 2025. | Series: Critical moments in American history | Includes bibliographical references and index.
Identifiers: LCCN 2024030984 (print) | LCCN 2024030985 (ebook) | ISBN 9781032483917 (hardback) | ISBN 9781032473826 (paperback) | ISBN 9781003388784 (ebook)
Subjects: LCSH: Pullman Strike, 1894. | Strikes and lockouts—Railroads—United States—History—19th century. | Labor movement—United States—History—19th century. | Industrial relations—United States—History—19th century. | United States—Economic conditions—1865–1918.
Classification: LCC HD5325.R12 1894 C563 2025 (print) | LCC HD5325.R12 1894 (ebook) | DDC 331.892/825230977311—dc23/eng/20240716
LC record available at https://lccn.loc.gov/2024030984
LC ebook record available at https://lccn.loc.gov/2024030985

ISBN: 978-1-032-48391-7 (hbk)
ISBN: 978-1-032-47382-6 (pbk)
ISBN: 978-1-003-38878-4 (ebk)

DOI: 10.4324/9781003388784

Typeset in Bembo
by Apex CoVantage, LLC

# Contents

# Series Editor Introduction

Welcome to the Routledge *Critical Moments in American History* series. The purpose of this series is to give students a window into the historian's craft through concise, readable books by leading scholars, who bring together the best scholarship and engaging primary sources to explore a critical moment in the American past. In discovering the principal points of the story in these books, gaining a sense of historiography, following a fresh trail of primary documents, and exploring suggested readings, students can then set out on their own journey, to debate the ideas presented, interpret primary sources, and reach their own conclusions—just like the historian.

A critical moment in history can be a range of things—a pivotal year, the pinnacle of a movement or trend, or an important event such as the passage of a piece of legislation, an election, a court decision, a battle. It can be social, cultural, political, or economic. It can be heroic or tragic. Whatever they are, such moments are by definition "game changers," momentous changes in the pattern of the American fabric, paradigm shifts in the American experience. Many of the critical moments explored in this series are familiar; some less so.

There is no ultimate list of critical moments in American history—any group of students, historians, or other scholars may come up with a different catalog of topics. These differences of view, however, are what make history itself and the study of history so important and so fascinating. Therein can be found the utility of historical inquiry—to explore, to challenge, to understand, and to realize the legacy of the past through its influence of the present. It is the hope of this series to help students realize this intrinsic value of our past and of studying our past.

*William Thomas Allison*
*Georgia Southern University*

# Illustrations

## FIGURES

## SIDEBARS



## DOCUMENTS

# Acknowledgments

I am so grateful to the many dedicated individuals and institutions that have played important roles in the realization of this book. Their support, guidance, and encouragement have been invaluable throughout this journey.

First and foremost, I want extend my sincere thanks to William Allison, the editor of this series, Critical Moments in American History, for his guidance in seeing this project from proposal to completed book. Likewise, I want to thank Editorial Assistants Allison Sambucini and Kimberly Smith at Taylor & Francis for their help in keeping me on schedule and guiding the manuscript to publication.

I am also deeply indebted to the staff at the Newberry Library in Chicago. Their professionalism and commitment to helping me to access the historical resources related to the Pullman Strike significantly enriched my research and greatly enhanced the book. Thanks also to librarian Jennifer Whelan (College of the Holy Cross) who provided indispensable help in tracking down several elusive sources.

I also want to thank the staff at BirchTree Bread Co. in Worcester, MA for keeping me fed and caffeinated while I sat at the counter working on this book.

Heartfelt thanks especially go to my wife, Stephanie, for her loving support. It goes without saying that I could not have written this book without it.

Finally, I am so grateful to my now several decades' worth of students whose enthusiasm for and curiosity about history have inspired me to write, in addition to books for scholarly and popular audiences, works such as this that are aimed at the undergraduate reader. It is with great pleasure that I dedicate this book to them, acknowledging the role they have played in inspiring me to be the very best teacher possible.

# Introduction

On May 11, 1894, the day at the Pullman Palace Car Company had begun just like any other. Several thousand employees filed through the factory gates and took their places for another day building or repairing luxury railroad sleeper cars. But by mid-morning one word could be heard throughout the cavernous works—Strike! Hard pressed by repeated wage cuts, harsh working conditions, and high rents in the midst of a national economic depression, the workers had had enough. They knew striking meant more hardship and possible loss of their jobs, but they were angry and desperate. By noon nearly all the employees had walked out. They had no way of knowing that in less than two months this localized dispute between one company and its employees would balloon into a massive nationwide railroad strike, the results of which would have repercussions for generations to come.

Several features of the Pullman Strike make it stand out as a critical moment in American history. First, the Pullman Strike—one of nearly 37,000 strikes between 1880 and 1900—reflected the conflicting visions of freedom that lay at the heart of Gilded Age labor–capital conflict. Capitalists like George Pullman insisted that they must have unfettered freedom to run their businesses as they saw fit. No one—especially workers, union leaders, or political officials—could tell them what to do regarding wages, hours, or workplace conditions. Employees were free to take their labor elsewhere if they were dissatisfied. On the other hand, workers argued that laissez-faire capitalism was enriching a small number of industrialists and bankers while simultaneously impoverishing them and undermining their freedom to live as independent republican citizens. One strike leader told a crowd of Pullman strikers, "You are striking to avert slavery and degradation."[1]

DOI: 10.4324/9781003388784-1

Additionally, the Pullman Strike exposed the limits of paternalistic capitalism popularized by magnates like Andrew Carnegie and George Pullman. The latter had earned wide praise for building his workers a model town featuring decent housing, clean streets, and parks. Yet when an economic downturn hit in 1893, Pullman slashed wages but refused to lower rents in company housing. And when workers responded with a strike, he refused to negotiate. Industrial benevolence, it turned out, was not nearly as important as profits. As labor leader Eugene V. Debs put it, the strike would "strip the mask of hypocrisy from the pretended philanthropist and show him to the world as an oppressor of labor."[2]

The strike also illuminated the struggle of workers to form and maintain unions in the face of intense opposition. The Gilded Age marked a significant period of successful labor organizing. Labor activists in the Gilded Age challenged the popular notion that individual struggle was the key to economic success. Confronted by powerful and ruthless employers, they preached solidarity and collective action, an ethos captured by the slogan of the Knights of Labor: "An injury to one is the concern of all." But the labor movement faced fierce opposition from employers, political leaders, and newspaper editors who denounced unions as dangerous, un-American institutions that threatened to destroy the free-market economy and impose godless socialism.[3]

The Pullman Strike also revealed the extraordinary power of big business to compel the federal government to use both the law and the military to smash the strike. Such actions ran counter to a widely held belief that the government ought to act as a neutral party to ensure a fair outcome in labor–capital disputes. The unchecked political influence of business interests alarmed not only wage earners, but also many middle- and upper-class Americans who viewed it as a threat to democracy. This concern explains the ubiquitous depiction in political cartoons of big-business tycoons as kings and autocrats.

Furthermore, the strike helped establish (via the 1895 U.S. Supreme Court decision, *In re Debs*) the court injunction as the preferred tool of big business for suppressing labor unions and strikes. Employers could now avoid the bad publicity of violence that often accompanied hiring strikebreakers and calling in the police or militia to break picket lines. Court-imposed injunctions, cloaked in the mystique and majesty of "the law," soared in popularity after 1895. They jumped from 122 in the 1890s to 328 between 1900 and 1909. By the 1920s, fully 25 percent of all strikes were stymied by court injunctions. The practice was sharply curtailed in 1932 with the passage of the Norris-LaGuardia Act which placed limits on when federal courts could issue injunctions in labor disputes.[4]

Finally, the Pullman Strike launched the storied career of Eugene V. Debs, who became an iconic labor leader and advocate of socialism for the next twenty-five years. Indeed, it was during his time in prison (for violating a court injunction during the strike) that Debs began his conversion to socialism. "I was to be baptized in socialism in the roar of conflict," he later recalled. "In the gleam of every bayonet and the flash of every rifle the class struggle was revealed." Debs popularized socialism by running for president on the Socialist Party ticket five times between 1900 and 1920. Debs rounded out his remarkable career by becoming a leading opponent of the US entry into World War I, a stance that led to his imprisonment for violating the Sedition Act (1917). Here again the U.S. Supreme Court ruled against him in *Debs v. United States* and upheld his ten-year sentence (he was later pardoned and released by President Warren G. Harding).

Chapter 1 establishes the context in which the Pullman Strike took place. The Gilded Age (1870–1900) was a period marked by a powerful duality: that of optimism and anxiety. This chapter focuses on the former which was fueled by a booming industrial economy, new technology like electric lighting and steel, westward expansion, and the rise of great cities like Chicago and New York. The one word ceaselessly invoked by politicians, business leaders, editors, and ministers to characterize the period was "progress." Railroads and other huge corporations emerged, as did the men who led them, so-called "Captains of Industry" like John D. Rockefeller (oil), Andrew Carnegie (steel), and George Pullman (luxury rail cars). These men were hailed for creating new industries, employing countless workers, and ushering in a new, modern era. Some like George Pullman sought to prove that industrial capitalism could generate enormous profits for investors, while also providing a decent living for workers. In 1881 he opened a model town named Pullman near Chicago that included a new manufacturing complex and new homes for his workers.

Chapter 2 examines the other aspect of the Gilded Age duality: anxiety. While many Americans were thrilled by the developments noted in Chapter 1, many others were unnerved by significant increases in poverty and inequality, as well as labor–capital conflict in the form of strikes and boycotts, some of which were attended by violence. Many were likewise alarmed by the rise of corporate power in the hands of people like Rockefeller, Carnegie, and Pullman. Sensational corruption scandals in the period revealed the extent to which powerful industrialists and bankers were using their wealth to bribe politicians and subvert democracy. This chapter also explores the ways that workers (via labor unions like the Knights of Labor) and farmers (via the Granger and Farmers' Alliance movements) organized to denounce what they viewed as an unfair economy and corrupt political system and to demand reform. In these efforts they faced vehement opposition from powerful business and political interests. The chapter also discusses rising discontent among Pullman workers who resented the high rents the company charged for housing and the tight social control it exerted over the town's residents.

Chapter 3 details the impact of the Panic of 1893, a nationwide economic collapse that led to the failure of thousands of businesses, banks, and farms, as well as a surge in unemployment and homelessness. This was the critical context that gave rise to the Pullman Strike in 1894. The discontent among Pullman workers increased dramatically as the company laid off several thousand workers and slashed the wages of those still employed. And yet, Pullman refused to reduce the rents he charged for company housing. In response, Pullman workers organized and made several attempts to convince Pullman to either rescind the wage cuts or to reduce rents. When the company refused, the workers walked out on strike on May 11, 1894. They soon received support from the American Railway Union (ARU), a new labor organization established by Eugene Debs. Initially this support took the form of advice on tactics and fiery speeches denouncing George Pullman for refusing to negotiate to resolve the strike.

Chapter 4 chronicles the escalation of the strike from a local dispute in Chicago between one company and its workers into a national railroad strike that threatened to paralyze the nation. The key moment was the decision by the ARU in late June to cast its support to the strikers by announcing its members would "boycott," or refuse to handle, Pullman cars which were attached to trains all across the country. In response, the heads of the twenty-six major railroads that passed through Chicago joined forces though an organization called the General Managers' Association (GMA) to oppose the ARU boycott and crush the union in the process. The GMA followed the course established by George Pullman and refused to negotiate with the ARU. Soon railroad traffic throughout the country began to stall and snarl. In Chicago, crowds of strike supporters began to stop trains and occasionally break railroad equipment. Nearly every newspaper in Chicago and nationwide published sensational and exaggerated accounts of the disturbances which helped diminish public support for the strike. Behind the scenes the GMA convinced the administration of President Grover Cleveland to use the full power of the federal government to end the strike. Soon federal judges issued injunctions that prohibited ARU leaders from engaging in any strike-related activity. Days later Cleveland ordered federal troops be sent to Chicago.

Chapter 5 explores the drama of the strike as it reached its peak in early July 1894. The arrival of more than 1,000 federal troops in Chicago was accompanied by alarmist claims by GMA officials and the local press that the city was under a reign of terror by violent strikers bent on overturning society. Violence and vandalism did increase in early July, resulting in significant loss of railroad property. But Chicago police, aided by the state militia, contained the disturbances and kept order throughout most of the city. Nonetheless, on July 8 President Cleveland issued a proclamation that effectively placed Chicago under martial law. In response, the ARU and many sympathetic labor unions in the city announced that due to the Pullman Company's continued refusal to negotiate with its striking employees, they would begin a general strike that would shut down the city and, they hoped, spread to other localities across the country. But the general strike failed to materialize as federal officials arrested Debs and other ARU officials for violating the injunction. Faced with the combined power of the GMA and the federal government, Debs soon conceded that the strike was lost.

Chapter 6 discusses the aftermath of the strike. The strike proved costly to the railroads, but most especially to the strikers, many of whom were fired and blacklisted. President Cleveland also came in for considerable criticism, prompting him to establish the United States Strike Commission which investigated the causes of the strike and issued a report that was critical of the actions taken by both the federal government, George Pullman, and the GMA during the strike. Debs and the ARU officers were tried in federal court and found guilty and sentenced to six months in prison. They appealed this case all the way to U.S. Supreme Court which upheld their convictions in the case *In re Debs* and affirmed the authority of the federal government to use any measures—including injunctions and federal troops—deemed necessary to quell domestic unrest.

The book concludes with an Epilogue that examines the several key legacies of the Pullman Strike. First, it exposed the tension between industrial capitalism and democracy, a tension that exists to this very day, and raised the question of what role the federal government should play in labor–capital disputes. In the wake of the strike a growing number of Americans, including influential politicians, civic leaders, and business leaders, called for greater intervention in and regulation of the economy by the government as necessary to reduce social turmoil and secure more peaceful and just outcomes in labor–capital disputes. Second, it called into question the use of federal troops to quell strikes. Notably, eight years after the Pullman Strike, President Theodore Roosevelt resisted calls for him to deploy the military to end a coal strike and instead used his influence to bring about a peaceful resolution. Third, the Supreme Court decision *In re Debs* opened the door to the widespread use of injunctions to stop strikes, consequently weakening the labor movement from the 1890s to the 1930s.

## NOTES

1 Almont Lindsey, *The Pullman Strike: The Story of a Unique Experiment and of a Great Labor Upheaval* (Chicago: University of Chicago Press, 1942), 124.
2 Lindsey, 124.
3 *Chicago Tribune*, July 5, 1894, 9.
4 James W. Wimberly Jr, "The Labor Injunction—Past, Present, and Future," *South Carolina Law Review*, vol. 22, no. 5 (1970), 3.

# CHAPTER 1

# The Stupendous Results of American Enterprise

The decades that followed the end of the Civil War were marked by spectacular economic growth, wealth creation, and technological innovation that transformed the United States from a mainly agricultural nation with a developing economy into the world's greatest industrial power by 1900. But those same years—known as the Gilded Age (ca. 1870–1900)—also witnessed unprecedented social turmoil that included a record number of strikes, popular protest movements, increased poverty and inequality, and rising concern over the power of big business. The name comes from the title of a book, *The Gilded Age: A Tale of To-Day*, co-authored by one of the period's most popular writers, Mark Twain. It captured perfectly the idea of an era of contrasts and contradictions, suggesting a "golden era," but also a disturbing superficiality to all the progress and prosperity, for beneath the veneer of gold lay ugly and disturbing realities.[1]

Those who welcomed the changes brought by the Gilded Age saw everywhere vivid signs of progress. It seemed nearly every industrialist, scientist, commencement speaker, and politician extolled the era as one of progress, prosperity, and innovation. "Our inventors are the true national builders, the true promoters of civilization," said the head of the United States Patent Office in 1892. "They . . . add to the sum of human knowledge, to the sum of human possessions, and to the sum of human happiness." Indeed, the number of patents issued grew from 4,589 in 1860 to 26,194 in 1890, an increase of more than 500 percent. One year later, President Grover Cleveland emphasized this optimistic theme of progress in his second inaugural address in March 1893: "[E]very American citizen must contemplate with the utmost pride and enthusiasm the growth and expansion of our country . . . the wonderful thrift and enterprise of our people, and the demonstrated superiority of our free government."[2]

DOI: 10.4324/9781003388784-2

Evidence of this progress—especially industrial progress—abounded. In 1860, the economy of the United States ranked well behind European nations like Germany, France, and Great Britain. Forty years later in 1900 the US economy was the largest in the world. That period witnessed the number of factories rise from 140,000 to 510,000, and the annual value of industrial output surge from $2 billion to $13 billion. Steel output jumped from 13,000 tons in 1860 to 10,382,000 tons in 1900 (a stunning increase of 9,762 percent).[3] "The prosperity which now prevails," said President James A. Garfield in 1881, "is without parallel in our history."[4]

Steel was at the heart of this booming industrial economy. Like the silicon chip in the mid- to late twentieth century, steel was the transformative product that changed nearly every aspect of nineteenth-century American life, from factory machinery and farm implements, to railroads and weaponry, not to mention architecture, furniture, and consumer goods. One vivid symbol of this transformation was the Brooklyn Bridge. Hundreds of thousands, including the President of the United States and many members of Congress, turned out for a massive celebration when it opened on May 24, 1883. It was the world's largest suspension bridge, so-called because the roadbed was suspended by a four massive steel cables draped over two stone towers. In his speech at the opening ceremonies, Congressman Abram Hewitt said the bridge reflected the "sum and epitome of human knowledge" and would forever stand as "the crowning glory of an age memorable for great industrial achievements."[5]

The man who supplied the steel for the Brooklyn Bridge was Andrew Carnegie, the nation's "steel king." Carnegie had come to America in 1848 as a penniless immigrant from Scotland with only a few years' formal education. He settled with his family in Pittsburgh and instead of attending school twelve-year-old Andrew was sent to labor in a bobbin factory where he earned $1.20 a week. Two years later the ambitious Carnegie landed a job as a message boy in a telegraph office earning $2.50 a week. Here he showed the focus, ambition, and innovativeness that would mark his rise to business success. For example, Carnegie taught himself telegraphy by closely watching the office telegraph operator and soon was promoted to the position at five dollars a week. One year later, he was hired by Tom Scott, president of the Pennsylvania Railroad and one of the most powerful men in America, to be his personal secretary. By 1859, Carnegie was running the western half of that railroad and earning tens of thousands of dollars in annual income. He was also learning all the techniques of business management being developed by the railroads. In 1865, he left railroads and started a thriving business building railroad bridges. Ten years later, he opened his first steel mill and went on to dominate the industry. He retired in 1901 with an estimated fortune of $200 million—equivalent to well over $100 billion in contemporary dollars.[6]

Other industries in the Gilded Age also became associated with certain "Captains of Industry" as they preferred to call themselves (their critics called them "Robber Barons"). John D. Rockefeller opened his first oil refinery in 1863 at the age of 24. In 1870 he established the Standard Oil company and proceeded to buy out nearly all his competitors.[7] By the early 1880s, Rockefeller controlled over 90 percent of the nation's oil-refining capacity. Elsewhere, John S. Pillsbury (flour milling), Philip D. Armour and Gustavus Swift (meatpacking), J.P. Morgan (finance), Cyrus McCormick (farm equipment), and Cornelius Vanderbilt and Jay Gould (railroads) emerged as dominant figures in their industries. While they came in for their share of criticism, especially from their employees, these business titans were lauded in the press for the business genius, contributions to national growth, and philanthropy.

They also embodied the ideal of the self-made man. Nearly every business leader in the Gilded Age presented their life story as one of rising from humble origins to riches through honesty, hard work, resilience, thrift, and intuition. Some like Andrew Carnegie did rise from poverty, but most business titans of the late nineteenth century were born into middle-class families. Nonetheless, the image they projected of rising from "rags to riches" helped promote the notion that *any* American could achieve success if they tried hard enough. This message was popularized further by writers like Horatio Alger who wrote more than one hundred short novels that told stories of boys overcoming great obstacles to achieve, if not riches, middle-class comfort and social respectability. Tobacco companies in this era had started including the first baseball cards with some of their tobacco products, but the Duke company also offered a series of cards titled "Histories of Poor Boys Who Became Rich and Other Famous People" that featured profiles of men like Rockefeller, Carnegie, and Vanderbilt.[8]

Along with the rise of industry and famous industrialists, optimists in the Gilded Age pointed to the development of many astonishing technological innovations. On September 4, 1882, Thomas Edison, who a few years earlier had invented the incandescent lightbulb (1879), threw a switch to illuminate a one-square mile area around Wall Street financial district in New York City. The event garnered headlines all across the country and made Edison a household name. It also led to the rapid spread of electric illumination of towns and cities, and eventually homes and businesses. At nearly the same time, Alexander Graham Bell invented the telephone (1876) and the new device spread rapidly into homes and businesses, changing dramatically the way Americans communicated.[9]

And there were still more ways to see evidence of American progress in the Gilded Age. The nation's population boomed as never before in this period, soaring from 31 million in 1860 to 76 million in 1900 (an increase of 142 percent). By contrast, Great Britain's population grew only by 10 million in the same period. A significant portion of the US population boom was due to mass immigration, as some 14 million immigrants arrived between 1860 and 1900. This tremendous influx of foreigners benefited the United States in many ways, most especially by providing a vast pool of cheap labor for the booming industrial economy.[10]

| Immigration to U.S. | |
|---|---|
| 1860–1869 | 2,081,261 |
| 1870–1879 | 2,742,287 |
| 1880–1889 | 5,248,568 |
| 1890–1899 | 3,694,294 |

But mass immigration in the Gilded Age, as has been true in every era of American history, also triggered a nativist backlash the demonized immigrants as a threat to American society. Nativists claimed immigrants weakened the U.S. by bringing crime, poverty, and disease. They also blamed immigrants for strikes and labor unrest, arguing they spread "foreign ideas" like socialism and communism among American workers. "Socialism not only centers in the city, but is almost confined to it," wrote Rev. Josiah Strong in a poplar book published in 1885. ". . . Here is heaped the social dynamite; here roughs, gamblers, thieves, robbers, lawless and desperate men of all sorts, congregate; men who are ready on any pretext to raise riots for the purpose of destruction and plunder."[11] Many nativists like Strong also articulated increasingly popular pseudoscientific claims that immigrants came from racially inferior "stock" and thus threatened to weaken the strength, intelligence, and health

Seventy percent of immigrants to America arrived in New York harbor and passed through the inspection facilities at Ellis Island. Officials there were charged with preventing any "undesirable" migrant from entering the United States. In most cases, immigrants were excluded if it was determined they were afflicted with a serious and incurable disease, impoverished, or a radical (e.g., communist, socialist, anarchist). Even so, only 2 percent of arrivals at Ellis Island were sent back to their countries of origin.

of the nation. These fears sparked demands for immigration restriction, resulting in the Chinese Exclusion Act of 1882 and the federal Immigration Act of 1891 that led to the establishment of Ellis Island and similar facilities in port cities to screen immigrants seeking entrance into the U.S.[12]

Closely tied to mass immigration was the spectacular rise of cities. In 1860, only 20 percent of Americans lived in the nation's 392 cities. By 1890, 35 percent of Americans lived in more than 1,300 cities, some of which were enormous and growing larger by the day. Americans who visited these cities were astonished not simply by their size, but also the soaring height of buildings called skyscrapers, the rapid forms of mass transit, the gaudy displays of wealth, racy forms of entertainment, and the bewildering mix of cultures. In 1890 Chicago's population exceeded 1 million; New York's topped 1.5 million.

Particularly impressive was the recovery and growth of Chicago. In October 1871 the city was devastated by the most destructive conflagration in American history. The flames incinerated approximately 3.3 square miles of the city, killing more than 300 people and destroying in excess of 17,000 buildings, including much of the central business district. Nearly 100,000 people were left homeless. Total damages were estimated at $222 million and many feared the city would never recover. But recover it did—and rapidly. Fortunately for the city, the fire left untouched the great stock yards and packing plants which were emerging as the center of American meat processing. Also largely undamaged were the city's railroad tracks, grain elevators, wharves, and mills, which allowed key processing, manufacturing, and transportation industries to quickly get back up and running. Preservation of the railroad infrastructure was especially important as it allowed Chicago to continue its emergence as the central hub of the nation's rapidly expanding railroad network.[13]

In coming years city residents, as well as the nation as a whole, took great pride in the reemergence of Chicago as the second largest city in the United States. The ceremonies in 1893 marking the 22nd anniversary of the fire, declared the *Chicago Tribune*, were intended

> to glorify over all that has been done since then—the unwearied energy and patience that took a district which was burned over till it was as bare as the palm of one's hand and made it what it is today, that raised handsome and colossal business blocks, and also built up universities and public libraries, that extended the bounds of the city for miles, that added enormously to its industries and multiplied its facilities for doing business.[14]

Many Americans in the Gilded Age also celebrated events west of Chicago. They saw in the migration of millions of white Americans, many of them immigrants, into the trans-Mississippi West as evidence the nation was fulfilling its "Manifest Destiny" to become a continental power stretching from the Atlantic to Pacific Oceans and connected by sprawling networks of railroads and telegraph wires. They deemed the expulsion by the U.S. Army of Native Americans from these lands and forced confinement on reservations as a tragic but necessary policy in the quest for national greatness. As one writer put it, "the Red Men are a doomed race . . . under what appear to be one of immutable laws of progress, the savage is giving place to a higher and more civilized race." After the many so-called "Indian Wars" raged in the 1870s and 1880s, this project was for all intents and purposes completed with the massacre of hundreds of Native Americans at Wounded Knee in South Dakota in 1890. As white Americans celebrated this conquest of the West, entertainers like Buffalo Bill popularized an image of cowboys, cavalry, and pioneers as noble and heroic figures.[15]

A related source of optimism was the perception that the nation that had nearly destroyed itself in a bloody civil war was in the decades after 1865 rapidly coming together. This unity was predicated on white Americans in the North and West accepting white southerners' systematic and violent overthrow of Reconstruction (1865–1877), the period in which four million formerly enslaved people won their freedom, full citizenship, voting rights, and equality before the law. By the 1890s white Southerners had succeeded through violence, intimidation, and racist laws in re-imposing white supremacy across the former Confederacy, forcing generations of African Americans to live under an oppressive system known as Jim Crow. "It seems to me that we are drifting, drifting back under the leadership of the slaveholders," wrote one African American leader in the South. "Our former masters are fast taking the reins of government."[16]

White southerners and northerners in this period essentially agreed to obscure this injustice with a false but alluring version of recent history known as the "Lost Cause" that presented slavery as a benign institution, denied slavery was the cause of the Civil War, and asserted the war demonstrated the extraordinary martial skill and courage of white southern soldiers who lost only due to the North's numerical and industrial supremacy. This deceitful history allowed Gilded Age politicians, business leaders, and editors to urge the nation to set aside the divisions that had led to war and work to strengthen the growing social and economic ties between the two regions. The "New South," as business promotors like Henry Grady claimed, had shed its backward slave labor system for an economy more like that of the North—"a hundred farms for every plantation, fifty homes for every palace—and a diversified industry that meets the complex need of this complex age."[17]

This celebratory spirit of national unity and optimism and faith in progress was especially evident at the world's fairs held in Philadelphia (1876) and Chicago (1893). The former, the Centennial Exposition in Philadelphia, commemorated the 100th anniversary of the signing of the Declaration of Independence. But its primary focus was on showcasing the wonders of American technological genius in a large Machinery Hall, what President Grant in a speech opening the fair described as "specimens of our attainments in the industrial and fine arts, and in literature, science, and philosophy, as well as in the great business of agriculture and of commerce." The main attraction was the Corliss Generator, a massive 1,400 horsepower engine that rose 45 feet high and weighed 650 tons. It powered all the machinery in the hall and the rest of the exhibition. It symbolized the rising industrial power of the United States.[18]

But the preeminent symbol of this new industrial age was the railroad. Railroads first emerged in the U.S. in the 1830s, but their greatest impact was not felt until after the Civil War. The national railroad network, the central hub of which was Chicago, spread in every direction in those years, but it was the Transcontinental Railroad (1863–1869) that garnered the most attention. It was a monumental undertaking by private railroad companies with massive financial assistance from the federal government to build a line of nearly 2,000 miles length from Omaha, Nebraska to Sacramento, California. To mark its completion on May 10, 1869, one of the railroad executives drove into the last rail a specially made golden spike with the inscription, "May God continue the unity of our Country as this Railroad unites the two great Oceans of the world." News that "the Continent is spanned" sparked exuberant celebrations across the country.[19]

The railroads transformed the nation in myriad ways. Between 1860 and 1900 total trackage in the US rose from 30,000 miles to 193,000, forming a vast transportation network. Because they offered speedy and inexpensive travel for people, goods, and information, the railroads played a key role in the development of the national industrial economy. Wherever they were built, railroads opened up new areas for settlement and development, including farmers, ranchers, and minders, eager to use the railroads to sell their products to the national market, as well as shopkeepers, tradesmen, professionals, and others who settled in the towns that developed at or near railroad junctions. Railroads also contributed to the national economy simply by growing, because they consumed massive quantities of steel, coal, and wood.[20]

Driving the growth of the national railroad network were giant corporations that became the first big businesses in America. Enterprises like the Pennsylvania Railroad, New York and Harlem Railroad, Union Pacific Railroad, and Missouri Pacific Railroad gobbled up smaller competitors to become the largest corporations in the world. Before the Civil War the largest businesses in America were mostly manufacturers with fewer than twenty-five employees. They were privately owned and serviced relatively small, local markets. In contrast, the railroads that emerged after 1865 were capitalized at hundreds of millions of dollars, much of it financed by stock traded on Wall Street. They also employed thousands of workers and operated over enormous stretches of territory.

Massive corporations like railroads were new features of American society and bore no resemblance to their late-eighteenth century predecessors. The corporation in America, like so many things, had its origins in England. The British crown created corporations to do certain things that would benefit society and the nation. For example, it created corporations like the East India Company to develop trade in Asia. It also created corporations to dig canals, construct roads, and establish ferries. In most cases, the corporation enjoyed special privileges or monopolies on their services that protected them from competition and allowed them to turn a profit for their investors. The goal was for these government-created corporations to prosper while also providing services that benefited society as a whole.[21]

In the United States, following the American Revolution, state governments granted corporate charters in a manner similar to that of Great Britain—mainly for projects seen as benefiting the public: construction of highways, canals, and railroads. But states also began to issue corporate charters for private, for-profit enterprises. At first the numbers were small: in 1800 there were just 100 of these types of corporations. But as the industrial revolution took hold in the nineteenth century, states began to issue hundreds and eventually thousands of corporate charters to private enterprise. By 1870, there were 100,000 such corporations and the numbers were rising. The most significant aspect of these new corporations was that, unlike their early American and British ancestors, they were almost entirely free of state control and they were focused exclusively on earning profits with almost no concern for the public good.[22]

In order to run these massive organizations efficiently and profitably, railroad managers pioneered the development of what became widely adopted modern business practices. For example, railroads led the way in incorporating and issuing stock which allowed a corporation to raise capital to expand its business. By the 1870s, an ever-growing number of companies involved in manufacturing, communications, mining, and finance had followed the lead of railroads and incorporated. Additionally, to manage these vast commercial operations, railroad executives developed complex structures of superintendents, managers, and clerks, as well as new systems of accounting, information management, and pricing. These practices also soon became standard among American corporations involved in manufacturing, mining, in retailing.[23]

Another important business practice popularized by the railroads was standardization of the design for equipment like couplers, signals, and brakes to allow for easier operation and maintenance of their giant fleets. In 1886, the nation's largest railroads collaborated to establish a "standard gauge" of 4 feet 8½ inches between the rails. This eliminated the expensive and time-consuming practice of having to transfer cargo between railroad lines that operated on tracks of different gauge size. The most notable example of standardization was the creation of national time zones. In 1883 the nation's major railroads established the four time zones that are still in use today. Prior to this innovation, "time" varied considerably from town to town and from region to region. Clocks in Chicago might read 12 noon, while in St. Louis they read 11:55 AM. But because trains traveled over complex networks, often sharing tracks and crisscrossing at junctions, a small difference in time could lead to costly delays and disastrous collisions. Standard time promised efficiency, predictability, and safety.

Not everyone was happy with this demonstration of railroad power to impose a new way of telling time. An editorial in the *Indianapolis Sentinel* lamented:

> Railroad time, it appears, is to be the time of the future. And so, people will now have to marry and die by railroad time. Ministers will preach by railroad time, and banks will be required to open and close by the same time. The sun is no longer the boss of the job.[24]

The most famous figures associated with the railroads were Cornelius Vanderbilt and his son William H. Vanderbilt, as well as Jay Gould, Edward Harriman, and Collis P. Huntington. They owned and operated vast railroad networks and were major figures on Wall Street. But many other entrepreneurs made sizable fortunes in the railroad industry without owning or operating a railroad. George Westinghouse, for example, became rich by inventing a highly effective braking system ("air-brakes") that made railroads much safer. James Buchanan "Diamond Jim" Brady made a fortune selling railroad equipment. And George M. Pullman became a millionaire manufacturing railroad sleeper cars.

Pullman was born in 1831, the third of ten children to a family living in the western New York state town of Brocton. His father James Pullman was a carpenter who worked on projects associated with the Erie Canal. He also found work raising and moving buildings, a service which was in demand due to the widening of the canal. James eventually invented and patented a wheeled device for moving buildings. George received a good education until at age fourteen when he left school to take a job as a clerk in a store. He later began working with his father in the building moving business, taking over in 1853 when his father died. Seeking greater opportunities, George relocated to Chicago where he started a successful business raising and moving buildings to allow for the installation of a new city sewer system.[25]

But Pullman soon saw greater opportunity in the booming railroad industry. At the time, the main focus of railroads was the moving of goods and commodities to market. They offered passenger cars, but they were more of an afterthought. As a consequence, travel on the nation's railroads was extremely uncomfortable. Pullman knew this from first-hand experience. Passenger cars were dirty, loud, and uncomfortable. He came to believe that there was a golden opportunity awaiting someone who managed to replicate for the railroads the comforts passengers enjoyed on steamboats. Accordingly, while maintaining his stake in the building-raising business, he formed a partnership with Benjamin Field whom he knew from New York. They managed to convince the Chicago, Alton, and St. Louis Railroad to allow them to convert two of its traditional railroad cars into beautifully appointed passenger vehicles. When the cars debuted in 1859, they earned wide praise from the public and media—in part because Pullman skillfully organized a demonstration journey for the press.[26]

In 1860, with business at a lull, Pullman and his partners decided to seek opportunity in the mania surrounding the discovery of gold in the Pike's Peak area in Colorado. He had no interest in prospecting for gold. Rather he went to Colorado to "mine the miners" by selling them lodging and supplies at high prices. Pullman returned to Chicago in 1863 with a lot of money and threw himself into building up his sleeper-car business.

He eventually realized that to build a truly comfortable passenger car, he would have to design and manufacture it himself, rather than converting existing cars.

Over the next few years Pullman perfected his designs and in 1864 began manufacturing his own luxury passenger cars. To offer greater stability and a smoother ride, Pullman cars rode on sixteen wheels, rather than the standard eight. They also featured double-paned windows to minimize noise and a special ventilation system that removed soot from the incoming air. Each car was decorated in high Victorian finery, with chandeliers, plush seating, paneling and brass fixtures, and lush carpeting. At night, one's berth easily converted into comfortable bedding with clean sheets.[27]

Each Pullman car also featured a dedicated porter whose job was to carry passenger luggage, shine shoes, run errands, clean and convert berths for overnight sleeping. From the start, Pullman hired only African American men as porters, many of whom had been born into slavery. Pullman's motives were not charitable: reflecting the racist attitudes of the day, he reasoned that Black porters were "naturally" inclined to be obedient servants who would cater to every whim of white passengers. And he could pay them the lowest possible wages—less than one-sixth those paid to white conductors. These porters worked incredibly long hours and had to endure all manner of racist taunts, including being called "George" (likely for George Pullman) regardless of their actual names. They endured these conditions because their low wages made them dependent on tips from customers.[28]

As orders for more cars came in, Pullman began building drawing-room cars, hotel cars, and dining cars. The latter offered food said to rival that of the finest restaurants in the nation.[29]

In 1867 Pullman formally incorporated the Pullman's Palace Car Company and issued $1 million in stock to raise capital needed for expansion.[30] By 1869 the Pullman company operated seventy cars on several railroad lines and orders for more continued to pour in.

Rather than sell his "Pullman Palace Cars" to railroads, he leased them, thereby earning fees from the leases and from a portion of the tickets sold to passengers who booked passage on them. Those tickets were expensive, but people were eager to pay for the experience of traveling in style, comfort, and luxury. By 1879, 464 Pullman cars were attached to trains from coast to coast, as well as railroads in England, Scotland, and Italy, earning George Pullman $1 million in profit annually. By 1885 the corporation's capitalization was just short of $16 million and its assets topped $28 million.[31]

Pullman's success made him a wealthy man. As was customary for Gilded Age tycoons, he built an opulent mansion for his family on Chicago's Prairie Avenue, a wealthy district that was home to other leading business figures like retailer Marshall Field and meatpacker Phillip D. Armour. Pullman's mansion cost between $350,000 and $500,000 and featured a theater that seated two hundred, a bowling alley, a pipe organ, and an ivory and gold drawing room. [32] The Pullmans were famous in the upper echelons of Chicago society for hosting lavish parties for four hundred guests. They also built a posh summer home at Long Branch, New Jersey, a summer retreat popular among the nation's rich and famous, plus another on an island in the Thousand Islands region of upstate New York.[33] The family also traveled extensively throughout the United States and Europe where they socialized with the Morgans, Vanderbilts, and other elite families. Pullman also dined with Presidents Ulysses S. Grant and Benjamin Harrison.[34]

In the late 1870s Pullman decided to consolidate his several manufacturing operations located in the Midwest and East into one large facility near Chicago. In addition, Pullman planned to build a town there to house his employees. In 1880 he quietly acquired 4,000 acres (6.25 square miles) of open land near Lake Calumet south of Chicago at a cost of $800,000. He soon initiated construction on both the new manufacturing facility and the town. Pullman, as it came to be known, was actually not an independent town, but rather a small section of a larger municipality named Hyde Park.[35]

The town reflected Pullman's desire to be thought of as a benevolent capitalist at a time when many of his contemporaries were criticized for exploiting their workers. Rather than simply construct cheap, ramshackle buildings, Pullman announced that his would be a model town that offered decent housing, clean streets, public parks, good schools, and more. But Pullman's motives were neither charitable nor philanthropic. His town had three purposes. First, he intended for it to earn a 6 percent annual profit derived from the rents charged the residents. Second, Pullman planned to exert paternalistic control over his workforce beyond the factory gates so that they would be afraid to strike or join a union. This control also included the moral lives of his employees as the town banned saloons, gambling halls, and brothels. Third, Pullman intended for the town to garner him fame as a model capitalist who earned stupendous profits while providing his workers with decent houses and apartments in a tidy community that seemed to offer everything a working-class family could desire.[36]

## Model Towns

George Pullman drew inspiration from an effort in the late 1870s to build model housing for workers in New York City. This initiative, which began years earlier in England, marked a new approach to the problem of working-class poverty. Previously, reformers had focused on changing the habits and lifestyles of the poor, cajoling them to stop drinking alcohol and become more thrifty. Model housing advocates, however, believed that the lives of the poor could be improved by changing their environment, rather than their habits. Alfred T. White, a man made wealthy in the fur trade, built two "model tenements" in Brooklyn with apartments that were vastly superior to the average tenement dwelling. They featured large, clean rooms with plenty of access to light and air. White said his project was inspired by a desire to do good works, and to earn a profit. His motto was, "Philanthropy, plus 5 percent," meaning he would earn a modest 5 percent profit from the rents he collected.

Pullman believed his model town would inspire his fellow industrialists to follow his lead in pursuing both profit and public accolades. "Capital will not invest in sentiment nor for sentimental considerations for the laboring classes," said Pullman. "But let it once be proved that enterprises of this kind are safe and profitable and we shall see great manufacturing corporations developing similar enterprises, and thus a new era will be introduced into the history of labor."[37]

The town of Pullman opened in January 1881 and over the next few years as it grew in size and population, George Pullman received the tributes he desired. Journalists, politicians, and ministers extolled his town as a monument to enlightened and benevolent capitalism. "As all the world knows," wrote a Chicago journalist, "[Pullman] is an industrial hive of many thousand busy workers, all placed in an environment unique and unmatched the world over for solid comfort and luxuriousness."[38] As a consequence, asserted another, "The disturbing conditions of strikes and other troubles that periodically convulse the world of labor would not need to be feared here."[39] The town was, according to the *Chicago Times*, "a living monument to the culture, philanthropy, enterprise and business capacity of [George Pullman] . . . and future generations will bless his memory."[40] Pullman loved the publicity and frequently organized tours of the town for dignitaries, journalists, and prominent figures.

*Figure 1.1* **"Manufacturing Town of Pullman, and Car Works Belonging to Pullman's Palace Car Company," ca. 1885. George Pullman garnered widespread praise for building a model town for both his sleeping car manufactury and decent housing for his workers.**

© Newberry Library in Chicago.

Pullman's town offered several types of housing. Common laborers lived in tenements, while skilled workers with higher incomes could rent small attached homes. Some distance away, Pullman managers and top administrators lived in large, comfortable homes. The streets of the town—many of them named by Pullman after famous inventors such as Eli Whitney and Samuel F. B. Morse—were laid out in a typical grid pattern and paved. A system of gutters to draw away rainwater and elevated, wooden plank and stone sidewalks enabled pedestrians to walk free of the muddy water and muck that characterized the streets of Chicago. Also unlike Chicago, the streets of the town were lined with trees.[41]

For recreation the residents could visit several parks and athletic fields. The town also included a train depot for the Illinois Central Railroad, the Florence Hotel (named for Pullman's daughter), and the Pullman School. The largest structure, aside from the factory works, was the Arcade which housed most of the town's mercantile businesses and public meeting rooms, as well as the Post Office, theater, bank, public library, doctor's offices, and town administrative offices. A nearby Market Place featured vendors selling meat and fresh produce, as well as public meeting rooms. Pullman only allowed one church in the town, a Gothic-style structure called the Green Stone Church on account of the green tinted stone of which it was constructed. Pullman envisioned that the community's various religious sects would rent the church for their services.[42]

Some of the produce sold at the Market Place was grown on the Pullman Farm. Like everything in the town, the farm was intended as a money maker for Pullman. In this case, it both saved and made him money. Instead of paying for a six-mile pipeline to Lake Michigan for the dumping of the town's sewage waste water, Pullman sent it to the farm where it was used as fertilizer. The farm itself proved productive and Pullman earned profits from produce sales in the town and Chicago.

The population of Pullman grew steadily in the 1880s. By 1885, four years after the first workers moved in, the town counted 8,500 residents, of whom 2,700 were employed by Pullman.[43] Slightly more than half the population was foreign born, a percentage that would continue to rise to 72 percent by 1892. In 1893 the town reached its peak population of 12,600, of whom 5,500 labored for George Pullman.[44]

The town's rapid growth reflected the expansion of the Pullman Palace Car Company. In the early 1880s it enjoyed robust profits and investors and analysts considered it one of the best-run companies in the nation.[45] But Pullman could not rest on his laurels. He faced serious competition from rival sleeping-car companies that sought to win contracts from railroads when ones he had previously signed neared expiration. Pullman also faced numerous lawsuits from his rivals, some over contracts and others over alleged patent infringements on sleeping-car technology and design. Pullman responded with many lawsuits of his own over the same matters. Through it all he expanded the company's reach and profits. He also followed the lead of many a Gilded Age business tycoon by buying out his chief rivals to reduce competition and increase his dominance in the sleeping-car business.[46] By 1893, 2,573 Pullman cars rolled along the nation's extensive railroad network. That year the company reported earnings of $11,400,000.[47]

The year 1893 also marked a key moment in Chicago's history: the opening of the massive, year-long World's Columbian Exposition, a world's fair to mark the 400th anniversary of Christopher Columbus' arrival in the Americas and to celebrate Chicago's astonishing recovery from the devastating fire in 1871. The city's leading business figures provided substantial financial backing for the event, including George Pullman who pledged $100,000.

> The exposition officially "opened" with great fanfare in October 1892 to coincide with the 400th anniversary of Columbus' 1492 arrival in the Americas. But due to delays in constructing the fairgrounds and buildings, it did not open to the public until the spring of 1893.

The city hired renowned architect and urban planner Daniel Burnham and gave him nearly 700 acres of waterfront property along Lake Michigan to lay out the exposition grounds. Burnham assembled an impressive team that included landscape architect Frederick Law Olmsted and architect Louis Sullivan. Together, they developed a master plan that called for a sprawling complex of more than 200 buildings. Like previous world's fairs in cities like Philadelphia and Paris, the Chicago Exposition was a celebration of technology, culture, and commerce. It contained thousands of exhibits on science, machinery, art, history, ethnic heritage, music, and theater. Thomas Edison offered demonstrations of his new kinetoscope, a prototype of a motion-picture projector. George Pullman displayed his famous luxury sleeper cars.[48]

But this world's fair was also a celebration of the American city and its possibilities. In many ways, the buildings and grounds were the main attraction. Olmsted designed a system of lagoons and waterways—fed by the waters of Lake Michigan—to serve as decorative reflecting pools, and waterways for transportation. Around the waterways, Burnham placed fourteen main buildings designed in the Beaux-Arts architectural style, which emphasized logic, harmony, and uniformity. The Court of Honor buildings lined a water-filled Grand Basin, forming the centerpiece of the exposition grounds. Covered in bright white stucco this "White City," as it was called, astonished the more than twenty-seven million visitors who arrived from every corner of the nation, many of them aboard Pullman sleeper cars. They saw not only abundant evidence of the greatness that America had achieved in the Gilded Age, but also hints of still greater glory to come, what President Grover Cleveland in his address opening the fair referred to as, "the stupendous results of American enterprise and activity and . . . magnificent evidences of American skill and intelligence."[49]

Many of those visitors also took side trips to other Chicago-area attractions. One of the most popular was an excursion to the model city of Pullman, just fifteen minutes by train to the south. Like the White City, Pullman offered an optimistic vision of the urban future. Visitors marveled at its neat brick houses, clean streets, tidy lawns, and seemingly happy residents. The town offered a stark contrast to the grim tenement districts of Chicago and other large U.S. cities.[50]

## NOTES

1 Mark Twain and Charles Dudley Warner, *The Gilded Age: A Tale of Today* (American Publishing Company, 1873).
2 Grover Cleveland, Second Inaugural Address, March 4, 1893; Report of the Commissioner of Patents to Congress for the Year ending December 31, 1892 USPTO https://www.uspto.gov/web/offices/ac/ido/oeip/taf/h_counts.htm
3 Jennifer Keane, Saul Cornell, and Edward T. O'Donnell, *Visions of America: A History of the United States*, 2nd edition (Upper Saddle River, NJ: Pearson, 2013), 470.
4 James A. Garfield, Inaugural Address, Friday, March 4, 1881.
5 Oration Address of Hon. Abram S. Hewitt at the Opening Ceremonies of the New York and Brooklyn Bridge, Delivered May 24, 1883.
6 David Nasaw, *Andrew Carnegie* (New York: Penguin Press, 2006), passim.
7 Ron Chernow, *Titan: The Life of John D. Rockefeller, Sr.* (New York: Random House, 1998), 119–242.
8 John G. Cawelti, *Apostles of the Self-Made Man: Changing Concepts of Success in America* (Chicago: University of Chicago Press, 1968), 101–164; Paulette D. Kilmer, *The Fear of Sinking: The American Success Formula in the Gilded Age* (Knoxville, TN: University of Tennessee Press, 1996), 1–21.
9 Randall E. Stross, *The Wizard of Menlo Park: How Thomas Alva Edison Invented the Modern World* (New York: Crown, 2008), 132–135.
10 Keane, et al., 500.
11 Josiah Strong, *Our Country: Its Possible Future and Its Present Crisis* (New York: Baker & Taylor, 1885), 132.
12 Erika Lee, *America for Americans: A History of Xenophobia in the United States* (New York: Basic Books, 2019), 75–146.

13 Carl Smith, *Urban Disorder and the Shape of Belief: The Great Chicago Fire, the Haymarket Bomb, and the Model Town of Pullman* (Chicago: University of Chicago Press, 1995), 34–63. See also Karen Sawislak, *Smoldering City: Chicagoans and the Great Fire, 1871–1874* (Chicago: University of Chicago Press, 1995).
14 *Chicago Tribune*, October 9, 1893, 12.
15 Ned Blackhawk, *The Rediscovery of America: Native Peoples and the Unmaking of U.S. History* (New Haven, CT: Yale University Press, 2023), 289–364; William Blackmore, Introduction to Richard Irving Dodge*, The Plains of the Great West and Their Inhabitants* (1877), liv.
16 Eric Foner, *Reconstruction: America's Unfinished Revolution* (New York: Oxford University Press, 1988), 444.
17 Gary W. Gallagher and Alan T. Nolan, eds., *The Myth of the Lost Cause and Civil War History;* Henry Grady, Speech to the New England Society in New York City, December 21, 1886.
18 *New York Times*, May 11, 1876, 1, 2.
19 *New York Times*, May 12, 1869, 1
20 Richard White, *The Republic for Which It Stands: The United States During Reconstruction and the Gilded Age, 1865–1896* (New York: Oxford University Press, 2017), 144–145, 216–217, 220–223, 590–598.
21 Tyler Hallloran, "A Brief History of the Corporate Form and Why it Matters," *Fordham Journal of Corporate & Financial Law* (November 18, 2018). https://news.law.fordham.edu/jcfl/2018/11/18/a-brief-history-of-the-corporate-form-and-why-it-matters/
22 Alan Trachtenberg, *The Incorporation of America: Culture and Society in the Gilded Age* (Hill & Wang, 2007, orig pub 1982), 82–86.
23 White, 247–251.
24 *Indianapolis Sentinel*, November 21, 1883.
25 Stanley Buder, *Pullman: An Experiment in Industrial Order and Community Planning, 1880–1930* (New York: Oxford University Press, 1970), 3–8.
26 Buder, 8–9.
27 Buder, 10–12.
28 Richard Schneirov, "The Pullman Strike" https://digital.lib.niu.edu/illinois/gildedage/pullman; Larry Tye, *Rising from the Rails: Pullman Porters and the Making of the Black Middle Class* (New York: Henry Holt, 2005), 2–3, 22–28.
29 Liston E. Leyendecker, *Palace Car Prince: A Biography of George Mortimer Pullman* (Denver, CO: University Press of Colorado, 1992), 86–87
30 Leyendecker, 81–83.
31 Almont Lindsey, *The Pullman Strike: The Story of a Unique Experiment and of a Great Labor Upheaval* (Chicago: University of Chicago Press, 1942), 24.
32 Jack Kelly, *The Edge of Anarchy: The Railroad Barons, the Gilded Age, and the Greatest Labor Uprising in America* (New York: St. Martin's Press, 2019), 73
33 Leyendecker, 111; Kelly, 74–75.
34 Leyendecker, 121.
35 Lindsey, 61–62; Richard Schneirov, "The Pullman Strike" https://digital.lib.niu.edu/illinois/gildedage/pullman
36 Buder, 42–45; Smith, 177–208.

37 Mrs. H. E. Starrett, "Pullman—A Social, and Industrial Study," *Weekly Magazine* (September 16, 1882). Cited in Richard Schneirov, "The Pullman Strike" https://digital.lib.niu.edu/illinois/gildedage/pullman

38 *Chicago Inter-Ocean*, September 6, 1888.

39 *Boston Herald*, September 1, 1881.

40 *Chicago Times*, October 23, 1881; Smith, 188; Steve Fraser, *The Age of Acquiescence: The Life and Death of American Resistance to Organized Wealth and Power* (New York: Basic Books, 2016), 166.

41 Buder, 49–76.

42 Lindsey, 44.

43 Lindsey, 24.

44 Lindsey, 50.

45 Leyendecker, 179–180.

46 Leyendecker, 179–199.

47 Annual Report of the Pullman Company, *Pullman Journal*, October 21, 1893, p. 4. Cited in Lindsey, 25.

48 Trachtenberg, 208–234.

49 Chicago *Inter-Ocean*, May 2, 1893, 5.

50 Buder, 147–148.

CHAPTER 2

# Millions Born to Suffering and Poverty

Even as the Gilded Age economy boomed and industrialists like George Pullman earned both fortunes and praise for their contributions to national progress, evidence abounded that there were serious social, economic, and political problems brewing. One major concern that emerged was the growth of poverty, especially in big cities like Chicago and New York. In large sections of these cities known as slums, hundreds of thousands of poor, working-class people—many of them immigrants—crowded into filthy tenement apartments that often lacked running water, toilets, or adequate ventilation. These neighborhoods suffered from high rates of crime and poor public health. In Chicago in 1891, where 15 percent of city residents lived in tenements, some 2,000 people died from typhoid fever and 4,300 from bronchitis and pneumonia. The city also saw some 10,000 to 12,000 children under the age of five die each year in the early 1890s.[1] The single-most important factor contributing to poverty were the low wages paid the most vulnerable and exploitable workers. In 1888 the *Chicago Times* published an exposé series under the headline "Life Among the Slave Girls of Chicago." It revealed that women worked for wages as low as 28 cents per day, a level of exploitation so extreme it forced thousands into prostitution.[2]

The dreadful conditions of the urban poor gave rise to the settlement house movement. Inspired by efforts by reformers in England to help the urban poor better their condition, Jane Addams and Ellen Gates Starr founded Hull House in a poor, immigrant neighborhood in Chicago in 1889. Over the next few years the institution developed a wide range

DOI: 10.4324/9781003388784-3

of programs to benefit residents of the neighborhood, from classes that taught English, civics, cooking, and hygiene, to concerts, art exhibitions, and vocational training. Gradually Hull House opened its door to labor organizers endeavoring to unionize workers. Addams and others also lobbied political leaders for improved tenement laws, increased street cleaning and garbage removal, expanded public education, improved factory safety, and a ban on child labor. Scores of settlement houses opened in cities across the country.[3]

Another related concern that emerged was the growing gap between the rich and poor. Most Americans in this era rejected calls for economic equality, but they also believed that *extreme* inequality ran counter to their understanding of an ideal republican society. When working-class and middle-class Americans looked about them in the 1870s and 1880s, they could see both colossal fortunes being accumulated by a small number of people with names like Rockefeller, Carnegie, Vanderbilt, and Pullman and grinding poverty spreading among increasing numbers of workers and farmers. By 1890, the top 1 percent of the U.S. population owned 51 percent of all wealth; the lowest 44 percent of population owned just 1.2 percent of all wealth.[4]

The anxiety produced by these extremes in wealth were captured in a drawing that appeared in *Harper's Weekly* in February 1876. Titled "The Hearth-stone of the Poor," it shows a wealthy, well-dressed family walking down the sidewalk past a group of poor, homeless people gathered about a steam grate for warmth on a cold winter's night. One child in the rich family notices the poor; the rest pass by oblivious to their suffering. The artist was presenting a scene not merely of callous rich people. The larger and more disturbing point was to present a shockingly un-American scene of haves and have-nots on a sidewalk—a scene most Americans associated with London and novels of Charles Dickens. Americans had long been conditioned to believe that victory in the American Revolution meant their society was immune to these European-style extremes of wealth and poverty. But now in the Gilded Age, it appeared that American society was trending in this direction and many Americans found this deeply disturbing. As the editor of a Boston newspaper put it in 1878, "What is the good of having a republic unless the mass of the people are better off than in a monarchy? Does not a real republic mean that all men have an equal chance and not millions born to suffering and poverty?"[5]

***Figure 2.1*** **"The Hearth-stone of the Poor" (*Harper's Weekly*, February 12, 1876). The artist who drew this magazine cover image endeavored to depict the popular fear that rising levels of inequality in the Gilded Age might indicate that the United States was becoming more like the nations of Europe.**

© Library of Congress.

This question about "monarchy" and the Dickensian "Hearth-stone" drawing indicated one of the great fears of Gilded Age Americans: that their nation was becoming Europeanized. This concern had nothing to do with ethnicity, as they understood that most Americans were of European ancestry. Rather, the notion of Europeanization focused on social and political concerns. Many Gilded Age Americans feared that their political culture was being transformed from a democracy based on republican values such as liberty, equality, and opportunity to a European-style society that featured monarchy, landed aristocracy, fixed classes, great gaps between the rich and poor, social upheaval, and incessant warfare. These were the very things Americans believed their ancestors had broken away from when they declared their independence in 1776. Now a century later the American republic appeared to be sliding toward monarchy, aristocracy, and poverty for the average citizen.

Those who feared Europeanization pointed to evidence that opportunities for advancement for the average American were rapidly declining.

This observation called into question one of the tenets of American political culture—the belief that everyone is born with the opportunity to better themselves. America did not guarantee everyone success, but opportunity abounded for those willing to work hard, make sacrifices, take risks, and play by the rules. Not everyone would enjoy success on the level of Andrew Carnegie, but everyone could be a self-made man. As Abraham Lincoln put it in 1854, "There is no class of permanent laborers amongst us. Twenty-five years ago I was a hired laborer. The hired laborer of yesterday labors on his own account to-day, and will hire others to labor for him to-morrow."[6]

But in the Gilded Age, increasing numbers of average Americans were coming to the conclusion that opportunity for the average person to rise was disappearing. These sentiments were captured in the testimony provided by workers who spoke to a Senate committee in 1883. This group of lawmakers held hearings at different locations around the country for the purposes of finding answers as to why there was so much unrest among American workers.[7]

Warning of Europeanization, Carpenter P. J. McGuire called attention to "the crystallization of society more and more into distinct classes, classes just as distinct as any that exist to-day in Europe, and a man born in one of them can never hope to reach the other." McGuire and other workers attributed this "crystallization" of fixed classes to the rapidly increasing power of monopolies and corporations to crush competitors and exploit workers. Brassworker John Finnerty testified that as late as 1870, a brassworker needed just $300–400 to start his own business. But now in the early 1880s, the emergence of large brassmaking companies had pushed the start-up cost to $5,000—far beyond the means of the average brass worker. The vast majority of workers like McGuire and Finnerty believed that a capitalist economy was inherently good and just. But in recent years, they charged, it had been corrupted by greedy monopolists who used their power to rig the economy to their advantage. "The poor unfortunate laborer is just like the kernel of wheat between the upper and lower millstone," express wagon driver Thomas McGuire testified, "in any case he is certain to be ground. He *produces* all the wealth while the men who produce nothing *have* all the wealth." Machinist John Morrison echoed this claim: "[Railroad magnate] Jay Gould never earned a great deal, but he owns a terrible lot."[8]

Anxious Americans also noted an important result of big-business titans owning "a terrible lot": they were using their wealth to corrupt American democracy. This was not a new concern, but rather one with deep roots in American political culture. Long before the Gilded Age, many Americans argued that corporations, especially those deemed "monopolies," posed a threat to republican liberty. Andrew Jackson, for example, rose to political prominence in the 1820s and 1830s by portraying himself as a "man of the people" who promoted the interests of average citizens while opposing those of elites and the wealthy. Jackson and the Democratic Party were especially opposed to granting state charters for corporations. They argued that such arrangements, even if supposedly in the interests of the common good, say, to build a railroad or canal, created a corrupt and undemocratic alliance between private interests and public officials. Only people with connections to state legislators—and the money to bribe them—stood to win corporate charters. Worse, these alliances over time would lead to the evolution of an entrenched American aristocracy and the undoing of American democracy. This explains why, in the 1830s, President Jackson expended so much political capital to eliminate the Bank of the United States.[9]

Decades later in the Gilded Age, evidence of the connection between monopoly power and political corruption abounded. The Credit Mobilier scandal (1864–1867) featured massively inflated contracts related to building the transcontinental railroad. The Whiskey Ring (1871–1876) involved politicians who colluded with the liquor industry to avoid paying excise taxes. The Black Friday scandal (1869), a failed attempt by Wall Street tycoons to corner the gold market, also involved high-level public officials, including members of President Ulysses S. Grant's family.[10]

Politics corrupted by business interests also thrived on the state level. The Pennsylvania Railroad enjoyed so much power and influence in Pennsylvania, it had its own office in the state Capitol building and its chief lobbyist was known as the 51st Senator. He used bribes and other inducements to compel the legislature to pass laws that benefited the railroad.

Corruption likewise abounded in cities which were often controlled by political machines like New York's Tammany Hall. In the early 1870s the city was rocked when it was revealed that the head of Tammany, William "Boss" Tweed, had raked in millions through a massive kickback scheme involving construction contractors. A decade later in 1886, twenty-two of twenty-four New York City councilors were indicted for taking bribes from a large streetcar company seeking to expand its control over the city's transportation system. Similar scandals erupted in Chicago involving bribery, kickbacks, and voter fraud schemes.[11]

With the political system at all levels in the Gilded Age awash in corporate money, lawmakers acted in the interests of corporations and rarely if at all on behalf of workers or farmers. This anxiety and anger over corporate money in politics was vividly expressed in a political cartoon that appeared in the popular magazine *Puck* in 1889. Titled "The Bosses of the Senate," it showed the US Senate chamber balcony filled with giant industrial monopolists shaped like moneybags. Each is labeled a particular industrial trust such as the Steel Beam Trust, the Sugar Trust, and the Coal Trust. Below are a group of much smaller US senators who seem filled with apprehension as the monopolists glower down at them with angry, menacing faces. A sign on the wall reads, "This is the Senate of the monopolies, by the monopolies, and for the monopolies." Another sign indicates that the monopolists have entered through a door labeled "Entrance for Monopolists," while in the background the "People's Entrance" is boarded shut. The message is clear: big business had captured American democracy, shutting out and defying the will of the people.

***Figure 2.2*** **"The Bosses of the Senate" (*Puck*, 1889). This cartoon captures the rising concern over the corrupting influence of corporate interests on American democracy. Note that the corporate titans enter through the "Entrance for Monopolists" while in the background the "People's Entrance" is barred.**

© Library of Congress.

Politicians beholden to business interests meant that judges appointed to the courts, from local courts to the Supreme Court, reflected a similar outlook. Legal decisions bearing on business in the late-nineteenth century overwhelmingly favored business over the public at large, or particular groups such as workers or farmers. Indeed, it was in this period that the Supreme Court ruled (*Santa Clara County v. Southern Pacific Rail Road*, 1886) that under the recently adopted 14th amendment—an amendment adopted to establish and protect the rights of recently emancipated African Americans—provided corporations with constitutional rights as though they were persons.[12]

Another closely related development in the Gilded Age that disturbed many Americans was the dismissive arrogance exhibited by some big-business leaders. In 1883 railroad magnate William H. Vanderbilt (son of Cornelius) answered a reporter who asked him whether he ran particular express trains to earn a profit or to accommodate the public by saying, "Accommodation of the public? The public be damned! We run them because we have to." This outburst was a gift to Vanderbilt's critics who quoted it and included it in political cartoons for the rest of his life. Another railroad titan Jay Gould, when asked if he was concerned about the rise of union activity among his workers, allegedly snarled, "I could hire one half of the working class to kill the other half."[13]

This arrogance also extended to the social lives of the super-rich in the Gilded Age. Ignoring a longstanding republican ideal of modesty and restraint, they built themselves palatial mansions on Fifth Avenue in New York, Lake Shore Drive in Chicago, and Nob Hill in San Francisco, as well as massive summer retreats places like Newport, Rhode Island and Long Branch, New Jersey. They also held many grand balls and dinners that put on display their spectacular wealth.

The most famous of these exhibitions was the 1883 Vanderbilt Ball. To celebrate the opening of her new mansion on Fifth Avenue, Alva Vanderbilt invited 1,000 of New York's wealthiest citizens to a costume ball. Some invitees came dressed as animals and others as figures from history or literature. But the most popular theme was to dress as European royalty—Louis the XIV, Marie Antoinette, and many more.[14]

This practice of building palaces and dressing up as European royalty was another sign of Europeanization that signaled a major shift in American political culture. Ever since the American Revolution, American political culture stressed the necessity of adhering to republican values of modesty and restraint and shunning anything that suggested monarchy and aristocracy, especially ostentatious displays of wealth and status. But in the 1880s the nation's richest families rejected the virtue of republican simplicity and embraced the lavish life of European elites, endeavoring self-consciously to transform themselves into an American aristocracy.[15]

The Vanderbilts inspired other wealthy Americans to imitate their example. In Chicago in 1886, for example, the wife of department-store magnate Marshall Field held an equally extravagant ball for the city's upper-crust families, including the Pullmans. The theme of this gala was the recent hit comic opera by Gilbert and Sullivan, *The Mikado*. The Fields decorated their mansion in the style of a Japanese castle, and guests wore Japanese costumes. "There was such a bewildering mass of rich and costly stuffs," gushed a *Chicago Tribune* reporter, "that no detailed description could be well given."[16]

Both the Vanderbilt and Field balls drew huge crowds of onlookers who gathered on sidewalks near the mansions to watch the arrival of

In 1899, after observing decades of the extravagant behavior of America's rich and famous, sociologist Thorstein Veblen coined the phrase "conspicuous consumption" to describe the phenomenon. He wrote, "Conspicuous consumption of valuable goods is a means of reputability to the gentleman of leisure."[18]

the guests. The rich in America had become celebrities and most newspapers now featured what they called "Society" pages that chronicled in breathless detail not only the lavish balls, but also the European tours of the Belmonts, Astors, and Lodges, the impending weddings of Morgans to the Satterlees and the Vanderbilts to the Whitneys. The scandals of high society—affairs, divorces, bankruptcies, and suicides—also received intense media coverage.[17]

Another very different trend—a sharp upsurge in labor–capital conflict—also seemed to suggest American society was becoming more and more like those in Europe. Strikes before the Gilded Age were small and relatively rare (only about 1,400 between 1741 and 1881). But between 1881 and 1900, the United States experienced an astonishing 36,757 strikes involving six million workers.[19] The sheer volume of strike activity was disturbing, but so too was the fact that many of these strikes were enormous and many involved violence and bloodshed. The Great Uprising Railroad strike of 1877, for example, was the first national strike and it was marked by stunning violence that led to more than 100 deaths of workers at the hands of federal troops, state militia, and local police, including 18 in Chicago.[20]

This seeming epidemic of strikes and violence challenged another cardinal principle of American political culture—that unlike Europeans, Americans lived in a society without fixed social classes. But the sudden explosion of strikes in the Gilded Age suggested that fixed classes were indeed forming in American society. Why were more and more American workers referring to themselves as members of a besieged "working class" who were oppressed by a greedy "upper class"? Many Americans wondered: Was this yet another sign of Europeanization?

It seemed that way to the great poet Walt Whitman. In the mid-nineteenth century there was no greater champion of America than Whitman. His poetry brimmed with optimistic odes to democracy, the common man, and the republic's bright future. America was, he wrote, the "Centre of equal daughters, equal sons." But by the late 1870s, he was worried about rising poverty and social unrest. In a speech he delivered in 1879, he gave voice to the concern that the U.S. was succumbing to Europeanization. He said:

> If the United States, like the countries of the Old World, are also to grow vast crops of poor, desperate, dissatisfied, nomadic, miserably-waged populations . . . then our republican experiment, notwithstanding all its surface-successes, is at heart an unhealthy failure.[21]

In referencing "surface successes" Whitman alluded to the Gilded Age metaphor—that beneath the great displays of wealth, growth, and technology were roiling and destructive social problems that threatened the future of the republic.

Evidence of rising social unrest was not confined to the nation's urban centers. Beginning in the mid-1870s, American farmers had begun to organize to resist the growing power of railroads, banks, and grain-storage companies that they believed used their monopoly power to charge exorbitant rates that impoverished them. In 1874, they formed what they called "Granger Parties" to challenge the Republican and Democratic parties they believed were controlled by the railroads and banks. That fall Granger party candidates swept to victory in many Midwestern states, winning controlling majorities in the state legislatures of Illinois, Wisconsin, Iowa, and Minnesota, and significant influence in several more states. They used their power to enact a series of "Granger Laws," which were some of the earliest regulations of powerful corporations, banks, and railroads—especially the railroads. Some Granger laws set maximum rates for transporting or storing grain. Others banned practices such as offering preferred customers special discount rates. Railroad executives denounced these efforts to curb their power and profit as unconstitutional and sued. The Supreme Court, however, in two key cases (*Peik v. Chicago and North Western Railroad*, 1876; and *Munn v. Illinois*, 1877) ruled that state legislatures did possess authority under the Constitution to regulate business.[22]

These regulations, along with a rise in farm product prices in the late 1870s, caused the Granger movement to diminish. But when low prices and hard times returned in the 1880s, farmer activism reappeared in the form of Farmers' Alliances. These were associations dedicated to combining the power of individual farmers (via cooperatives) against commodity buyers who paid them inadequate prices for their goods and railroads that charged extortionate rates to move these goods to market. By the mid-1880s the Farmers' Alliances had more than 6 million members. Another one million African American farmers, excluded from the main alliances, joined a Colored Farmers' Alliance.

As Americans came to believe that their country faced a host of serious problems related to big business, corruption, poverty, extreme inequality, and social unrest, reformers emerged to offer solutions. One of the most notable was Henry George, a California journalist and editor who in the 1870s—a decade marked by a severe economic depression—grew increasingly concerned over the growth of inequality and unrest in America. He responded by writing a book titled *Progress and Poverty* (1879) that became an international bestseller. The book's driving question was: Why, amidst so many signs of economic and technological progress, did poverty appear to be increasing while a small handful of individuals like William K. Vanderbilt, George Pullman, and Andrew Carnegie reaped vast fortunes?[23]

George's answer was rising monopoly power. By monopolizing land, resources, and large sectors of the economy, rich and powerful interests were becoming richer and more powerful. As they did, they became more powerful than democratically elected leaders. In effect, they were becoming a new American aristocracy every bit as privileged and entrenched as that in Europe. At the same time, working-class and middle-class Americans were finding themselves cut off from opportunity, left to lead lives of poverty and despair. This inequality, he argued, was not "natural" but rather it was a product of structural flaws in the economy facilitated by misguided public policy. "In our time," wrote George, ". . . creep on the insidious forces that, producing inequality, destroy Liberty."[24]

To save the American republic, George argued that the government needed to be empowered to enact measures that would reduce inequality and promote the common good. He acknowledged that the Founders believed limiting government power was essential for the preservation of republican liberty. But he contended that Madison, Jefferson, Washington, and the others thought as men living in a small-scale, rural eighteenth-century society where it made sense to have a weak government. But now, a century later, the U.S. was a modern industrial society. And in that context, a weak, laissez-faire government was no longer appropriate as it allowed the greedy and unscrupulous heads of massive corporations and banks to oppress the people. To stop this dangerous trend, the power of the government needed to be increased to protect and promote democracy and republican ideals. For Henry George, this meant instituting what he called a "single-tax" on land values. But understood more broadly, Henry George—along with many other early progressive thinkers—helped popularize the idea that government was no longer a threat to liberty. Government in the age of big business was liberty's protector.

Another response to the challenges of the Gilded Age was the labor movement. American workers had formed early versions of labor unions as far back as the late eighteenth century. But they grew in popularity in the years after the Civil War. Most were organized by specific trades of skilled, native-born male workers. The Amalgamated Association of Iron and Steel Workers, for example, was comprised of men skilled in puddling, rolling, and molding. Because steel companies like those owned by Andrew Carnegie could not make steel without these skilled workers, the latter had the power to negotiate for higher wages, shorter hours, and safer conditions. Excluded from membership in the union were the low-skill workers who shoveled coal into blast furnaces and loaded finished metal products onto rail cars for delivery. Skilled workers tended to look down on these men, many of them immigrants, seeing them as uneducated and unreliable union members.

In the 1870s a more inclusive form of labor organizing began to gain popularity. Industrial unionism called for the organization of *all workers*, regardless of skill or ethnicity, into one big union. Advocates argued that all workers had shared interests and that steady advances in industrial technology were fast erasing the distinction between skilled and unskilled workers. The best-known and most powerful industrial union to emerge was the Knights of Labor (KOL). Founded in 1869 in Philadelphia by a small group of tailors, its slogan captured the spirit of solidarity that lay at the heart of the movement: "An injury to one is the concern of all."[25]

Originally the KOL was a secret organization because the workers rightly feared their employers would fire them for joining. Secrecy and a severe economic depression in the 1870s sharply limited the growth of Knights membership, but by the late 1870s the union had several thousand members. In 1878 the Knights drew up a constitution that neatly summarized its philosophy and goals, among them securing for workers "a proper share of the wealth that they create," equal pay for men and women, the establishment of the eight-hour workday, and the abolition of prison labor and child labor.

In the early 1880s the Knights dropped secrecy and came out into the open. Membership soared, especially after the Knights won several high-profile railroad strikes. Knights' members also played a key role in establishing Labor Day as a holiday to honor workers and call attention to the threats they faced. The first Labor Day was celebrated on September 5, 1882 in New York City. Between 5,000 and 10,000 workers marched in a grand parade up Broadway. Many held signs with messages that expressed workers' solidarity ("Eight Hours for Work—Eight Hours for Rest—Eight Hours for What We Will" and "Liberty, Equality, Fraternity"), as well as demands that workers receive a proper share of the wealth they created ("Labor Creates All Wealth") and calls for labor to exert more influence in politics ("Labor Built this Republic. Labor Shall Rule It" and "Strike with the Ballot").[26]

The idea of an annual "Labor Day" holiday and parade quickly gained popularity and by 1886 it had spread nationwide. Nearly 20,000 workers marched in Manhattan, and another 10,000 in Brooklyn, while 25,000 turned out in Chicago, 15,000 in Boston, 5,000 in Buffalo, and 4,000 in Washington, D.C. That same year, the Knights boasted a membership of more than 700,000, making it the largest labor union in the world at the time.[27]

It is important to note that some American workers saw unionism as an ineffective protection against the exploitation by business owners. They turned more radical alternatives like socialism, communism, and anarchism that promised not to reform American capitalism, but rather to replace it altogether with a new system of production and social organization that would offer workers a full share of the wealth they created and a truly democratic voice in both the running of businesses and politics. The number of workers drawn to these radical visions of the future was small—probably no more than 10 percent—but the influence of socialist, communist, and anarchist ideas on labor activists was considerable.

Despite its impressive growth in this period, the labor movement faced significant obstacles. For one, there were no laws establishing the right of workers to form and join labor unions. In fact, many states had laws on the books that made conspiracies to harm an individual or institution illegal. Opponents of labor unions claimed—and judges and juries often agreed—that strikes and boycotts by workers constituted conspiracies to harm an employer, leading to the arrest, conviction, and imprisonment of union officials. Workers also had to contend with the fact that nearly all the nation's newspapers were decidedly anti-union and anti-strike. Labor activism was routinely denounced as dangerous and misguided. As one worker bitterly observed, "Whenever a man undertakes to advocate the cause of the working people, the papers come out and denounce what he says as the 'ravings of a demagogue.'" Workers did establish labor newspapers, but most were small (four pages), short-lived, weekly publications with tiny circulations. Labor unions also lacked strike funds that could allow their members to pay rent and buy food during long strikes. Striking workers, noted one worker, have "nothing to combat capital with except their empty stomachs, while the capitalists have had unlimited financial resources and have been able to starve the workingmen into submission."[28]

Opposition to the labor movement peaked in 1886, a year marked by hundreds of strikes and massive demonstrations for reforms like the eight-hour day. One event in particular became the pretext for suppressing the labor movement: the Haymarket Bombing on May 4, 1886 in Chicago. The city's labor movement in the 1880s was strong and active. Just three days before the bombing, more than 30,000 Chicago workers took part in a one-day nationwide strike for the eight-hour day. Two days later Chicago police shot and killed a striker outside the McCormick Harvesting

Machine Company factory. In response, city labor leaders, led by a group of self-identified anarchists, called for a rally in Chicago's Haymarket Square on May 4.

That evening a large crowd listened for hours to speeches denouncing the police and the exploitation of workers by unscrupulous capitalists. When the rally ended and the crowd began to disperse, a large squad of Chicago police moved in. Suddenly, a bomb landed among them and exploded. The blast and ensuing panic left seven policemen dead or dying, some from "friendly fire" by fellow officers, along with six workers.[29]

Anti-union politicians, ministers, editors, and businessmen—including George Pullman—seized upon the bombing as an opportunity to denounce *all* organized labor, a sentiment that was captured in the hysterical headlines in newspapers all across the nation that proclaimed that revolution was at hand. In the *New York Times*, for example, the headline read: "Anarchy's Red Hand: Rioting and Bloodshed in the Streets of Chicago." The accompanying article claimed, "The villainous teachings of the Anarchists bore bloody fruit in Chicago tonight and before daylight at least a dozen stalwart men will have laid down their lives as a tribute to the doctrine of [anarchism]."[30] Chicago police soon arrested eight men, all self-proclaimed anarchists, and charged them with murder—even though there was no evidence connecting them to the bomb. The drama of their subsequent trials and eventual convictions dominated headlines for the rest of the year. In the end, four of the anarchists were hanged and one committed suicide in his cell. The remaining three remained in prison awaiting their appeal to the Illinois State Supreme Court. They were eventually pardoned and released by Illinois governor John Peter Altgeld who said they had been victims of "hysteria, packed juries, and a biased judge."[31]

But anti-labor forces were not content with simply denouncing unions. They wanted to destroy them and the fearful atmosphere after Haymarket seemed to provide an ideal opportunity. In the spring and summer of 1886, all across the nation public officials jailed labor leaders on charges of conspiracy. In New York City alone, over 100 labor union leaders were jailed for calling strikes or boycotts. In response, workers in more than 200 cities and towns across the U.S. formed independent labor parties and ran pro-labor candidates for office. This included the workers of New York City who formed a United Labor Party and nominated Henry George as its candidate for mayor. That November George stunned observers when he finished a close second to the winner, former Congressman Abram Hewitt and ahead of Republican Theodore Roosevelt.[32]

At that moment George, labor activists, and Knights of Labor leaders believed they were on the verge of a revolution in American politics.

It seemed certain that the hundreds of labor parties that formed in 1886 would coalesce into a national third party that would challenge the Republican and Democratic parties they believed were in the pockets of big business. This new party would fight for the interests of everyday American workers and farmers, seeing to it that reforms like the eight-hour day and the regulation of corporations and banks were enacted.

But both the labor party insurgency and the Knights of Labor fell apart in the coming years, done in by the combined anti-labor efforts of business, political leaders, and the courts, as well as infighting and disagreements over strategy. The latter played a key role in the decision of skilled trades workers to form a new labor organization, the American Federation of Labor (AFL), in December 1886. In recent years it had come to resent anti-trade-union hostility from some KOL leaders and a lack of trade-union autonomy within the KOL. They also wanted to distance themselves from the radicalism (especially in the aftermath of Haymarket) and independent Labor Party efforts associated with the Knights. Led by a cigarmaker named Samuel Gompers, the AFL committed itself to pursuing a more conservative agenda of higher wages, shorter hours, better work conditions, and union recognition. Gompers called it "pure and simple" unionism, a catch phrase that set the AFL apart from the KOL which was dedicated to the transformation of society and the economic system. By the mid-1890s, the AFL would boast a membership of over 500,000 workers. The KOL membership plummeted to 100,000, but it remained an important—if diminished—labor organization into the 1890s.[33]

The decline in the Knights and independent labor party activity did not signal an end to the spirit of popular insurgency in the Gilded Age. Workers continued to organize, strike, and demand political leaders heed their demands for pro-labor legislation. And in rural America, farmer activism in the form of Farmers' Alliances surged in the late 1880s.

By 1890, the Farmers' Alliances had united into one National Alliance that had a combined membership of more than five million. That summer Farmers' Alliance delegates gathered in Ocala, Florida and drew up a manifesto listing their grievances and proposed reforms. Months later in the fall of 1890, Farmers' Alliance-backed political candidates swept to victory at the polls in twelve Western and Midwestern states, winning complete or partial control of their state legislatures and electing six governors. They also sent fifty pro-farmer representatives and three senators to Congress.[34]

These impressive results convinced many Farmers' Alliance activists that they needed to form a third political party and run a slate of candidates, including a presidential nominee, in the upcoming 1892 election. They held a convention in St. Louis in early 1892 that led to the formal creation of the People's Party. It also adopted a preamble to the party's platform that captured the mood of despair then gripping workers and farmers:

> [W]e meet in the midst of a nation brought to the verge of moral, political, and material ruin. Corruption dominates the ballot-box, the Legislatures, the Congress, and touches even the ermine of the bench. The people are demoralized . . . The fruits of the toil of millions are boldly stolen to build up colossal fortunes for a few, unprecedented in the history of mankind; and the possessors of those, in turn, despise the republic and endanger liberty. From the same prolific womb of governmental injustice we breed the two great classes—tramps and millionaires.[35]

The People's Party convention gathered in July 1892 and nominated former Union Army veteran James B. Weaver for president and former Confederate veteran General James G. Field of Virginia for vice-president. The convention also adopted a platform listing demands that fell into three broad categories, beginning with several antimonopoly initiatives such as the elimination of absentee ownership of land and national banks. It likewise called for a far greater role for the federal government regulating the economy to ensure fairness and widespread opportunity, including government ownership of railroads and telegraphs. It also demanded the adoption of a graduated income tax to make the rich pay a greater share of the tax burden, and free silver coinage to increase the money supply to help debtors. Another set of demands called for measures to restore to the people their democratic voice in politics, including the popular election of senators and introduction of the referendum and initiative. And in an attempt to create a national base of support among all struggling people, not just farmers, the platform also included several planks that expressed sympathy with industrial workers and denounced the use of private armies like the Pinkerton's in labor disputes and uncontrolled immigration that they claimed led to unfair job competition.

## Pinkertons

Pinkerton agents were employed by the Pinkerton National Detective Agency, a private police force founded in 1850 by a former deputy sheriff named Allan Pinkerton. He named it a detective agency because he fancied himself an expert in the art and craft of crime solving. The organization originally focused on assisting railroads by providing agents ("detectives") to protect trains from theft and apprehending those who stole freight, baggage, or passengers' valuables. During the Civil War Pinkerton earned fame for operating a spy network for the Union war effort, and allegedly thwarting an assassination attempt on President Abraham Lincoln. In 1866 Pinkerton's agency solved the case of a $700,000 theft from the Adams Express Co. But in the 1870s Pinkerton began to offer his services to businesses seeking to break strikes and crush labor-union activity. Pinkerton's were hired to spy on labor organizations and to employ force—often deadly—against workers. By the late 1870s the Pinkerton agency was the largest and best-known strikebreaking and union-busting outfit in the nation. They were despised by workers who denounced them as the private (and therefore illegitimate) army of big business.

In the end, the People's Party was no match for the established parties. Democrat Grover Cleveland won the election of 1892 with 46.1 percent of the vote to Republican incumbent Benjamin Harrison's 43 percent. Yet the Populists polled more than one million votes, accounting for 8.5 percent of the total. Their candidate, James B. Weaver, won Kansas, Colorado, Idaho, and Nevada, garnering twenty-two electoral votes. Results on the local level were even more impressive, as Populists elected 1,500 candidates to state legislatures, three governors, and five senators and ten representatives to Congress.[36]

In the face of so much criticism and protest, American business leaders responded by rejecting the claims of reformers and workers. The American capitalist system, they argued, was working just fine. The source of all labor–capital conflict was the embrace by workers of several misguided notions, many of them un-American ideas spread by recently arrived European immigrants. For example, many workers believed they had a right to influence the setting of wages and hours in their place of employment. Business leaders dismissed this idea, asserting that they—and only they—had the right to set wages and hours. They would not be "dictated" to by workers or their appointed leaders. Workers had only one right: to sell their labor to any employer willing to hire them. Labor, they insisted, was a commodity like grain or coal and "the market" set wage rates. Further, the idea of a "fair" or "living wage" was a dangerous, anti-capitalist fiction. So, too, was the claim that workers had the right to form unions that employers were bound to recognize and negotiate with. "The day of the inauguration of trades unions and labor organizations in this country," raged one writer, "was a day the blackest and fullest of menace to the popular prosperity and peace that ever dawned upon the nation. They have been an unmitigated curse to employers and employed alike."[37] These unions, and the dangerous ideas they propagated, proclaimed business leaders, were the cause of the surge in strikes and boycotts. Claims that employers exploited workers, crushed competitors, and corrupted politicians were utterly untrue. Industrial capitalism was bringing to the American people unprecedented wealth, prosperity, and comfort.[38]

No industrialist was more active in defending the status quo than steel magnate Andrew Carnegie. In a widely read 1889 article titled "The Gospel of Wealth," Carnegie asserted the poor in late-nineteenth-century America lived better than kings and queens of the past. The fact that some individuals such as himself had accumulated extraordinary fortunes was no cause for concern. Such fortunes were "inevitable" and, besides, men like him used their wealth to fund philanthropic projects like museums, universities, and libraries "from which the masses of their fellows will derive everlasting advantage." In another article, Carnegie positioned himself as a friend of the American worker, going so far as to claim that the right of workers "to combine and to form trades-unions is no less sacred than the right of the manufacturer to enter into associations . . . with his fellows."[39] And for proof Carnegie could point to the high wages and good conditions he provided his unionized workers at his largest steel works at Homestead, PA.

But Carnegie's rosy depiction of labor–capital relations and his professed warm attitude towards labor unions collapsed in the summer of 1892 when workers at his Homestead, PA steel works staged a strike. The dispute stemmed from Carnegie's decision to break the workers' union in order to gain complete control of wages, hours, benefits, and work rules. The company's skilled workers, most of them American-born men of Irish, English, and German descent, were members of the Amalgamated Association of Iron and Steel Workers, a powerful craft union formed in 1876. Proud of their skills and fiercely loyal to their trade union, they enjoyed high wages and decent living conditions. They won strikes in 1881 and 1889, both times by mobilizing most of the townspeople to their side (some 3,800 of Homestead's 11,000 residents worked for Carnegie). Carnegie, dependent on the Amalgamated men for their specialized steelmaking knowledge and skill, had no choice but to agree to the workers' terms.[40]

But as new technology became available in the late 1880s that made these skills obsolete, it freed employers like Carnegie to break unions and hire less skilled workers to whom they could pay lower wages and demand longer hours. The contract signed with the Amalgamated after the 1889 strike was set to expire on June 30, 1892 and Carnegie and his hard-nosed business partner, Henry Clay Frick, decided the time had come to get rid of the union and its demands for high wages, strict work rules, and resistance to the introduction of labor-saving machinery. "The mills have never been able to turn out the product they should," Carnegie wrote in frustration to Frick, "owing to being held back by the Amalgamated men."[41]

While the decision to break the union was in keeping with the cutthroat business practices of the day, it ran counter to the public persona of the benevolent capitalist Carnegie had worked for years to develop, a persona similar to that of George Pullman. To protect this image, just before the strike, Carnegie left the country for an extended vacation in Scotland, leaving Frick behind to take care of the dirty work.

In June, with the contract expiration deadline looming, Frick prepared for the showdown by building a twelve-foot-high wall around the mill complex and topping it with barbed wire. Then on June 29, the day before the contract expired and workers were likely to declare a strike, Frick announced a lockout and closed the mills.

## Lockouts

During labor disputes, increasing numbers of business owners in the 1880s and 1890s began to use the tactic of a lockout. That is, rather than wait for workers to call a strike, they would abruptly close their worksites, factories, and mines, locking workers out of their place of employment and stopping their pay. The goal of a lockout was to pressure workers to accept the wages, hours, and other terms being offered by the employer. Most unions in that era did not have strike funds, and most wage earners did not have significant savings, so their ability to hold out for better terms was severely limited. In addition, a lockout was often coupled with an effort to hire replacement workers, thus raising the prospect of permanent job loss.

Over the next week, tensions remained high as workers believed Frick intended to bring in non-union replacement workers, along with a large force of the most hated figures in late-nineteenth-century labor struggles: heavily armed professional strikebreakers of the Pinkerton Detective Agency. In the early morning hours of July 6, 1892, a gun battle broke out between the townspeople and hundreds of Pinkertons aboard two barges trying to land at the Homestead complex on the Monongahela River. The carnage claimed six strikers and five Pinkertons killed, with scores injured.

The next day, in a move that indicated the political power of Frick and Carnegie, state officials released the Pinkerton men, despite promises to the townspeople to charge them with murder. They also ignored the objections of the local sheriff and sent 2,000 soldiers of the state militia to Homestead to take control of the town and Homestead mills. Frick hired hundreds of replacement workers and on July 15, just two weeks after the lockout began, steel production resumed in the Homestead mills.

The national press gave extensive coverage to the strike and its tone in many instances was surprisingly pro-worker, probably due in part to the negative reputation of the Pinkertons. But public opinion soon shifted against the strikers after an anarchist named Alexander Berkman shot Frick several times on July 23. Remarkably, Frick survived the assassination attempt. Even though Berkman had no connection to Homestead or the Amalgamated, his actions brought widespread condemnation down upon the strikers very similar to that triggered six years earlier by the Haymarket bombing.[42]

The strike soon began to falter. By August more than 1,000 replacement workers were employed at the mills. Blacklisted and unable to find work, hundreds of steelworkers left town. In late September state officials charged thirty-three union leaders with treason against the state. Two months later, on November 20, 1892, the Amalgamated formally ended the strike. The Amalgamated went into a steep decline.

The Homestead strike revealed the power differential between labor and capital in the Gilded Age. Industrialists like Carnegie had the financial resources to withstand a long work stoppage, while his workers gradually faced starvation as the strike wore on. Industrialists also could rely on military and legal assistance from the state government to end strikes and prosecute labor leaders. And while his reputation took a hit, Carnegie had the time and fortune to build it back up again through a decades-long campaign of high-profile philanthropy.

By the time of the Homestead strike in the summer of 1892, there was ample evidence of rising worker discontent across the nation, including in the seemingly idyllic town of Pullman. While workers appreciated the fact that their housing and surroundings were superior to those in working-class neighborhoods of Chicago, they resented the near total control the Pullman Company exerted over their daily lives. Pullman owned everything and he refused to allow residents to purchase their own homes. The rents the company charged were high compared to neighboring towns. Pullman also charged

> Carnegie once summed up his belief that the wealthy must donate their fortunes to philanthropic causes by writing, "the man who dies rich, dies disgraced." When he sold his steel company to financier J. P. Morgan for close to $400 million, he spent the rest of his life giving it away to various causes, including the construction of Carnegie Hall in New York, Carnegie-Mellon University in Pennsylvania, and several thousand public libraries in the United States and Europe.

much higher fees for water and gas compared to nearby Kensington or Roseland. The Pullman Company also controlled everything. There was no local government, no independent newspaper, or any other semblance of democracy. Instead, the town was managed by a town agent appointed by George Pullman. And because he believed alcohol undermined worker morality and productivity, the town prohibited the sale of intoxicants—except to people wealthy enough to patronize the bar at the town's swanky Florence Hotel.[43]

Equally vexing to employees was their treatment within the Pullman works. Most employees, aware that Pullman deployed a network of spies and informants among their ranks, were afraid to complain about work conditions for fear of dismissal. But some did speak to journalists off the record, recounting how the company's arrogant managers and foremen made life miserable for most workers. "They would talk to the men as though they were dogs," said one veteran worker. At least one threatened violence when workers questioned his orders. Some foremen also delayed the start of work on a project, causing men to wait for hours for which they were not paid.[44]

These grievances were not of recent origin. As far back as 1885, just four years after the town opened to residents, economist Richard T. Ely published a long article about Pullman in *Harper's Weekly*, one of the nation's most prominent and influential magazines. The article opened with glowing descriptions of the town's beautiful and varied architecture, its tree-lined streets and groomed parks, as well as its marketplace, theater, library, bank, schools, and church. "Contrary to what is seen ordinarily in laborers' quarters," wrote Ely, "not a dilapidated door-step nor a broken window, stuffed perhaps with old clothing, is to be found in the city." But Ely then shifted his focus to the town's disturbing features and discontented workforce. While the town of Pullman appeared to outsiders to be a magnificent American success story, Ely concluded bluntly that it "is un-American . . . It is benevolent, well-wishing feudalism."[45]

Pullman workers had few options but to endure the conditions dictated by Pullman. But occasionally they reached their breaking point and walked off the job. In February 1882, some 1,000 employees walked off the job to protest the announcement that the Pullman Company would only cover half the cost of their railroad transportation to and from Chicago (the town was still under construction, so many workers commuted) instead of the full cost as had been customary. Pullman refused to budge and the strike quickly failed.[46] A little over two years later, in 1884, more than 150 freight-car builders struck in protest over a wage cut that they said left them unable to feed and house their families.

Pullman responded by dismissing their claims and filling their positions with strikebreakers.[47]

A larger strike took place in May 1886 when Pullman workers, most of whom worked a 10- to 11-hour day, participated in a nationwide strike for the eight-hour day. Two years in the making, the protest on May 1 saw 350,000 workers across the country walk off the job, including more than 30,000 in Chicago. It was intended as a one-day event, but many workers—including those at Pullman—stayed out on strike. In addition to the eight-hour day, they also demanded a wage increase of 10 percent.[48] George Pullman rejected these demands outright, insisting that workers had no right to any say whatsoever in the management of the company. He then called in the local police and re-opened his shops. Fearing the loss of their jobs and income, workers began returning to the Pullman works and the strike collapsed. Two additional walkouts by small groups of workers, one in January 1888 in another in January 1891, also failed in the face of Pullman's intransigence. Workers were informed that if they did not return to their positions by a certain date, they would be fired.[49]

Pullman's response to union activity and strikes was similar to that of most of his fellow industrial capitalists. He rejected workers' claims that they had a right to a living wage. Labor was a commodity like lumber or steel. Wages and hours were determined by the "the market." Or as George Pullman preferred to put it, "The wage question is settled by the law of supply and demand." Workers enjoyed freedom of contract; they were free as individuals to sell their labor to the highest bidder. If they were dissatisfied, so the argument went, they were free to take their labor elsewhere.[50]

Pullman's handling of labor disputes also reflected his personality which contemporaries described as arrogant and irritable. He had built his company and no one—not a government official, worker, or union representative—had the right to interfere with his running of it. Despite his paternalist pretenses, beneath the surface there lurked an authoritarian impulse. He loved to show off the town of Pullman to visitors in a manner his critics likened to a feudal lord. Indeed, when he received a patent of nobility from the King of Italy he frequently carried it with him and displayed it for people to admire.[51]

But to the general public, Pullman enjoyed a reputation as a brilliant entrepreneur, benevolent employer, and generous philanthropist. In April 1891, Pullman, joined Thomas Edison, George Westinghouse, and Cyrus Field as celebrity inventors at a reception in Washington, D.C. celebrating American inventiveness. Eight months later he returned to the capital for a reception at the White House. By then Pullman had been selected to serve on the committee charged with organizing the World Columbian Exposition, a year-long world's fair in Chicago set to open in fall 1892. In July 1892, when he received a patent for a new air-filtration system, the *Tribune* gushed, "[N]o man, in the railway or financial world, could make a great big grab into fortune's bag and have more folks glad of his luck than George M. Pullman."[52]

## NOTES

1 "Epidemics," *Encyclopedia of Chicago*, http://www.encyclopedia.chicagohistory.org/pages/432.html#:~:text=The%20city%20simply%20had%20to,under%20five%20died%20in%20Chicago; *Carroll Wright, The Slums of Baltimore, Chicago, New York, and Philadelphia* (Washington, D.C.: United States Congress, 1894), 18–19.

2 "Life Among the Slave Girls of Chicago," *Chicago Times*, July 30, 1888. For a sensational examination of Chicago's slums, see George Wharton James, *Mysteries of Chicago* (Chicago: Craig Press, 1893).

3 Louise W. Knight, *Jane Addams: Spirit in Action* (W.W. Norton, 2010), 65–103.

4 Walter Licht, *Industrializing America* (Johns Hopkins University Press, 1995), 183.

5 *The Boston Pilot*, November 2, 1878.

6 Abraham Lincoln, September 17, 1859, in Roy P. Basler, ed., *The Collected Works of Abraham Lincoln*, Volume 3, (New Brunswick, NJ: Rutgers University Press, 1953), 463.

7 Edward T. O'Donnell, *Henry George and the Crisis of Inequality: Progress and Poverty in the Gilded Age* (New York: Columbia University Press, 2015), 130–134.

8 Testimonies of Thomas McGuire, Joseph Finnerty, and John Morrison, *Report of the Committee of the Senate upon the Relations between Labor and Capital* (Washington, D.C.: Government Printing Office, 1885), vol. 1, 740–746, 760, 775.

9 Kenneth Lipartito, "The Antimonopoly Tradition," *University of St. Thomas Law Journal*, vol. 10, no. 4 (Spring 2013), 991–1005.

10 Richard White, *The Republic for Which It Stands: The United States During Reconstruction and the Gilded Age, 1865–1896* (New York: Oxford University Press, 2017), 118–119, 205, 247, 255–260, 266, 273.

11 "Political Culture," Encyclopedia of Chicago http://www.encyclopedia.chicagohistory.org/pages/987.html. See also "Policing" and "Gambling" and "Vice Districts."; O'Donnell, 182–187.

12 Adam Winkler, *We the Corporations: How American Businesses Won Their Civil Rights* (Liveright, 2018).

13 Matthew Josephson, *The Robber Barons: The Great American Capitalists, 1861–1909* (New York: Harcourt, Brace and Company, 1934), 187.

14 *New York Times*, March 27, 1883, 1.

15 Sven Beckert, *The Monied Metropolis: New York City and the Consolidation of the American Bourgeoisie, 1850–1896* (New York: Cambridge University Press, 2001), 257; Edwin G. Burrows and Mike Wallace, *Gotham: A History of New York City to 1898* (New York: Oxford University Press, 1999), 1071–1072.

16 *Chicago Tribune*, January 2, 1886, 1.
17 O'Donnell, 73–74.
18 Thorstein Veblen, *The Theory of the Leisure Class: An Economic Study in the Evolution of Institutions* (Macmillan, 1899).
19 Carroll D. Wright, *Sixteenth Annual Report of the Commissioner of Labor, 1901: Strikes and Lockouts* (Washington, D.C.: Government Printing Office, 1901).
20 White, 345–355; Richard Schneirov, *Labor and Urban Politics: Class Conflict and the Origins of Modern Liberalism in Chicago, 1864–97* (Urbana, IL: University of Illinois Press, 1998), 69–76.
21 Walt Whitman, *Specimen Days and Collect* (Philadelphia: David McKay, 1883), 330.
22 White, 257–258, 362–363, 373–375; Heather Cox Richardson, *West from Appomattox: The Reconstruction of America after the Civil War* (New Haven, CT: Yale University Press, 2008), 160–164.
23 O'Donnell, 33–68.
24 Henry George, *Progress and Poverty: An Inquiry into the Cause of industrial Depressions and of Increase of Want with Increase of Wealth* (New York: D. Appleton & Co., 1879), 548.
25 Craig Phelan, *Grand Master Workman: Terence Powderly and the Knights of Labor* (Westport, CT: Greenwood Press, 2000), 70–72; Robert E. Weir, *Beyond Labor's Veil: The Culture of the Knights of Labor* (University Park, PA: Penn State University Press, 1996), 8–13
26 Kim Voss, *The Making of American Exceptionalism: The Knights of Labor and Class Formation in the Nineteenth Century* (Ithaca, NY: Cornell University Press, 1993), 72–80; *New York Times*, September 5, 1882, 1; September 6, 1; September 7, 2; *Irish World*, September 16, 1882.
27 Jonathan Grossman, "Who Is the Father of Labor Day?," *Labor History*, 14, no. 4, (1973): 612–623.
28 Testimony of John S. McClelland, *Report of the Committee of the Senate upon the Relations between Labor and Capital* (Washington, D.C.: Government Printing Office, 1885), vol. 1, 152, 209
29 James Green, *Death in the Haymarket: A Story of Chicago, The First Labor Movement, and the Bombing That Divided Gilded Age America* (New York: Anchor Books, 2006), 174–191.
30 *New York Times*, May 6, 1886, 1.
31 Green, 3–11, 192–208.
32 O'Donnell, 169–239.
33 Voss, 78–79, 185–228.
34 Richardson, 240–242.
35 "People's Party Platform," *Omaha Morning World-Herald*, July 5, 1892.
36 White, 747–748, 755–756.
37 *Scribner's Monthly*, October 1877, 853.
38 William E. Forbath, *Law and the Shaping of the American Labor Movement* (Cambridge, MA: Harvard University Press, 1991), 65–66.
39 Andrew Carnegie, "An Employer's View of the Labor Question," *Forum*, 1886, 119.
40 Paul Kahan, *The Homestead Strike: Labor, Violence, and American Industry* (New York: Routledge, 2014), 40–55.

41 Kahan, 57–65.
42 Kahan, 66–99; *The Nation*, July 28, 1892.
43 Jack Kelly, *The Edge of Anarchy: The Railroad Barons, the Gilded Age, and the Greatest Labor Uprising in America* (New York: St. Martin's Press, 2019), 101; Almont Lindsey, *The Pullman Strike: The Story of a Unique Experiment and of a Great Labor Upheaval* (Chicago: University of Chicago Press, 1942), 61–63; Rev. William H. Carwardine, *The Pullman Strike* (Chicago: Charles H. Kerr & Company, 1973), 15–26; United States Strike Commission, *Report on the Chicago Strike, June–July 1894* (Washington, D.C.: Government Printing Office, 1895), 437, 439–440. [Hereafter referred to as USSC.]
44 *Chicago Tribune*, May 14, 1894, 1; USSC, 436–437, 439–440, 443.
45 Richard T. Ely, "Pullman: A Social Study." *Harper's Magazine* 70 (February 1885): 452–466.
46 *Chicago Tribune*, February 15, 1882, 8; February 16, 1882, 10; and February 17, 1882, 8. Lindsey, 28–29.
47 *Chicago Times*, March 5, 1884, 8; March 6, 1884, 8. Lindsey, 29.
48 White, 539–542; Schneirov, 194–199.
49 Lindsey, 29.
50 USSC, 556–557.
51 Lindsey, 30–31, 34; Kelly, 74.
52 *New York Times*, March 22, 1891, 15; *New York Times*, January 13, 1892, 4; *Chicago Tribune*, July 31, 1892, 11.

CHAPTER 3

# Striking to Avert Slavery and Degradation

George Pullman enjoyed two years of tremendous profits and labor peace following the 1891 strike. By January 1893, Pullman and the city of Chicago focused on the impending opening of the World's Columbian Exposition that would bring millions of visitors to the city and many thousands to tour the famous Pullman works and model town. But as May 1 approached, the day of the fair's official opening ceremonies, signs of an economic downturn were evident everywhere. In February the once mighty Philadelphia & Reading Railroad collapsed under a mountain of debt, shaking the confidence of investors on Wall Street. This in turn prompted many Americans to run to their banks and withdraw their deposits in gold, a trend that dramatically reduced the U.S. Treasury's gold reserves. Three days after the fair opened another major U.S. corporation failed. The National Cordage Company had been flying high in early 1893, with a stock price of $75 per share in February. But like the Philadelphia & Reading Railroad it was seriously overextended and deeply in debt. Its failure on May 4, 1893 caused the collapse of three prominent Wall Street investment firms which sent shockwaves through the national economy. They reached Chicago on May 9 with the announcement that the Chemical National Bank of Chicago had failed, followed by the Columbia National Bank two days later.[1]

The Panic of 1893, as it came to be known, was the most severe economic depression in U.S. history to that point. It lasted four years and caused the failure of 600 banks and 15,000 businesses, seventy-four of them railroads.[2] The collapse sent the economy into a deflationary spiral that saw prices plummet for everything from steel to wheat. Employers also slashed wages in order to remain solvent. For example, in late July

DOI: 10.4324/9781003388784-4

1893 the Westinghouse Air Brake Company laid off four hundred workers and cut the wages of its remaining employees by 15–20 percent.[3] As the economy contracted, manufacturing orders declined, as did railroad expansion. Railroad mileage construction fell from 4,579 miles of track in 1892 to 1,989 in 1895.[4]

As jobs disappeared, the unemployment rate soared to 20 percent—and often double that in big cities like Chicago and New York. The jobless quickly burned through what meager savings they may have accumulated and then, because so many of their friends and family were likewise destitute, they turned to churches and other charitable organizations which likewise soon ran out of money and food. Reports of widespread hunger emanated from all corners of the nation. In Buffalo, New York, one journalist wrote that 5,000 Polish immigrants were in "imminent danger of starvation." Untold thousands in mining camps, ranching operations, and farms packed up what they could and headed for the nearest city in search of food and shelter, swelling the ranks of homeless people to unprecedented numbers, including as many as 200,000 in Chicago alone.[5] "Men and women, deprived of work," commented New York Governor Roswell P. Flower, "see destitution and misery confronting them. . . . How vast this army of unemployed is nobody can accurately estimate."[6]

It was the latest in a series of economic meltdowns that marked the nineteenth century, including the Panic of 1837, the Panic of 1857, and the Panic of 1873. In each of these economic catastrophes, political leaders agreed that the best policy was: do nothing. They compared depressions to bad weather or illness. Wait long enough, they insisted, and the good times would return. The most irresponsible thing the government could do was provide assistance to the people because, so the logic went, that would only foster dependence and lead the U.S. down the path to socialism. As President Grover Cleveland put it in his second inaugural address, in March 1893, "The lessons of paternalism ought to be unlearned and the better lesson taught that while the people should patriotically and cheerfully support their Government its functions do not include the support of the people."[7]

> Economic collapses in the nineteenth century were called "panics" because they all prompted investors to panic when they learned that businesses, banks, and investment firms had begun to collapse. Many ran to banks to withdraw money or to brokerage firms to sell their stocks only to find that they were too late. In the twentieth century, likely due to the rise of the field of economics, financial downturns were described in more technical terms as recessions or depressions.

Cleveland was beginning his second term in office when the economy collapsed. He was born in Caldwell, New Jersey in 1837, as the fifth of nine children. His father was a Presbyterian minister who later relocated the family to upstate New York. Cleveland's father struggled financially and died when Grover was eighteen, forcing him to leave school to find work. He soon relocated to Buffalo, New York where his uncle helped him get a clerk position at a law firm. He studied law, passed the bar in 1859, and commenced a successful law practice. He served a term as sheriff of Erie County (1871–1873) and later won election as mayor of Buffalo in 1881. He quickly developed a reputation as a fiscal conservative and reformer dedicated to rooting out political corruption. His success helped him win election as governor of New York in 1882 and growing national attention for his fiscal conservatism and anticorruption initiatives.[8]

Just two years later, Cleveland was nominated by the Democratic Party for President of the United States. He won the election, making him the first Democrat to win the presidency since James Buchanan in 1856. As in his previous positions, Cleveland pursued pro-business policies of fiscal conservatism, vetoing legislation he deemed wasteful, corrupt, harmful to business, or fostering among the American people dependency on the government. In 1887, for example, he vetoed a $10,000 appropriation by Congress to provide seeds to farmers in drought-ravaged Texas. "I do not believe that the power and duty of the general government," he wrote, "ought to be extended to the relief of individual suffering." And yet during that same year he signed a bill providing $26 million in subsidized loans for railroads.[9]

Cleveland lost reelection in 1888 to Benjamin Harrison, but four years later he made a stunning comeback, winning the nomination and the election in 1892, becoming the only president to serve non-consecutive terms. He viewed his second term as an opportunity to resume his pro-business approach to governance and accordingly filled most of his cabinet with people who held similar views.[10]

As the economy worsened in the spring of 1893, Cleveland decided that his conservative economic principles allowed for government intervention in one particular realm—federal currency policy. On June 30, he called for a special session of Congress to address the "alarming and extraordinary business situation, involving the welfare and prosperity of all our people." His goal was to repeal the 1890 Silver Purchase Act that required the government to buy 4.5 million ounces of silver per month, thereby restoring the nation's gold reserves and boosting confidence among businessmen and investors. As an added benefit, said Cleveland, it would help the vulnerable wage earner who "relies for work upon the ventures of confident and contented capital." The special session convened August 7 and in short order repealed the Silver Act. Cleveland would soon commence a push for tariff reform.[11]

## Silver vs. Gold

Cleveland's repeal of the 1890 Silver Purchase Act was deeply unpopular with American farmers and others who supported the burgeoning Populist movement and People's Party. They favored the abolition of the gold standard (which tied the value of U.S. currency to the price of gold), arguing it favored the wealthy and banks by keeping the money supply tight and inflation low.

Gold, farmers and Populists contended, was the metal of elites and Wall Street. Silver, on the other hand, was presented as the metal of the common man. Switching to a currency based on the free, or unlimited coinage of silver would benefit debtors (most farmers had mortgages on their farms) by putting more money into circulation, and thus lowering the value of a dollar backed exclusively by gold. In 1896, Democratic Party candidate for President William Jennings Bryan delivered an impassioned speech in favor of silver, declaring to the wealthy and their political allies, "you shall not crucify mankind upon a cross of gold!"

Historically, economic depressions hit labor unions hard, as surging unemployment left many workers unable to pay union dues and employers with leverage to lower wages due to fierce job competition. But in the summer of 1893, as the nation's economy imploded, railroad workers defied this trend and established a new national railroad union. The leading figure behind the founding of the American Railway Union (ARU) was an experienced railroad man and labor activist, Eugene Victor Debs. He was born in 1855 in Terre Haute, Indiana to parents who had immigrated to the United States from France. His father was a successful textile manufacturer and meat retailer, so Debs grew up in a comfortable lower-middle-class home. He left school at age fourteen to take a job as a cleaner of machinery on the Vandalia Railroad, eventually working his way up to the position of painter and car cleaner. In December 1871 he filled in for an absent locomotive fireman and remained in that well-paid position for the next three and a half years.

At the urging of his mother, in 1874 he gave up his job as a locomotive fireman in favor of an accounting clerk position at a large wholesale grocery firm. But Debs maintained a fondness for his former railroad position and his fellow workers, so in February 1875 he joined and became an active member in the trade union, the Brotherhood of Locomotive Firemen (BLF). By day he worked in the grocery business, but at night and on weekends he participated in BLF meetings and functions. In 1877 the members of his local lodge elected him delegate to attend the BLF's national convention. The following year the national membership elected him associate editor of the union's monthly journal, *Locomotive Firemen's Magazine*.

As Debs' rise indicates, people who encountered him found him intelligent, sincere, and engaging. Although his formal schooling ended at age fourteen, he pursued self-education and self-improvement through membership in a local literary society. He also took an interest in local politics, winning election as City Clerk of Terre Haute in 1879 and again in 1881. In 1884 he won election as state representative to the Indiana General Assembly. All the while, Debs remained active in the BLF. He rose to editor of the *Locomotive Firemen's Magazine* in 1880, the same year he was elected the BLF's Grand Secretary and Treasurer.[12]

At this time, railroad brotherhoods like the BLF enjoyed high wages, decent working conditions, and a great deal of pride in their position as highly skilled workers who were valued and respected by the railroads that employed them. As a consequence, these organizations took a conservative approach to labor–employer relations, emphasizing cooperation over confrontation. That was certainly the case with Eugene Debs who had developed a friendship with a leading local businessman and civic figure, William Riley McKean, who owned a large stake in the Vandalia Railroad, the road upon which Debs worked from 1870 to 1874. Debs saw men like McKean not as ruthless capitalists who exploited their employees, but rather as admirable entrepreneurs who respected the men who labored for them. Debs and most brotherhood members shared the view that a railroad worker who failed to get ahead had only themselves to blame and not an abusive employer. They believed failure was due invariably to poor choices and a weakness for alcohol. Hence the railroad brotherhoods' emphasis on the development of personal virtues like hard work, sobriety, thrift, and benevolence as the keys to personal success and upward mobility. As Debs wrote in 1879, "to give our superior officers [employers] trained and intelligent labor, shall be our highest aim. We believe that then they in return will recognize our merits."[13]

This mindset set the railroad brotherhoods apart from many other trades. Unlike many unions of workers in fields like the building trades, mining, and manufacturing, railroad brotherhoods opposed strikes, including most notably the Great Uprising railroad strike of 1877. "The mission of the Brotherhood of Locomotive Fireman is not to antagonize capital," wrote Debs. "Strikes do that; hence we oppose strikes as a remedy for the ills of which labor complains."[14] Debs' BLF operated for fifteen years (1873–1888) before authorizing its first strike.

That dispute, the Burlington Railroad Strike of 1888, marked an important turning point in the history of railroad brotherhoods and in Debs' understanding of labor–capital relations. In the 1880s, as railroads grew larger and more powerful, their owners and directors viewed the powerful brotherhoods as impediments to high profits and as a consequence they took an increasingly hardline position on wages, hours, and conditions on the job. At the same time, the Knights of Labor and its brand of inclusive industrial unionism was growing more powerful and influential among American workers, including some members of the railroad brotherhoods. By the mid-1880s, many held dual memberships in their brotherhoods and the Knights as they became more sympathetic to the latter's call for labor solidarity across different trades and levels of skill. Much of the leadership of the brotherhoods, however, including Debs, remained hostile to the Knights.

Trouble on the Burlington line erupted in February 1888 when representatives of the engineers and firemen brotherhoods submitted a list of demands to the Burlington management, the most important of which was to be paid by the mile as was customary on other competing railroads, rather than by a complicated rate system that resulted in lower pay. When management rejected this demand, the brotherhoods broke with their tradition of comity and called for a strike. The railroad executives responded by recruiting strikebreakers and hiring Pinkertons to intimidate and fend off strikers. The railroad brotherhoods then called upon their brethren employed on regional lines to boycott any Burlington freight cars. Most, however, refused, seriously weakening the position of the strikers. The Burlington management, in a move that would become standard operating procedure in the coming years, requested that a federal judge issue an injunction to force several railroads where the boycott had taken hold to handle Burlington cars. The judge sided with the railroads and within a month the Burlington was running at near full capacity. The strike was all but over at this point, but the brotherhoods kept it going another ten months before admitting defeat in January 1889.[15]

This incident marked a turning point in Debs' thinking about labor–capital relations. Gradually he became convinced that skilled railroad men could no longer rely on individual brotherhoods that shunned less skilled railroad workers and clung to the belief that railroad managers and executives respected them as partners with shared interests. What was needed in this new, more hostile labor-management environment, thought Debs, was a single union for *all* railroad workers, regardless of skill. In January 1889, as the Burlington strike officially ended, Debs officially embraced the industrial unionism of the Knights of Labor, as well as strikes and boycotts as tactics necessary in the struggle for justice.[16]

By then Debs had also observed other disturbing trends that pointed to the imperative for greater worker solidarity. Anti-union sentiment had surged in the mid-1880s, especially in the wake of the Haymarket Bombing in May 1886. Even more alarming, local and state political leaders were increasingly willing to provide business leaders with support during labor disputes, both in the form of court injunctions and intervention by police and state militia.

It was in this context, beginning in 1891, that leaders of several of the railroad brotherhoods began discussing the need for a new labor union that would unite them all against the increasingly hostile railroads. What they had in mind initially was a union of the brotherhoods; that is, a union of organizations representing only elite and skilled railroad workers. These leaders and the organizations they represented had long guarded jealously their independence from each other and expressed only disdain for the struggles of unorganized and low-skilled workers.

Debs became involved in the discussions in the spring of 1892 and began to use his influence to steer them toward a bolder plan: a union of *all* railroad workers. All the railroad brotherhoods combined, Debs noted, would only organize about 25 percent of railroad workers.[17] He urged them to see that over the past five years the railroad owners and executives no longer acted as their "partners," but rather bitter as enemies. This new reality called for a new approach to labor organizing, one that reflected the spirit of the Knights of Labor. Debs proposed forming an American Railway Union that, as an industrial union, would bring together all railroad workers, from skilled engineers and firemen to less-skilled freighthandlers and trackmen, as Debs put it, "into one, compact working force for legislative as well as industrial action." Debs' vision prevailed (although the brotherhoods opted out) and by June 1893 the ARU had a provisional constitution, an executive board, and a president: Eugene V. Debs.[18]

As word of the new union spread across the country, the ARU headquarters in Chicago was flooded with letters from railroad workers seeking information about membership and soon 125 locals had been organized. They were motivated by a growing belief that business leaders, especially those who controlled railroads, sought to exploit and degrade them to a status below that of true republican citizens. Many also were drawn to the ARU as a welcome alternative to the brotherhoods that excluded most railroad workers and spent so much time fighting among themselves.

Additionally, railroad workers sensed that the rapidly declining national economy meant that layoffs and pay cuts were on the horizon.[19]

In late August, 1893 Chicago hosted a "Labor Congress" as part of the World's Columbian Exposition festivities. The list of speakers included reformer Henry George, Populist organizer Mary Elizabeth Lease, and Populist Senator William A. Peffer of Kansas, as well as notable labor leaders like Samuel Gompers and Eugene Debs.[20] "This labor Congress is looked upon with considerable interest," observed the *Ann Arbor Register*, "on account of the great number of unemployed people, and the general situation and depression in labor circles just now."[21]

Debs' address on August 30 was aimed not simply at his fellow workers, but also the business and political establishment. Drawing upon the Bible and symbols of American democracy, he laid out the case that the health and fate of the nation was to be measured by the degree of prosperity and security enjoyed by American workers who created nearly all the wealth. He conceded that while workers had suffered setbacks at the hands of their "enemies"—"entrenched in wealth" with its political connections—they were working toward "their full emancipation."[22]

> The time is coming, fortunately, when we are hearing less of the old paternal pharisaism. "What can we do for labor?". . . [and instead] our ears are regaled by another and a more manly query, an interrogatory permeated with the spirit of liberty and independence, which is, "What can labor do for itself?" The answer is not difficult. Labor can organize, it can unify, it can consolidate its forces. This done, it can demand and command. Such are the possible and the practical things labor can do, is doing, and will continue to do, until constitutions and courts and laws, based upon principles of eternal justice, make no distinction in dealing with the people.

Debs' broader, unspoken message was clear: the labor movement was not inspired by foreign, radical, or dangerous ideas as was alleged by many politicians and business leaders, but rather commonsense American principles. Those leaders who rejected labor's call for fair wages and just treatment were the true source of labor discontent and strikes. "[W]hen labor is honestly paid," Debs concluded, "communities and states feel at once the vivifying influence; consumption keeps pace with production; trade and commerce proceed on lines of security and wide prosperity, and rewards are equitably distributed. To secure these blessings is the paramount purpose of organizations of workingmen."

Eight weeks after the labor conference concluded, the World's Columbian Exposition in Chicago closed on October 30, 1893. The millions of visitors drawn to the Fair had temporarily boosted the city's economic fortunes while the rest of the nation wallowed in the deepening depression. But its closure meant no more revenue from fairgoers and a surge in unemployment as thousands of Fair workers lost their jobs. And as shorter days and cooler temperatures set in during the last weeks of the fall, evidence of worsening unemployment, homelessness, and hunger abounded. "[W]e are sunk under a mass of the unemployed morning, noon, and night," reported Ellen Starr at Hull House.[23] In Pullman, the workforce had been slashed from 5,800 in early 1893, to 2000 by November. Pullman also imposed a sharp reduction in wages upon those still employed.[24] Across the city people begged for money or food on street corners and encampments of homeless people sprang up everywhere, including in the now abandoned buildings of the recently closed White City. The latter situation seemed to embody the great duality of the Gilded Age: what had stood recently as a proud symbol of American prosperity and progress now exemplified poverty and failure. Hundreds were living on the fairgrounds by January 8, 1894 when a fire broke out and began spreading rapidly. Within a few hours several White City structures had been reduced to smoldering ruins.[25]

In the early months of 1894, worker unrest surged across the nation, fueling the anxiety among middle- and upper-class Americans that some form of social revolution was in the offing. On January 23 coal miners in Kanawha Valley, Ohio struck over a cut in their wages. It was a prelude to a much larger strike of coal miners that would begin in April.[26] Two days later, 8,000 potters in Trenton, New Jersey walked out over a reduction in wages.[27] In February and March strikes over wage reductions broke out seemingly everywhere, including gold miners in Cripple Creek, Colorado, textile workers in Lawrence, Massachusetts,[28] ice cutters near Peekskill, New York,[29] silk ribbon weavers in New York City,[30] boilermakers in Elizabeth, New Jersey,[31] freighthandlers in New London, Connecticut,[32] carpenters in Chicago,[33] and printers at three Brooklyn, New York newspapers.[34] In several cities unemployed workers staged large rallies to demand elected officials provide public works jobs.[35]

All of these strikes were local but unrest among coal miners and railroad workers raised the prospect of large strikes spread out over several states and involving tens of thousands of laborers. In March 1894 workers on the Great Northern Railroad received word that their already meager wages would be cut again—the third time since August 1893. This decision would decrease the earnings of the average worker to less than $40 per month—well below the cost of rent, food, and coal.[36]

Many of these workers, especially the less skilled who did not belong to the railroad brotherhoods, had joined the ARU and they wrote to the union for help. Debs dispatched ARU organizer James Hogan to St. Paul, Minnesota to confer with workers. When Great Northern managers learned of Hogan's presence, they fired all known union members. Hogan relayed this information to Debs, along with his assessment that the Great Northern workers were in desperate straits, but also unified and prepared to strike.[37]

At 6:00 a.m. on April 13 the ARU sent a message to the Great Northern Railroad's general manager, C.W. Case, demanding that wages be restored to the rate paid prior to the first cut in August 1893, or the workers would strike at 12:00 noon. When Case rejected the demand, thousands of Great Northern workers left their positions and the railroad ground to a halt. Remarkably, given the long-standing divisions among railroad workers, men of every department and skill level joined the strike. When Debs arrived in St. Paul on April 18 to take charge of the strike, he found great enthusiasm and unity among the strikers. He also heard from the mayors and townspeople who lived along the railroad's route that, despite the disruption to their lives caused by the stoppage, they supported the strike.

The head of the Great Northern was James J. Hill, a hard-charging veteran railroad man known to many as "the Empire Builder." He owed his success to his shrewd and ruthless dealings with fellow railroad titans, Wall Street financiers, and politicians, as well as his unbridled hostility toward unions. Trying to appear reasonable to the public, Hill agreed to meet with Debs and other ARU officials. He offered to send the dispute to an arbitration board that included representatives of the conservative railroad brotherhoods, many of which opposed the strike and the ARU. Debs rejected the offer out of hand, saying he would agree to arbitration but only if it included just one organization representing the workers, the ARU. Hill's next move was to wire the U.S. Attorney General Richard Olney—a man with deep ties to the railroad industry—to draw his attention to the strike which was, according to Hill, orchestrated by outside agitators, "men not in the company's employ." This message was a prelude to Hill's telegram to President Grover Cleveland on April 28 requesting he send in federal troops to break the strike because, he claimed, the work stoppage interfered with the movement of the U.S. mail (it did not).

When Cleveland declined his request, Hill invited Debs to present his case to the Saint Paul Chamber of Commerce, a body of powerful businessmen Hill was confident would side with the Great Northern. But Debs, a talented and persuasive speaker, so impressed Hill's business allies that they insisted the matter be decided by a board of arbitration that did not include the anti-ARU railroad brotherhoods. Both Hill and Debs agreed and after each had made their case, the board ruled in favor of the ARU, granting them a restoration of 97.5 percent of their wage demands. After just eighteen days, Debs and the ARU had won an astonishing victory over one of the more powerful corporations in America.[38]

By then another massive strike was underway involving coal miners in five states. Coal mining had been one of the hardest hit sectors of the economy during the depression. Because so much of the economy ran on coal, everything from locomotives and steamboats to factories and electricity generators, demand for coal plummeted with the downward spiral of the economy. Coal-mine operators responded with wage cuts in 1893 and again in 1894. Seeing so many of its members destitute and hungry, the United Mine Workers union called for a work stoppage on April 21, 1894. The response was overwhelming, as more than 180,000 miners in states from Pennsylvania to Colorado struck.[39] Some mine operators made token adjustments to their wage scales, but most dug in their heels and rebuffed the miners' demands. They also hired more guards and appealed to local sheriffs to create possies of deputized men in order to intimidate strikers and protect strikebreakers. Violence broke out in several locations between strikers and strikebreakers and between strikers and guards and sheriff's deputies.[40] The miners held out for nearly two months, but by mid-June the strike had been crushed.

Despite this surge of labor unrest across the country and the continued increase in the ranks of homeless and hungry Americans in the winter of 1893–1894, public officials and business leaders remained steadfast in their commitment to maintaining a laissez-faire approach to the depression. The wisest policy of the government, they insisted, was to ride out the hard times. But many Americans rejected this response to the crisis. They argued that the federal government (as well as state and local governments) had an obligation to adopt measures to help everyday Americans survive the economic distress. A laissez-faire government might have made sense back in the late-eighteenth century when the United States took form, but it was disastrous in an age of industry, wage work, mass immigration, huge cities, and giant corporations. Government intervention in the form of public works projects and moratoriums on evictions and foreclosures, they asserted, would not lead to socialism. They were merely temporary programs to help people find work that would allow them to feed, clothe, and shelter their families. When the economy recovered, the programs would end.

One person who held that view was Jacob Coxey. He was a successful farmer who also bred horses for sale and owned a sand-quarry business. In the 1880s, he had gotten involved in the burgeoning Populist movement which called for greater federal government intervention in and regulation of the economy to protect the interests of workers and farmers from the depredations of big business.

When the economy collapsed in 1893, Coxey proclaimed that the severity of the depression necessitated the federal government abandon its traditional commitment to laissez-faire and create a massive public works road-building program to provide jobs to the unemployed. Financing for such an unprecedented endeavor would come from $500 million in paper money issued to state and local governments in exchange for non-interest-bearing bonds issued by those governments. This "Good Roads Bill," as Coxey dubbed it, would alleviate mass unemployment, hunger, and homelessness, while also carrying out a long overdue upgrade to the nation's roadway system. "[P]eace and plenty," said Coxey, would "take the place of panic and poverty." To fend off critics who branded his plan socialism, Coxey emphasized that it was a temporary expedient. The moment the national economy recovered the program would wind down and disappear.[41]

To draw attention to this idea, the forty-year-old Coxey did something unprecedented: with the help of a likeminded man named Carl Browne, he organized a march of unemployed workers from his hometown of Massillon, Ohio to Washington, D.C. to demand that Congress take up his plan. To promote the idea, Coxey invested $2,000 of his savings to publish and distribute a pamphlet detailing his scheme and calling upon people to come to Massillon. Coxey hoped to gather 100,000 men for the march, but he had to settle for about one hundred unemployed industrial workers and farmers. He and Browne believed their numbers would swell as people along the march joined the ranks. On Easter Sunday, March 25, 1894, this "petition to Washington with boots on," as Coxey termed it, set off for the nation's capital.

The decision to commence on Easter Sunday was no accident. Coxey and Browne cast the march in religious terms, calling the assemblage the "Commonweal of Christ." They also endeavored to present the marchers as patriotic Americans exercising their right to petition the government. Many, including an African American named Jasper Johnson who walked at the head of the marchers, carried American flags. They also gave their encampments names associated with the American Revolution like Camp Lexington and Camp Washington.[42]

But most journalists covering the march presented it as an absurd venture of what the *New York Times* said were "tramps, cranks, and malcontents."[43] The *Chicago Tribune* ran the headline "The Coxey Crank Movement."[44] Despite numbering only in the hundreds at its height, reporters dubbed the marchers "Coxey's Army" led by "General Coxey."

Journalists also fixated on some of the colorful, eccentric characters that joined the movement. Browne, a man with a long career as an activist, editor, and orator on behalf of labor interests, emerged as a charismatic leader. But reporters fixated on his Buffalo Bill-esque fringed buckskin outfit and large sombrero, as well as his espousal of the principles of Theosophy, a fringe religious movement that emphasized the reincarnation of the soul (what one writer termed "an Oriental anti-Christian faith"[45]). They also played up figures like cowboy Oklahoma Sam, astrologer Cyclone Kirtland, labor and Native American rights activist Honoré Jaxon (who dressed as a Metis Indian), and a mystical figure known only as The Great Unknown, who traveled with his veiled wife and dog Nero.[46]

While many journalists wrote mainly mocking or bemused characterizations of the Coxeyites, others combined derision with suggestions that "the mob" posed a great danger to the republic. Politicians, business leaders, editors, and other public figures raised the alarm. "In spirit and in morals, if not yet in law," declared the *New York Tribune*, 'it is the highest of crimes for any mob in this country to assume to be 'the people.'"[47] Celebrity Gilded Age detective Thomas F. Byrnes of New York denounced Coxey's followers as, "idle, useless, dregs of humanity" whose efforts to intimidate Congress constituted a "movement . . . the most dangerous this country has seen since the Civil War."[48]

Adding to the hysteria was news that other Coxey-inspired "industrial armies" of the unemployed were emerging across the country and heading for Washington, D.C., suggesting a serious threat to order and property. "Eight or ten other contingents from different parts of the country between New York and Seattle," Major General O. O. Howard wrote ominously, "calling themselves companies or divisions of the Industrial Army or the Army of the Commonweal, are to-day marching or bivouacking along the different railroads which intersect our extensive country. There is little variation of allegation of grievance or remedy among them for the ills they suffer."[49] In Los Angeles, Lewis C. Fry and Arthur Vinette led separate contingents, while Charles T. Kelley (San Francisco) and Anna F. Smith (Oakland) led marchers from northern California. Out of the Pacific Northwest came groups headed by S. L. Scheffler (Portland, OR) and Frank T. "Jumbo" Cantwell (Tacoma, WA). In Montana five hundred unemployed miners were led by William Hogan.[50]

The alarmist media coverage soon drew the attention of the Cleveland administration, in particular Attorney General Richard Olney. Born into a wealthy Boston family, Olney enjoyed a childhood of comfort and privilege. Highly intelligent, he excelled at Brown University and Harvard Law School, before starting a long and successful career in the burgeoning field of corporate law, especially that relating to the largest and most powerful corporations in the world, railroads. Olney represented and advised railroads, and served on their boards of directors, including for the New York Central, the Chicago, Burlington & Quincy, and the Atcheson, Topeka and Sante Fe railroads.[51]

In 1893, newly re-elected president Grover Cleveland surprised political observers when he named Olney as his Attorney General. The fifty-eight-year-old Olney had never held political office, nor did he have any history with Cleveland. But the president must have been drawn to Olney's reputation for intelligence, hard work, thick skin, and the dogged protection of corporations and property rights. Olney agreed to accept the position of Attorney General with one condition: he be allowed to continue to represent his railroad clients and receive their fees. Cleveland acceded to this demand, even though the Department of Justice was very likely to become involved in legal disputes involving railroads which would lead to accusations of conflict of interest.[52]

But Olney's first test as Attorney General involved not railroads per se, but rather some of the Coxeyite groups in western states. Unlike Coxey's collection of Commonwealers in the east whose march toward Washington, D.C. was proceeding peacefully, some groups in the west appeared to Olney more desperate and dangerous.[53] The most notorious incident occurred on April 24, 1894 when a group of two hundred men led by William Hogan, most of them unemployed miners but some of them railroad workers, commandeered a Northern Pacific train in Montana to hasten their journey to Washington, D.C. They managed to travel 350 miles, successfully fending off attempts by deputy marshals to seize the train. When Montana's governor wired Washington requesting federal troops, Olney convinced President Cleveland to issue the order. Those troops eventually stopped the train at Forsyth, Montana. Hogan and scores of other men were arrested and sent to the state capital where they stood trial. Convicted of contempt of court for defying a federal injunction, Hogan was sentenced to six months in jail, while the others received shorter sentences.[54]

Sending federal troops to quell a domestic disturbance was rare. The legal justification for doing so against the Coxeyites rested on a technicality: railroads like the Northern Pacific had gone bankrupt at the outset of the economic depression and had come under "receivership" of the federal government (similar to Chapter 11 bankruptcy in our time) that allowed the railroad executives to run the company but under the oversight of a government-appointed receiver, often a federal judge. Because this technically meant the government was the custodian of these railroads, it could use all its powers to stop interference by Coxeyites. Federal judges issued injunctions that required Coxeyites to cease all activity interfering with a particular railroad's trains. Federal marshals and deputy marshals were dispatched to enforce the injunctions and arrest anyone who violated them. When in some instances they proved unable to do so, Attorney General Olney instructed them to wire President Cleveland requesting he send federal troops to restore order. Subsequently federal troops were sent to several locations besides Forsyth, Montana. In cases involving Coxeyite interference with railroads not in receivership, Olney introduced another method of suppression: because the federal government was obligated by the Constitution to ensure delivery of the mail and nearly every train carried U.S. mail, Coxeyites were arrested for "obstructing and retarding the passage of the mails."[55]

Olney's embrace of injunctions in the name of protecting the movement of the U.S. mail laid the legal and political groundwork for his response to the Pullman strike in June and July. Likewise, his success in urging President Cleveland to dispatch federal troops to states to enforce injunctions—often without being requested by state legislatures or governors as stipulated by the Constitution—created the precedent for similar action on a grander scale in the coming Pullman strike.[56]

While Olney tried to contain the Coxey-inspired marchers in the west, Coxey and his followers continued their trek to Washington, D.C. Extensive press coverage ensured that residents of towns all along the route knew when the Commonwealth of Christ would pass through. Thousands of supporters and curiosity seekers traveled long distances to see the rag-tag protest march by. They saw hundreds of men and some women on foot, but also key figures like Browne and The Great Unknown mounted on horses, and Coxey and family in a carriage. Supply wagons featured large cartoons drawn by Browne and banners with slogans like "The Farmer Leads for He Feeds." And to boost spirits and attract attention, a brass band played popular songs.[57]

In many places the Coxeyites were greeted by enthusiastic supporters who offered food, clothing, and encouragement. In Canton, Ohio residents provided dinner and dry hay for bedding.[58] Residents in Columbiana, Ohio collected two storerooms of supplies for the marchers.[59] "They may be wrong," observed one supporter. "They say their scheme is only an experiment. If it succeeds, every laboring man will be benefitted."[60] Debs likewise lauded their campaign:

> Out of work, out of money and without food, ragged, friendless and homeless, these Commonwealers began their march to the capital city of the nation . . . [to] petition Congress to enact

> laws . . . that rekindle the last remaining spark of hope, that their future would be relieved of some of the horrors of hunger and nakedness.[61]

In other places, acting on media-driven fears that Coxey and his followers were dangerous radicals who sought to overthrow society, local law enforcement met the marchers at the outskirts of some towns and forbade them to linger or set up camp. In Allegheny City, Pennsylvania, Coxeyites were allowed to stay, but local police refused to allow them to leave their encampment to receive supplies from locals. They arrested sixty-eight men who tried.[62] Coxey countered the claims that the Commonwealers represented a threat to the nation by arguing that theirs was a campaign to *save* the republic and honest capitalism from the clutches of corporate trusts, banks, and the politicians they controlled.

Nonetheless, fears of violence and revolution mounted as they approached the capital. "The intention is to mob Congress into the issuing of millions of bonds to be used in giving employment to people who do not care to work," declared the *New York Commercial*. "The mob, if sufficiently strong and infuriated, may conclude to sack the Capital."[63] "PREPARING FOR AN EMERGENCY" proclaimed a *New York Times* front-page headline. "Washington's Protective Force Largely Increased—White House Guarded." Hundreds of extra police were put on duty and U.S. Marines at the Washington Naval Yard conducted riot drills.[64]

Despite the hyperbolic headlines and a massive presence of police and federal soldiers deployed by panicked government officials, Coxey's Army of about 400 peacefully paraded into Washington, D.C. on May 1, 1894. As Coxey approached the U.S. Capitol where he intended to deliver a speech calling upon Congress to act to save the people, police on foot and horse attacked the crowd, clubbing people indiscriminately and arresting several. In the mayhem Coxey attempted to mount the steps of the Capitol, but was seized by police.[65] As he was being led away, Coxey handed his speech to a journalist in the hopes that it would be published. Several newspapers did publish it and a sympathetic member of Congress read it into the *Congressional Record*. It was an impassioned plea for federal lawmakers to cease doing the bidding of monopolists and financiers and to attend to the many needs of the people they ostensibly represent.

> We stand here to-day in behalf of millions of toilers whose petitions have been buried in committee rooms, whose prayers have been unresponded to, and whose opportunities for honest,

remunerative, productive labor have been taken from them by unjust legislation, which protects idlers, speculators, and gamblers: we come to remind the Congress here assembled of the declaration of a United States Senator, "that for a quarter of a century the rich have been growing richer, the poor poorer, and that by the close of the present century the middle class will have disappeared as the struggle for existence becomes fierce and relentless."

Fifty years to the day from when he was arrested and jailed in Washington, D.C., Jacob Coxey returned to deliver his speech on the steps of the U.S. Capitol. Much had changed in the nation since 1894 and his ideas about public works projects to provide work and income to unemployed Americans had been enacted on a massive scale during the Great Depression in the 1930s. Most Americans no longer viewed Coxey's ideas as radical or dangerous and he gave the speech with the official blessing of Congress.

In the end, Coxey was fined $5 for illegally walking on the Capitol grass. He also was sentenced to twenty days in jail for carrying partisan banners on Capitol grounds.[66] Upon his release Coxey returned to Massillon, Ohio a hero and then went on a fundraising speaking tour. Many of his followers remained in Washington into the summer, occasionally staging protest marches. Their numbers swelled as sympathizers and other Coxey-inspired protest marches arrived. But when donations of food, clothing, and cash dried up, they began to leave for home. By early fall Coxey's army was no more.[67]

As the nation followed the alarmist coverage of Coxey's arrival in Washington, D.C. and the ongoing coal-miner strike, a new crisis was emerging in the town of Pullman. In January 1894 Pullman had imposed another wage cut, the third in the past year.[68] Men in the car building shop who had been earning $2.65–2.80 per day in 1893, now earned just $1.25 per day. Women seamstresses who were making $2.25 per day in 1893 now earned $.70–$.80 per day.[69] All the while, George Pullman refused to lower rents, or the fees townspeople paid for water and gas. To circumvent a state law prohibiting the company from deducting these fees directly from workers' paychecks, Pullman issued workers two checks on payday, one for the amount owed in rent and fees and another for whatever was left over. Workers were pressured to sign over the first check to the Pullman company on the spot. Some refused, but those who acceded walked away with only a dollar or two, including workers with large families to feed.[70]

In March Pullman workers wrote to the ARU seeking help and advice. They were eligible to join the ARU because the Pullman Company operated a small railroad around its shops to send new cars off to buyers and bring in older cars for repairs. By the ARU's capacious definition, this meant they qualified as railroad employees. Debs sent George Howard, the ARU vice-president, to Pullman to assess the situation and encourage workers to join the union. Both Debs and Howard wanted to avoid a strike, fearing that neither the ARU nor the Pullman employees possessed enough resources to win.

Enthusiasm for the ARU ran high, especially when workers learned of the great victory earned by Debs and the ARU over the Great Northern Railroad on May 1. Many wondered, if the ARU could defeat a man so powerful and ruthless as James J. Hill, could it not help them do the same against George Pullman? By early May, a sizeable majority of the Pullman Company's workers had joined the ARU as members of nineteen locals.[71]

Emboldened by this surge in membership and compelled by their worsening circumstances, they formed a grievance committee of forty-one men and five women to call upon Thomas H. Wickes, second vice-president of the Pullman Company. On Monday May 7, dressed in their Sunday-best attire to emphasize their respectability and seriousness, the forty-six committee members and ARU vice-president Howard arrived at the imposing Pullman office building on Michigan Avenue in downtown Chicago.[72]

Wickes had long enjoyed a good reputation among Pullman company workers.[73] The forty-nine-year-old executive had been born in England and he struck those he encountered as smart, educated, dignified, and friendly. A Pullman Company employee for twenty-six years, he acted as George Pullman's right-hand man.[74] He received the delegation of workers with respect and an apparent willingness to hear them out.[75]

The committee's spokesman, a fifty-eight-year-old car-builder named Thomas W. Heathcoate,[76] opened by stating their demand that wages be restored to the level paid in May 1893, before the cuts were imposed. Workers' pay had been slashed to such a degree over the past year that many struggled to feed their families. Pullman, they insisted, must raise wages by one-third and offer double time for work performed on Sundays.[77]

Wickes listened politely and then responded in a tone that implied both sympathy and resolute firmness. It was impossible to raise wages, he said, because the car-manufacturing unit was losing money due to the economic downturn. It actually made economic sense for the company to close the factory, but Pullman benevolently kept it open, he claimed, to keep the workers employed. Restoring wages to the May 1893 level was out of the question. To do so would impose unacceptable financial losses on the company, including, for example, a $20,000 loss on a recent contract to build cars for the Long Island Rail Road. The Pullman Company was also losing money on $4 million worth of cars standing idle due to the depression in the yards, depreciating in value with every passing day.[78]

Heathcoate challenged Wickes' claim that keeping the plant open benefited Pullman workers. Had the company closed the works they could have found employment elsewhere, moved out of Pullman, and secured cheaper housing. At present, said Heathcoate, he was feeding his family on just eight cents per meal and they could not afford new clothing.[79]

Wickes responded that the Pullman Company was not responsible for these hard economic times. And yet, he continued, even though Pullman residents owed some $70,000 in back rent, the company refrained from pressing anyone to pay and carried out no evictions. Several committee members then spoke up to say they had been pressed by the company to pay up, citing the example of one man who succumbed to pressure on pay day to sign over the check to cover his rent and fees, leaving him to feed a family of eight on the remaining two dollars.

If the company would not raise wages, the workers asked, would it lower rents? No, replied Wickes, it was "utterly impossible to lower rent one penny," because the Pullman Company was only receiving a paltry 3 percent return on its real-estate investment. Wickes said he was "sorry . . . but powerless" to meet their demands.[80]

Acknowledging the impasse, Heathcote shifted the conversation to another grievance: many foremen in the shops were abusive and tyrannical and manager Harvey Middleton did nothing to stop them. Wickes replied that it was not in the interest of the Pullman Company to employ abusive foremen, but he would investigate these charges. He asked the committee to write up their complaints against the foremen and bring them to him in two days. With this small measure of progress, the meeting concluded with many workers feeling hopeful and Howard relieved that they seemingly had averted a strike.[81]

Two days later, on Wednesday May 9, the committee again traveled to the Pullman Building to speak with Wickes. Also in the meeting with Wickes were manager Harvey Middleton and several Pullman executives. Over the next two hours, Heathcote and the other committee representatives spelled out their grievances regarding shop foremen and supervisors, detailing numerous specific incidents of abusive language, threats of violence, incompetence, and withholding piece-rate prices until a job was nearly completed. Wickes took copious notes and when asked if any workers would face retaliation by the company for membership in the ARU and service on the grievance committee, he said no.[82]

Then in a bit of carefully stage-managed drama, George Pullman suddenly appeared. The intent of this stunt seemed to be to intimidate the workers, while at the same time convince them that Mr. Pullman cared deeply about them and their welfare. Reading from a prepared statement, Pullman said he was sorry about the hard times, but claimed he was doing everything in his power to provide work for them. All the recent contracts he signed for new cars were at a loss to the company. Cars built for the Northwestern Railroad, for example, cost $12 per car over the price paid. Cars built for the Lake Street Elevated Railroad cost $79 more. Raising wages was impossible.[83]

As for rents, here Pullman deployed a convenient fiction: the real-estate business of renting homes in the town, he claimed, was utterly separate from the business of manufacturing and repairing of railroad cars. There was no direct relationship between wages paid and rents charged. He could not lower rents in his separate real-estate business to compensate for wage rates paid in his manufacturing operations. Besides, the latter was doing poorly, earning only a 3.82 percent return on its investment (versus a desired 6 percent) in the town. "It will be readily understood," said Pullman, echoing the claims of Wickes, "that there is no room for reduction under these circumstances." For good measure he added that Pullman residents should appreciate the fact that they did not have to pay for street cleaning or garbage removal. If they wanted, they could inspect the company's books to see for themselves the financial constraints he was up against. Their wellbeing was his top priority because he thought of them as his "children." But in closing, the paternal Pullman struck an ominous tone, warning them to think twice about calling a strike, implying that he would play hardball and they would regret it. His ultimatum was clear: get back to work at the current wage rate or find employment elsewhere.[84]

Just before the meeting broke up, George Howard asked Pullman if he would promise, as had Wickes, that no one on the grievance committee would face any reprisals by the company. Pullman assured him that there would be none. At 6:00 PM the committee members headed back to Kensington, the town adjacent to Pullman where it was safe to hold a union meeting. A capacity crowd of ARU members filled Turner Hall to receive an update on the meeting in Chicago. Howard said they received a full hearing from Wickes and Pullman and that they now had to wait while the company conducted its promised investigation into the abuses they described. "You may have to be a little patient for a while," he said, noting that it was not a good time for a strike. "My advice is to go back to the shops tomorrow."[85]

The next day the *Inter-Ocean* ran a story under the headline "Strike Is Averted," while a similar story in the *Tribune* was headed "Pullman is Serene."[86] Pullman employees showed up at 6:30 AM like any other day and commenced working. But soon word began to circulate throughout the works that three members of the grievance committee had been sent home after having been told that there was no work for them that day or for the foreseeable future. Most workers concluded that Pullman and Wickes had gone back on their word and had the men fired. The workers remained at their posts, but their mood steadily darkened as the day wore on.

That evening the grievance committee met at the Dew Drop Tavern in Kensington. Many workers said the apparent firing of the three grievance committee members was the last straw. They should strike, even if they stood no chance of winning. But Howard urged calm and said that Debs wanted them to be patient and not act rashly. They should wait for the results of the company's investigation into their complaints. Ignoring this plea, the committee took a vote on a resolution to strike. It passed by a margin of forty-two to four. More debate and another vote ensued into the early hours of the morning. A third vote was unanimous in favor of a strike. But before any walkout occurred, the members of the grievance committee were instructed to report to work where they could poll the workers in the various Pullman shops they represented on the question of striking.[87]

On the morning of Friday, May 11, the day at the Pullman Palace Car Company works began as any other. Workers filed in, took up their positions and tools, and got to work. But the atmosphere in the shops that morning was filled with tension and apprehension. Word of the unanimous strike vote taken just a few hours earlier had spread throughout the factory complex. So too had many rumors, including one that George Pullman planned to preempt a strike by, as Carnegie had done two years prior in Homestead, summarily closing the works at noon and locking out the workers.

Then it happened. At 10:30 AM word spread throughout the Pullman complex: We strike! Very deliberately, workers put their tools away, turned off machinery, and walked out. Out on Florence Avenue, where a growing throng of strikers gathered, men and women who had begun their day anxious and subdued, now beamed and talked excitedly with each other. Occasionally the air was punctuated with cheers sent up when specific groups of workers emerged. An especially loud one greeted Jennie Curtis and 400 women primarily from the upholstery and laundry shops. After weeks of talking about a strike they had finally done it. A spirit of solidarity and collective purpose swelled as the crowd grew. By midday, 2,500 workers were out, with only 600 remaining at their posts, a good many of them managers, foremen, and clerks. One of them emerged to hang a sign on the front gate that read: "These shops will be closed until further notice"[88]

That evening at Turner Hall in Kensington, workers established a Strike Committee with representatives from all the ARU locals at the Pullman Company. Thomas Heathcoate was selected as chairman. Heathcoate then addressed the assemblage, stating the workers' demands for wages to be restored to the May 1893 rate and for relief from abusive foremen. Knowing reporters were present, he cited specific figures concerning reduced wages, noting for example, that woodworkers who made $2.50 in 1893 now made $2.00, while painters had seen their wages cut from $2.75 to $2.00. When rent and fees for water and gas were deducted, workers were left with so little money they could only spend eight cents per meal per person in their families. "All we ask is sufficient wages to live on," said Heathcoate.

**_Figure 3.1_ "The Condition of the Laboring Man at Pullman" (_Chicago Labor,_ July 7, 1894). While many Americans opposed Debs and the ARU for launching a strike that triggered railroad tie-ups and incidents of violence and vandalism, many also condemned George Pullman for abusing his workers and refusing to negotiate with them.**

But the strike was not solely about wages. It was also about dignity and self-respect. They would stand up for themselves even if it meant fighting a losing battle:

> We do not expect the company to concede our demands. We do not know what the outcome will be, and in fact we do not care much. We do know we are working for lower wages than will maintain ourselves and families and the necessities of life. And on that proposition we absolutely refuse to work any longer.

Heathcoate concluded by urging the workers to stay away from the Pullman works and to break no laws.[89]

Theodore Rhodie, president of the Painters' Union, then addressed the crowd. Pullman and Wickes, he said, could not be trusted. Their pledge to fully investigate the grievances laid out by the committee was a sham. So, too, was their claim that the company was taking contracts at a financial loss. Pullman had made similar claims in the past to stymie requests for higher wages. Rhodie called upon the workers to stay away from the Pullman works because they would be fighting the company "from a distance," relying upon fellow ARU members refusing to handle Pullman cars. This was the first mention of the "boycott" that would commence six weeks later.[90]

ARU vice-president George Howard then stepped forward. It was absolutely crucial, he said, that the strikers conduct themselves peacefully. If they allowed themselves to be goaded into clashing with strikebreakers, the police, or thugs hired by the Pullman Company to stir up trouble, the strike would be doomed. His words reflected an awareness that labor–capital conflict in recent years had shown that employers could call upon the state to smash strikes, all while enjoying newspaper coverage that denounced strikers and unions. All they needed was a pretext. "If you violate any law," said Howard, "the police will have a right to call in the Sheriffs and if they are not enough the militia will be brought and that means defeat." Howard also urged the strikers to avoid drinking alcohol as it might cloud their judgment and lead to rash actions. "[K]eep sober and straight, and every laboring man in the country will be with you."[91]

Howard also commented on Pullman's arrogance. He told the workers that he had spoken with him the day before and Pullman had laughed about the possibility of a strike, claiming the workers grievances "didn't amount to anything." Pullman also reminded him that the workers owed him $70,000 in back rent. "If that is so," asked Howard of the strikers, "how long will it be before he owns you soul and body?" Pullman, he said, was out of touch. He had not done an honest day's work in many years and had no experience with privation or exploitation. If Pullman had done as he promised and come down to the works to talk face-to-face with his employees, the strike would have been avoided.[92]

The meeting adjourned and workers headed out into the night for their homes. They knew they faced a long, hard struggle against a wealthy, powerful, and stubborn George Pullman and that even if they could hold out for weeks or months, they still might lose the strike and their jobs. That had been the grim fate of the workers in Homestead, Pennsylvania who less than two years prior had taken on the mighty Andrew Carnegie and lost everything. But the Pullman workers had one major advantage over Carnegie's employees: they were members of a large, powerful, and, lately, spectacularly successful union, the ARU.

Over the next few days, the strike committee set up various subcommittees and began making decisions. It established a daily 9:00 AM meeting open to all to hear reports from various subcommittees charged with mediation, raising money, distributing food, and communicating with other unions. They also discussed the progress of the strike and voted on key policy decisions. To emphasize the law-abiding nature of the strike, the committee posted patrols of three hundred strikers around the Pullman works to protect it from vandals or "toughs from the city," as Heathcoate put it. Likewise emphasizing their peaceful intentions, union representatives emphasized that these patrols would not prevent replacement workers from entering the works. They maintained this round-the-clock vigil—even as George Pullman falsely claimed it was a picket line—until federal soldiers sent to break the strike arrived on July 4.[93]

This emphasis on peace and lawfulness was a crucial part of their strategy. They were keenly aware that winning—and maintaining—public sympathy was critical to winning the strike. Any acts of violence or vandalism, they knew, would be seized upon by the city's many daily newspapers that consistently expressed hostility towards unions and strikes. As one member of the strike committee put it when warning workers about speaking to reporters, "The papers are all in the employ of Pullman."[94]

Equally aware of the need to present a positive image before the public, George Pullman invited reporters to his home on the evening of the first day of the strike. He presented himself as the wronged party, the father figure who, despite all he has done for them, found himself falsely accused of abuse by his children. News of the strike, said Pullman, came as "a most unpleasant surprise," one that "pained me, for I have taken a great interest in keeping the men employed." Now that the factory was closed, he was "exceedingly anxious for the welfare of the men."

Other Pullman officials were on hand and they repeated the claim that they had offered to let the employees examine the company books to prove that they were operating at a financial loss in order to provide them with jobs. They also said they had been conducting a thorough investigation into the allegations of abusive behavior by managers and foremen when the workers walked out. Plant manager Harvey Middleton, the man accused by the grievance committee of ignoring workers' complaints about abusive foremen, dismissed the alleged cause of the strike. The laying off of the three members of the grievance committee, he said, had been due to a scarcity of work, not union activity. The three workers were lying about their dismissal. Another official on hand, E. F. Bryant, cashier of the Pullman Loan and Savings Bank, challenged the workers' claims that their wages were inadequate to cover rent and food. He said Pullman workers had saved $677,000 before the economic downturn which caused the savings to drop to $473,000 by January 1, 1894. But since that time, he claimed, savings had started to rise, indicating that workers' fortunes were improving and "that if they had not struck they were on the road to prosperity." Just as Pullman had hoped, the next day the city's main newspapers gave substantial space to the company's version of events.[95]

Such coverage was not surprising. Newspapers in this era depended on advertising revenue from other businesses for a large percentage of their profits. Accordingly, in most cases their coverage of labor–capital conflict consistently promoted a pro-business and anti-union position. But because newspapers also relied on working-class and middle-class readers to purchase their product, they often framed their critique of strikes in such a way that expressed sympathy with workers' complaints about low wages, long hours, and abusive bosses, while also declaring strikes ill-advised, short-sighted, and harmful to workers' interests and the wellbeing of their families. The *Chicago Record*, for example, deemed the strike "a grave mistake" and chided the strikers that it, "is not themselves alone they have to consider. Their wives and their children are, of course, the first objects of their care."[96] The *Tribune* ran an editorial on May 16 under the headline "Wild Demands of the Pullman Men." Frequently, they softened their critique of the workers by saying they were "led astray" by "outsiders" by which they meant labor activists. In the case of the Pullman strike, this suggestion referred to ARU leaders like Debs and Howard who were not Pullman employees. Only the *Chicago Times* expressed support for both the workers and their decision to strike.[97]

Pullman likewise enjoyed the public support of ministers and priests who said much the same thing as the newspaper editors, expressing sympathy for workers but condemning the strike as misguided. On Sunday May 13, just two days into the strike, Rev. E. C. Oggel presided over a service in the Pullman-owned Greenstone Church in which he chastised the strikers for their rash action. "Strikes in nine cases out of ten injure the employee far more than the employer." It was, he claimed, "precipitated by outsiders" before the grievance investigation had been concluded. He would rejoice to see wages raised and rents reduced but, he said invoking the language of immutable economic "laws" popularized by industrialists and economists, "this is not a matter of sentiment but of business." Given the hard economic times, he said, it was impossible for Pullman to raise wages or cut rents. "There is no industrial community in the world where men can do better than here." Those who are dissatisfied are free to leave and take their chances elsewhere.[98]

Of prime concern to the strike committee was the prospect of hunger and eviction in Pullman. Given their reduced wages, many residents had been battling hunger long before the strike. Many workers routinely skipped meals, causing some to collapse at their work stations. Even so, deeply engrained notions of shame and self-recrimination associated with poverty regardless of its cause led many Pullman workers to resist offers of food relief. "[T]hey are proud," noted the *Tribune*, ". . . and many of them are enduring pangs of hunger rather than let their condition be known." To overcome this shame, the Relief Committee sent canvassers out into the community to ascertain people's true needs and then—after swearing confidentiality—made arrangements to provide relief.[99]

Lacking a strike fund, they appealed to the community for help and the response was remarkable. Between mid-May and mid-July, the people of Chicago donated $15,000 to aid the Pullman strikers.[100] This included donations of $909.75 from some Chicago firemen, $50 from a Swedish singing society, $100 from a Kensington saloonkeeper, and $50 from Knights of Labor Lodge No. 8246.[101] Many business owners sent food, including a freight car of flour from the Siegel-Cooper department store and 300 pounds of meat from a group of South Chicago merchants. Baker W. H. Briggs, who operated a bakery in Pullman, sent hundreds of loaves of bread. Another merchant offered the use of a storeroom to serve as a relief distribution center.[102]

The most high-profile contributor was the city's mayor, John Patrick Hopkins. A successful merchant with strong sympathy for wage earners and a potent dislike for George Pullman (in 1888 Hopkins was a highly regarded employee at Pullman when he was fired for his support for the Democratic Party), he donated $1500 in food and supplies, including 2,500 pounds of flour and 2,000 pounds of meat, along with $100 in cash. He also urged the people of Chicago to donate whatever they could. Donations also came in from unions and other sympathetic groups across the country.[103]

ARU President Eugene Debs arrived in Chicago on Monday, May 14. He had been riding high after the victory over the Great Northern Railroad on May 1. But news of the strike at Pullman just ten days later alarmed him, and he immediately set off for Chicago. His concern stemmed not from any doubts about the justice of the Pullman workers' grievances, but rather from the weakness of their position. A strike called by workers with few resources against a mighty and ruthless capitalist like George Pullman was likely to fail. Debs was also concerned that the strike posed a grave danger to the ARU. He knew from reports from Howard that the workers at Pullman hoped the ARU would endorse the strike and order its 150,000 members across the country to refuse to handle Pullman cars. Such a move would wreak havoc on the nation's railroad network and likely bring a legal and possibly military response from the federal government.

To protect the ARU, Debs expressed support for the strikers, highlighted their grievances, and denounced George Pullman, while fending off questions about ARU officially joining the conflict. He visited Pullman to interview workers and their families and to witness their poverty and hunger. The experience convinced him fully that they were a cruelly exploited workforce that had been pushed to the brink by a greedy and unscrupulous employer. The dispute was partly about wages, but also about defending their rights as free republican citizens. In his first speech on May 14 he noted that as a general rule he was against strikes, "but when the only alternative to a strike is a sacrifice of rights, then I prefer a strike. There are times when it becomes necessary for a man to assert his manhood."[104]

Two days later Debs delivered another address to a large crowd where he lambasted Pullman as a man who posed as a philanthropist while plotting to enslave his workforce. "I believe a rich plunderer like Pullman is a greater felon than a poor thief," said Debs, noting that one of the goals of the ARU was "to strip the mask of hypocrisy from the pretended philanthropist and show him to the world as an oppressor of labor." Pullman deserved none of the accolades he had received for his model town. "The paternalism of the Pullman," declared Debs, "is the same as the interest of a slaveholder in his human chattels. You are striking to avert slavery and degradation."[105]

For his part, George Pullman's strategy was to ignore the accusations of Debs and the strikers while downplaying the significance of the work stoppage. He also refused to negotiate with the strikers or their ARU representatives claiming, in what became his mantra over the next two months, there was "nothing to arbitrate." He knew time and the company's vast cash reserves were on his side. The last two decades of labor–capital conflict had shown that there were limits to how long workers could hold out, especially if a company succeeded in hiring replacement workers. Time would also allow Pullman to work behind the scenes to rally the nation's major railroads to his support, since they all wanted to destroy the ARU. When Pullman or other company officials were asked about the strike, they brushed it off as "unfortunate" but not something that threatened the vitality of the corporation. When asked about the need to fulfill existing contracts for orders, one manager said, "the strike will not affect us. For all of them [contracts] have strike clauses in them." Wickes voiced a similar lack of alarm. "The loss will fall heaviest on the men. It will not inconvenience the company to have the shops idle at this time."[106]

The sound financial health of the company was revealed four days into the strike when it announced that it had paid a 2 percent quarterly dividend to its shareholders amounting to $720,000. How could the company pay out such a sum, people asked, when it claimed to be operating at a loss?[107] Company officials responded that the company as a whole was very profitable, but the car-manufacturing division was losing money. To the strikers this explanation was a convenient accounting fiction. Pullman's claims that he could not raise wages due to financial losses were only plausible if one pretended there was a wall separating the manufacturing division from the repair and service divisions, as well as the revenue stream from the fees charged the railroads.[108]

Despite the efforts of the relief committee, hunger remained a serious problem in Pullman. A *Tribune* reporter toured the town on May 16 and presented case after case of destitution, debt, and hunger. John Granowski, a cabinetmaker at Pullman, lived in a two-room tenement with his wife and two young children. They had no food in the house. His income for the previous year amounted to only $75, a sum that did not cover the $7.60 he owed each month for rent, let alone expenses for food, clothing, and medicine. The Miller family living in the same building offered a similar portrait of suffering. Through tears Mrs. Miller explained that there was "nothing to eat in the house, [and that] many a time last winter they had all gone to bed hungry and got up with nothing to eat." Mr. Miller, also a cabinetmaker, earned only about $5.00 per month, leaving him unable to pay the $9.10 monthly rent. "I do not want to live this way any longer," said Mrs. Miller. "Sometimes I think I will take the children and jump into the lake."[109]

By the last week of May the relief committee reported that it was nearly out of food to distribute to the strikers. In an act of solidarity and community support, representatives of the Chicago Trade and Labor Assembly and the Chicago Building Trades Council met on May 27 to devise a plan for providing relief for the Pullman strikers. Thomas Heathcote spoke defiantly to the gathering. "We intend to stay out until the American Railway Union is ruined or George M. Pullman is a pauper." Heathcoate also spoke to the suffering caused by the strike, saying, "Our wives and children are starving, yet they have been our staunchest supporters in the fight." This last point was an explicit rejection of the claims by the Pullman Company and the newspapers that the workers had irresponsibly imperiled their families by striking.[110] The Chicago Trade and Labor Assembly responded by issuing an appeal to the people of Chicago that included a scathing rebuke of George Pullman:

> The people of Pullman are destitute and starving. Over 5000 human beings are in dire necessity and appeal to the liberal-minded people of Chicago for help. Their unfortunate condition is not due to any fault of theirs. They have been noted for their thrift, sobriety, and industry. The fault lies in the hard times and a hard task master. Forced for years to work on starvation wages so that dividends could be paid on watered stock, they have at last struck against a soulless corporation which sought to fatten on the very marrow of their bones. They struck against slavery worse than that of the negroes of the South. . . . the slaves of Pullman . . . could not earn enough to clothe and feed themselves decently—hardly enough to keep body and soul together. Now that they have struck for living wages, for a fair day's pay for a fair day's work, they find themselves penniless with gaunt famine and despair staring them in the face. . . . Their cause is the cause of humanity. Their struggle is the struggle of honest industry against corporate greed.[111]

The Assembly created a committee of seven to solicit donations from unions and union workers.[112] Additional revenue came from about two hundred Pullman employees who had left the city and found work elsewhere. They sent half their pay to their families and half to the relief committee.[113] On June 4 the relief committee received word that the Board of Cook County had voted to send them $500.[114] These funds were welcome, but inadequate to meet the growing need. On the same day of the Cook County vote, the *Tribune* published another dire account of the strikers and their families. Despite 1,000 families receiving aid, "Squalor and sickness reign in the tenements of Pullman." Outbreaks of malaria and other forms of sickness, many exacerbated by malnutrition, kept the sick committee working non-stop.[115] On June 6 a group of strikers sought permission to start fishing in Lake Calumet to ease their hunger.[116]

As they struggled to survive, the Pullman strikers likewise grappled with the question of the strike's likely outcome. On the one hand, there was cause for pessimism. The strike was now four weeks old and George Pullman remained as obstinate as ever. He seemed impervious to criticism for, as the Trade and Labor Assembly put it, "his heartless treatment of his employees whom he starved into striking and with whom he now refuses to arbitrate."[117] Pullman even rejected a plea on June 1 from the Chicago Civic Federation—a body comprised of prominent business leaders, public officials, and reformers—to agree to arbitration.[118] It was evident that Pullman's plan was to starve the strikers into submission while simultaneously hiring replacement workers.[119] And there were rumors that he had gone to Washington, D.C. to confer with the heads of several large railroads to form an alliance against the ARU.[120]

And yet there were developments that for strikers raised hopes of success. For one, to date the strike had remained peaceful and no workers had been arrested. Likewise, the strikers' spirits were buoyed by the support they received from the people of Chicago and elsewhere in the nation. Additionally, some evidence appeared that suggested the Pullman Company was struggling. George Howard told a large gathering on June 7 that he had received a communication from an ARU official in St. Paul who said the Pullman Company had just sent a carload of wheels to be repaired to the railroad shop of the Chicago, Milwaukee, and St. Paul railroad. Howard told his listeners that this meant the company was getting desperate.[121]

On Saturday June 9, Mayor Hopkins, with the blessing of the City Council, issued a proclamation asking the citizens of Chicago to donate money, food, and clothing to assist the struggling people in Pullman.[122] That same day 2,000 strikers and their families gathered behind a marching band outside Turner Hall in Kensington and began parading toward Gardener Park for a massive picnic. The event was intended as a fundraiser for the strike relief fund, as well as a much-needed day of joy and fun. There was ample food, plus sporting events and dancing in the evening. In total some 6,000 people turned out and the event raised $1,500. "We are as solid as a Stonewall," said Heathcoate reflecting the optimistic mood. "We never had so much food in our lives."[123]

Another source of optimism was an awareness that in just three days, on June 12, the first-ever national conference of the American Railway Union would convene in Chicago. Hundreds of delegates from locals all across the country would gather to discuss and vote on all manner of union business. But everyone knew that one question loomed above all others: would the ARU membership vote to support the striking Pullman workers by "boycotting" or refusing to handle any Pullman cars attached to trains from Boston to Sacramento? Such a move would cause turmoil on the nation's rail system which might force George Pullman to the negotiating table. Or it might trigger a repressive response from the federal government. The fate of not just the Pullman strike, but possibly the ARU itself would ride on that vote.

## NOTES

1 Jack Kelly, *The Edge of Anarchy: The Railroad Barons, the Gilded Age, and the Greatest Labor Uprising in America* (New York: St. Martin's Press, 2019), 12–14.
2 Nick Salvatore, *Eugene V. Debs: Citizen and Socialist* (Urbana, IL: University of Illinois Press, 1982), 114.
3 *New York Times*, July 29, 1893, 8.
4 Douglas Steeples and David O. Whitten, *Democracy in Desperation: The Depression of 1893* (Westport, CT: Praeger, 1998), 46, 51–53.
5 Sidney L. Harris, "Class Conflict and the Suppression of Tramps in Buffalo, 1892–1894," *Law and Society Review*, vol. 11, no. 5 (Summer, 1977), 897.
6 Roswell P. Flower, speech at the State Fair, Syracuse, NY, September 16, 1893, Public Papers of Roswell P. Flower, Governor, vol. 2 1893 (Albany, Argus, 1894), 351. Cited in Benjamin F. Alexander, *Coxey's Army: Popular Protest in the Gilded Age* (Baltimore, MD: Johns Hopkins University Press, 2015), 37.
7 Grover Cleveland, Second Inaugural Address, March 4, 1893.
8 Troy Senik, *A Man of Iron: The Turbulent Life and Improbable Presidency of Grover Cleveland* (New York: Threshold Editions, 2022), 1–73.
9 Kelly, 115–116; Jack Beatty, *Age of Betrayal: The Triumph of Money in America, 1865–1900* (New York: Knopf, 2007), 194–195.
10 Senik, 220–222.
11 Grover Cleveland, Special Session Message, August 8, 1893 https://millercenter.org/the-presidency/presidential-speeches/august-8-1893-special-session-message; Senik, 222–232.
12 Ray Ginger, *The Bending Cross: A Biography of Eugene Victor Debs* (New York: Russell & Russell, 1949), 3–34.
13 Salvatore, 13–18, 30.
14 Eugene V. Debs, "The Mission of the Brotherhood," *Locomotive Firemen's Magazine*, May 1884, 8; quoted in Salvatore, 49.
15 Salvatore, 72–79; Ginger, 55–58.
16 Salvatore, 79–80; USSC, 152–153.
17 Salvatore, 115.
18 Salvatore, 115; Almont Lindsey, *The Pullman Strike: The Story of a Unique Experiment and of a Great Labor Upheaval* (Chicago: University of Chicago Press, 1942), 109–10.
19 Lindsey, 110–114.
20 *Chicago Tribune*, August 29, 1893, 8;
21 *Ann Arbor Register*, August 31, 1893 source: https://aadl.org/node/525387
22 Eugene V. Debs, "The Organization of Working Men: Speech to the Chicago World's Fair Labor Congress," August 30, 1893. https://www.marxists.org/archive/debs/works/1893/930830-debs-organizationofworkingmen.pdf

23 Kelly, 91.
24 *Chicago Inter-Ocean*, May 10, 1894, 1.
25 *Chicago Tribune*, January 9, 1894, 1.
26 *New York Times*, January 24, 1894, 11.
27 *New York Times*, January 25, 1894, 3.
28 *New York Times*, February 13, 1894, 1.
29 *New York Times*, February 18, 1894, 2.
30 *New York Times*, February 16, 1894, 1.
31 *New York Times*, March 1, 1894, 3.
32 *New York Times*, March 16, 1894, 6.
33 *Chicago Tribune*, February 21, 1894, 5.
34 *New York Times*, April 1, 1894, 16.
35 *Chicago Tribune*, February 21, 1894, 5.
36 USSC, 134; Salvatore, 119; Ginger, 102–107.
37 Eugene V. Debs, *Eugene Debs: His Life, Writings and Speeches* (Honolulu, HI: University Press of the Pacific, 2002), 8; Salvatore, 120.
38 Salvatore, 119–123; Kelly 22–26.
39 *New York Times*, April 22, 1894, 1.
40 W. T. Stead, "Incidents of Labor War in America," *The Contemporary Review*, vol. LXVI, no. 1, July 1894, 65–74.
41 Alexander, 3–4, 45
42 Alexander, 46–47.
43 *New York Times*, March 26, 1894, 1.
44 *Chicago Tribune*, April 2, 1894, 6. See also *Chicago Tribune*, March 28, 1894, 1; March 26, 1894, 1; April 8, 1894, 29; April 22, 1894, 36.
45 O. O. Howard, "The Menace of 'Coxeyism'," *The North American* Review, vol. 158, no. 451 (June 1894), 688.
46 *Chicago Tribune*, March 26, 1894, 1.
47 *New York Tribune*, May 7, 1894 quoted in O. O. Howard, "The Menace of 'Coxeyism'," *The North American Review*, vol. 158, no. 451 (June 1894), 687–705.
48 O. O. Howard, 687–705. See also Toledo *Blade* quoted in *Chicago Tribune*, April 5, 1894, 6.
49 O. O. Howard, 692.
50 Alexander, 76–96.
51 Gerald G. Eggert, *Richard Olney: Evolution of a Statesman* (University Park, PA: Penn State University Press, 1974), 1–32.
52 Lindsey, 148–49; Eggert, 47–51.
53 *Chicago Tribune*, May 20, 1894, 5.
54 Alexander, 87–92.
55 Lindsey, 13–14.
56 Eggert, 115–132.
57 Alexander, 47.
58 Alexander, 52.
59 *Chicago Tribune*, March 30, 1894, 7.
60 Kelly, 28
61 Lindsey, 13; Eugene V. Debs, President's Keynote Address to the 1st National Convention of the American Railway Union: Ulrich's Hall, Chicago, June 12, 1894, 7.

62 *Chicago Tribune*, April 6, 1894, 5.
63 *New York Commercial*, quoted in *Chicago Tribune*, April 23, 1894, 3
64 *New York Times*, April 28, 1894, 1
65 *New York Times*, May 2, 1894, 1–2.
66 *New York Times*, May 22, 1894, 1.
67 Alexander, 97–116.
68 USSC, 434.
69 USSC, 434, 436, 458.
70 USSC, 426.
71 Salvatore 127, USSC, 6, 129–130, 432.
72 Kelly, 63, *Chicago Tribune*, May 8, 1894, 8.
73 USSC, 7; Buder, 155.
74 USSC, 570.
75 *Chicago Inter-Ocean*, May 8, 1894, 7.
76 USSC, 416.
77 USSC, 423; *Chicago Tribune*, May 8, 1894, 8.
78 *Chicago Inter-Ocean*, May 8, 1894, 7; *Chicago Tribune*, May 8, 1894, 8.
79 *Chicago Tribune*, May 8, 1894, 8.
80 USSC, 417, 419, 423, 435; *Chicago Tribune*, May 8, 1894, 8.
81 USSC, 445.
82 *Chicago Tribune*, May, 10, 1894, 1; *Chicago Inter-Ocean*, May 10, 1894, 1.
83 *Chicago Inter-Ocean*, May 10, 1894, 1.
84 *Chicago Inter-Ocean*, May 10, 1894, 1.
85 Kelly, 79; "Report of a Meeting Held under the Auspices of the American Railway Union," Newberry Library, 8, 10.
86 *Chicago Inter-Ocean*, May 10, 1894, 1.
87 Buder, 157.
88 USSC, 586; *Chicago Tribune*, May 12, 1894, 1.
89 *Chicago Inter-Ocean*, May 12, 1894, 2.
90 *Chicago Tribune*, May 12, 1894 1; USSC, 436.
91 *Chicago Tribune*, May 12, 1894 1; *Chicago Inter-Ocean*, May 12, 1894, 2.
92 *Chicago Tribune*, May 12, 1894 1.
93 *Chicago Tribune*, May 13, 1894, 6 and May 14, 1894, 1; USSC, 586; Lindsey, 123.
94 *Chicago Tribune*, May 13, 1894, 6.
95 *Chicago Tribune*, May 12, 1894 1, 6; *Chicago Inter-Ocean*, May 12, 1894, 2.
96 *Chicago Record*, May 12, 1894, 4, May 18, 1894, 4. [Cited in in Lindsey, 125.]
97 *Chicago Tribune*, May 16, 1894, 6.
98 *Chicago Tribune*, May 14, 1894, 1.
99 *Chicago Tribune*, May 14, 1894, 1; May 17, 1894, 8; June 4, 1894, 1.
100 Lindsey, 125; Cawardine, 41–44; *Chicago Times* May 28, 1894, 2; June 1, 1894, 1; June 15, 1894, 2.
101 Kelly, 89, *Chicago Inter-Ocean*, June 21, 1894, 8; *Chicago Tribune*, May 17, 1894, 8; June 5, 1894, 8.
102 *Chicago Tribune* May 17, 1894, 8
103 Kelly, 89.
104 *Chicago Tribune*, May 15, 1894, 8.
105 Lindsey, 124.
106 *Chicago Tribune*, May 12, 1894, 6 and May 16, 1894, 7.

107 USSC 424.
108 *Chicago Tribune*, May 16, 1894, 7.
109 *Chicago Tribune*, May 17, 1894, 8
110 *Chicago Tribune*, May 28, 1894, 2.
111 *Chicago Inter-Ocean*, May 29, 1894, 7. See also reports of hunger in Chicago *Tribune* June 1, 1894, 2.
112 *Chicago Tribune*, June 3, 1894, 11.
113 *Chicago Tribune*, June 4, 1894, 1.
114 *Chicago Tribune*, June 5, 1894, 8.
115 *Chicago Tribune*, June 4, 1894, 1.
116 *Chicago Tribune*, June 6, 1894, 3.
117 *Chicago Tribune*, June 4, 1894, 2.
118 USSC, 459–460, 590.
119 *Chicago Tribune*, June 9, 1894, 4.
120 *Chicago Tribune*, June 8, 1894, 7.
121 *Chicago Tribune*, June 8, 1894, 7.
122 *Chicago Tribune*, June 10, 1894, 6.
123 *Chicago Tribune*, June 9, 1894, 4 and June 10, 1894, 6.

CHAPTER 4

# To Battle Such an Extended Evil

On Tuesday, June 12, 1894 the American Railway Union convened its first national convention. The choice of Chicago made sense from a logistical standpoint, as it was one of the great centers of the American railway system. But it also possessed tremendous symbolic value, as it was the home of the ongoing Pullman strike, a labor dispute that was gaining national attention and raising fears that it might escalate into a major tie-up of the railroads. The question of the hour was: Would the ARU, as was rumored, call upon its members to boycott Pullman cars in support of the Pullman strikers?

More than four hundred delegates representing 150,000 members of 415 locals nationwide gathered in Chicago's Uhlich Hall. ARU president, Eugene Debs, welcomed them with a stirring keynote address. He began by extolling the establishment of their union just one year earlier as a new kind of union, "an order with new formulas, new policies, new purposes, and new shibboleths." Whereas previous railroad unions and brotherhoods had proved "dismal failures," the ARU was strong and growing rapidly. Open to all railroad workers, it was garnering members from the "thousands of railway employees . . . who were left out in the cold [by the exclusive brotherhoods] to endure the pitiless storms of corporate power."[1]

Debs tempered these enthusiastic claims by sounding a note of caution. The economy had been buffeted by "cyclonic disturbances [that] fall with crushing force upon labor." Corporate power remained unchecked. As a consequence, the ARU had been designed "like a modern battleship." When conditions were good, it was content to sit peacefully at anchor enjoying "peace and prosperity." But the ARU was "built for war" and was always ready to engage the enemy in defense of its membership. Previous railroad unions and brotherhoods were not constructed for battle and thus were always sunk when confronted by "a corporation battleship."

DOI: 10.4324/9781003388784-5

Debs also spoke in flowery terms laced with references to scripture and literature. "The men who resist tyranny in labor affairs are fighting the battles of workingmen now and in all future time." In like manner he extolled the ongoing valiant march of the Coxeyites and harshly criticized Congress for refusing to listen to their grievances. "Oh, my fellow workingmen, there must be no slavery in this land of 'the star spangled banner.'"

When he turned to the matter of the Pullman strike, Debs pulled no punches. George Pullman, he said, was in league with the devil, working together "to rob and degrade working men and women." He was "greedy as a horse leech" and had "a soul so small that a million of them could dance on the little end of a hornet's stinger." Pullman had pushed his employees to the point of desperation and so they walked out, knowing full well the hardships that awaited. The Pullman Strike, said Debs, "is a terrible illustration of corporate greed, and heartlessness, and pharisaical fraud for which years has prevailed in this country."

> The many references to slavery by labor leaders like Debs was quite common in the Gilded Age. They came of age in the North in the Civil War era when slavery was denounced as incompatible with American notions of freedom and democracy. Claiming American workers were in danger of being reduced to slavery by unscrupulous employers became an irresistible form of hyperbole for speakers defending unions, strikes, and pro-labor laws.

Debs concluded on an upbeat note, "A phenomenal success, so far, has attended [these] efforts. The strides of the American Railway Union have been gigantic. It is rapidly encompassing the great republic from ocean to ocean."

For the rest of that first day and the next two, ARU delegates undertook the business of transforming their prototype organization established a year before by a small group of activists led by Debs into a formal organization where every feature was approved by the body of delegates. One committee was tasked with drafting a permanent constitution that set forth the union's structure, offices, and procedures. Other committees were established to work on finances, legislative outreach, resolutions, and the union's life insurance benefits. Delegates also approved a proposal for the ARU to formally affiliate with the Knights of Labor.[2]

While Debs and the delegates undertook this business, a committee of striking Pullman workers worked on an appeal to the ARU that they intended to present to the body on Friday, June 15, 1894. They recognized the extraordinary opportunity presented by having the ARU convention in Chicago. Their strike against the Pullman Company was now more than a month old with no sign of a resolution in sight. George Pullman intended to starve them into submission. Their only hope was for the ARU to join the conflict by instructing its members across the nation to boycott all Pullman cars. The ensuing sharp decline in his company's revenue, they believed, would bring George Pullman to accept arbitration.

On Friday, June 15, 1894, ARU delegates spent the morning working on committees and hearing reports. At 11:30 AM, the convention transformed into a committee of the whole and welcomed a delegation of striking Pullman workers. Everyone present knew that this was potentially a big moment in the ongoing struggle. Debs opened this session with a speech in which he lambasted Pullman as a "monumental monster, a pirate on the high seas of labor, and a robber who has robbed, starved, and oppressed men, women, and children for years." The time and come to stand up to him and it would be "a fight to the finish."[3]

The appeal presented by the strikers opened with an emotional entreaty for support.

> We struck at Pullman because we were without hope. We joined the American Railway Union because it gave us a glimmer of hope. Twenty-thousand souls, men, women, and little ones, have their eyes turned toward this convention to-day, straining eagerly through the dark despondency for a glimmer of the heaven-sent message you alone can give us on this earth.[4]

That hoped-for message, of course, was a declaration of a boycott on Pullman cars.

The appeal then presented a detailed summary of their grievances against the Pullman company, including multiple reductions in "our miserable wages" with no corresponding reduction in high rents and extortionate rates for water and gas. They were being exploited "to make a millionaire a billionaire." They rejected Pullman's claim that the wage reductions were necessary to keep the company solvent, pointing out that it recently paid out hundreds of thousands of dollars in dividends to its stockholders. The strikers likewise challenged his claim that he had taken on railroad car construction contracts at a loss in order to help out his workers, noting that it was cheaper for him to keep his shops open at a small loss than to close them and lose his skilled workforce which he would need when good economic times returned. To counter Pullman's assertion that his workers were the best paid in the country, the strikers included detailed tables on wages that showed Pullman paid well below his competitors and businesses employing people for similar work. They also related the "abuse and tyranny" they suffered from foremen and forewomen who lorded their power over them. Their situation was desperate. The only reason the strikers and their families were not starving was due to the generosity and sympathy of the people of Chicago, while George Pullman "is patiently seated beside his millions waiting for what? To see us starve."[5]

Their appeal also situated their struggle as emblematic of the wider Gilded Age struggle of American workers to escape exploitation and degradation from greedy employers. "Pullman, both the man and the town, is an ulcer on the body politic." The fight for justice at Pullman was a fight for all workers and for the future of the nation.[6] If Pullman's "merciless, soulless, grasping corporation" triumphed, it will embolden other industrialists to pursue similar tactics:

> Know this, brother delegates, is what the Pullman system will bring us all to if this situation is not faced fairly and squarely in the American way, for Americans, by the American Railway Union. It is victory or death. And so to you we confide our cause. Do not desert us as you hope not to be deserted . . . Every man of you, every honest heart among you, every willing hand stands ready. You know you can; will you?[7]

Some of the ARU delegates had in the past few days toured the town of Pullman and spoken with strikers about their treatment at the hands of the company and the hardships they were enduring on account of the strike. Now all had the opportunity to hear them speak. One worker, the father of four, described his struggle to provide for his family. "[W]hen a man is sober and steady, and has a saving wife . . . and after working for two and a half years for a company he finds himself in debt for a common living, something must be wrong." Another lamented the extraordinary power the company held over its workers. "We are born in a Pullman house, fed from the Pullman shops, taught in the Pullman school, catechized in the Pullman Church, and when we die we shall go to the Pullman Hell."[8]

The most stirring words came from nineteen-year-old Jennie Curtis. A seamstress, she described the grueling work she and the other women in the shop performed to produce the opulent upholstery, drapes, tapestries, and carpeting for Pullman sleeper cars. Despite their hard work and quality output, Pullman cut their wages repeatedly. Even more affecting was her story about the Pullman Company's response to the death of her father, a company employee for thirteen years. The company demanded that she pay $60 in back rent owed by her father. She had tried, she explained, to satisfy this debt with a $3 payment each month. Given her starvation wages, she struggled. "Many a time I have drawn nine and ten dollars for two weeks' work, paid seven dollars for my board and given the Company the remaining two or three dollars on the rent." On those occasions when her pay was so low she could not afford the three dollars, "I would receive slurs and insults from the clerks in the bank." Curtis closed by echoing the conclusion of the strikers' appeal: "We ask you to come along with us because we are not just fighting for ourselves, but for decent conditions for workers everywhere."[9]

The strikers' appeal and speeches before the convention stirred sympathy and anger among the assembled delegates. A motion was put forward that the ARU declare a boycott against Pullman cars. Debs urged caution and suggested the convention form a committee to call upon vice-president Wickes to inquire about arbitration. That same afternoon, at 4 PM, this committee comprised of six members of the Pullman strike committee, including Jennie Curtis, and six delegates from the ARU convention, met with Wickes. They asked him to restore wages to the 1893 rate before the reductions, to which he responded that he would entertain no propositions put forth by representatives of the ARU. They then asked, "Will you arbitrate?" and Wickes replied with what by now had become the company's stock response, "We have nothing to arbitrate." Would he be willing to meet tomorrow with a delegation comprised only of striking Pullman workers? Yes, he replied, but only as individuals and not as members of the ARU. With that, the committee left.[10]

The next day, Saturday June 16, 1894, a committee of six members of the Pullman strike committee arrived at the Pullman building in Chicago. They were hopeful that the absence of ARU delegates, plus word that Wickes had communicated with Mr. Pullman since their last meeting, would yield a more positive outcome. The company vice-president quickly disabused them of that notion. When they asked if he would arbitrate the question of raising wages, he repeated that there was "nothing to arbitrate." When they pressed him on restoring wages to the 1893 rate, he snapped that they had no right to even ask that question, as they were all ex-Pullman employees on account of their strike. They stood in "the same position as the man on the sidewalk."[11]

When the committee reported Wickes' haughty and obstreperous response to the convention, delegates were incensed. Both Howard and Debs grew concerned that this justifiable anger would lead the convention to vote to declare a boycott on the Pullman company. While they understood this anger, they also appreciated the great risk such a declaration would create for the ARU. Certainly it had enjoyed a very successful first year in existence, especially its victory over the Great Northern Railroad, and its membership numbers were soaring. But it was still a young organization with very few resources. A boycott would not merely entail a struggle with the powerful Pullman Company, but also the many large and formidable railroads that attached its sleeper and dining cars to their trains. Additionally, they had to consider public opinion. At the moment there was widespread public sympathy for the Pullman strikers and scorn for George Pullman for his obstinate refusal to agree to arbitration. But there was no telling how the public would respond to a boycott if it led to snarled railroad traffic and economic hardship.

Howard spoke to the convention and urged caution. The delegates needed to wire their locals to update them on the Pullman situation and solicit their sentiments on how to proceed, including whether or not to announce a boycott. Only then could the convention consider a vote on a boycott. "Let us play as Mr. Pullman plays," Howard advised, "reserving our best cards." Soon thereafter, the convention adjourned until Monday morning.[12]

On Monday June 18 delegates took up the contentious question of whether or not to admit African-American railroad workers to the ARU. It arose during the process of finalizing the wording of the organization's permanent constitution. The preamble to the original document declared that any railroad worker "born to white parents" was eligible for membership in the union. One delegate rose to propose that these four words be struck, thereby opening membership up to Blacks. According to a journalist present, a "great uproar" ensued, leading to a raucous debate. Debs came out strongly in favor of admitting African-Americans. Given the virulent racism at the time, he phrased his support carefully. "I am not here to advocate association with the negro," he said, clarifying that he did not advocate social equality between the races. But he did call for solidarity among railroad workers regardless of race. "I am ready to stand side-by-side with him, take his hand in mine, and help him whenever it is in my power." He also urged delegates to view the question in practical terms, arguing that exclusion "will be used against us" by employers using non-union Black workers as strikebreakers.[13]

But Debs' position faced fierce opposition. One delegate opposed Black membership, declaring Black railroad workers lowered wages and were used as strikebreakers. Another from Colorado claimed that the ARU would lose 5,000 white members in the west if Blacks were admitted. On and on it went for eight hours until it was decided to defer action on a vote. The next day, ARU delegates voted to maintain their exclusion of Black workers.[14]

By then hundreds of telegrams had poured in from ARU locals across the country, most of them expressing strong support for, as one put it, "an aggressive action" against the Pullman Company.[15] To buy a little more time, Debs established a committee of five to formulate "a suitable line of action" for the union.[16] Delegates also approved a measure advocated by Howard to send ARU organizers to Pullman facilities in St. Louis, Missouri and Ludlow, Kentucky. These were profitable operations, so a work stoppage would inflict financial pain on the Pullman Company, perhaps enough to convince George Pullman to relent and agree to arbitration.[17]

On Friday, June 22, while delegates awaited the report from the committee of five, they responded to reports that the Pullman strikers were nearly out of relief supplies by voting to donate $2,000 to the cause and to impose a monthly fee of ten cents per member to provide continued support.[18] Then came the much-anticipated report from the committee which turned out to be a succinct, two-sentence recommendation to the convention. "Unless the Pullman Palace Car Company does adjust the grievances before 12 o'clock on Tuesday, June 26, 1894, the members of the American Railway Union shall refuse to handle Pullman cars and equipment." Additionally, it recommended that a strike be declared immediately at Pullman shops in St. Louis and Ludlow. The convention approved the recommendation "amid wild shouts of applause" and then dispatched a committee of three to deliver the ultimatum personally to Thomas Wickes who met them but "flatly refused to enter upon any negotiation." The committee returned to the convention where they were greeted with loud cheers.[19]

When asked by reporters if he was worried about a potential boycott, Wickes said he was not. The Pullman Company, he said, was blameless in this conflict. Besides, the boycott "is not a matter that concerns us" as the company built cars and did not operate railroads. The vice-president went further, saying he doubted railroad workers would initiate a "disturbance" when jobs were scarce.[20] Railroad executives echoed Wickes' lack of concern, saying they doubted their employees would risk their jobs to support the Pullman strikers. "They have not forgotten their experience in the Burlington strike," said one executive in a thinly veiled threat, ". . . The men let out then never got [their jobs] back, and those who took their places are not going to repeat the experience."[21]

Little of note occurred in the days following the issuing of the ARU's ultimatum. On Saturday June 23, Debs brought the ARU convention to a close with a final speech that implored delegates to return to their locals as "missionaries" in the cause of labor. That afternoon, the ARU sponsored a picnic in Burlington Park to raise money for and provide a welcome distraction to striking Pullman workers and their families. On Sunday Chicago was quiet, but anxiety over the looming boycott deadline was on the rise. The anti-labor *Tribune* predicted that if the ARU boycott received support from other railroad unions it would "breed serious complications, eventuate in ruinous strikes and possibly in widespread disorder."[22]

The next morning, unbeknownst to anyone but a handful of railroad executives, a crucial emergency meeting that would have a direct bearing on the outcome of the Pullman strike took place in the Rookery building in the city's financial district. In attendance were general managers of the twenty-six major railroads headquartered in or with significant ties to Chicago. They were members of the General Managers Association (GMA), a body founded in 1886 ostensibly, in its words, to address "problems of management arising from the operation of railroads." Behind these bland, bureaucratic words lay the real goal: to collectively develop a unified strategy against labor unions and to establish a system for keeping wages uniformly low across the industry. Despite its rabid anti-unionism, the GMA was, in effect, a "union" every bit as much as the ARU. The one key difference was that the GMA possessed staggering financial and political resources with which to combat the fledgling ARU. The member railroads comprised $818 million in capital and owned 40,000 miles of rail. Their directors had direct access to the most powerful politicians in the nation. Its goal was not simply to defeat the boycott, but rather to utterly destroy the ARU.[23]

Out of this first meeting the GMA issued a resolution. Without specifically mentioning the Pullman Strike it denounced the impending ARU boycott as "unjustifiable and unwarranted." The railroads were not involved in the Pullman Strike. The purpose of the boycott, the managers claimed, was to inconvenience the public and financially harm the railroads in the hope that this would somehow put pressure on the Pullman Company to settle the dispute. The railroads and only the railroads, they declared, will determine what cars they will handle or not handle. Railroad employees must not, out of sympathy for "supposed wrongs" against Pullman employees, take actions that would harm the railroads and inconvenience passengers. The resolution closed with a firm declaration by the railroads to resist the boycott "in the interest of their existing contracts, and for the benefit of the traveling public."[24]

One person in attendance at the GMA meeting was Thomas Wickes of the Pullman Company. He would later claim—in an effort to fend off accusations of collusion between the company and the GMA—that he simply observed the proceedings and did not participate. Both Wickes and Pullman later admitted that they communicated with GMA officials during the boycott, but only "casually." The truth of these claims is impossible to ascertain. But there is no denying that the GMA was pursuing a course of action that aligned perfectly with the desires of Wickes and Pullman.[25]

The next morning, June 26, even though the ARU's deadline was 12 noon, the city of Chicago woke up to identical headlines in the *Tribune* and *Inter Ocean*: "BOYCOTT IS ON TODAY."[26] Given each side's seemingly inflexible positions, no one was surprised when the deadline came and went. But concerning questions hung in the air. Would railroad employees refuse to handle Pullman cars? Would this action cause delays and tie-ups on the railroads? Would George Pullman succumb to the pressure? Would violence break out?

Initially it looked as though there was no boycott in effect. All afternoon trains left Chicago with Pullman cars attached. It turned out that most of these trains, in an effort by railroad officials to thwart the boycott for at least one day, had been assembled prior to the deadline. This included the "Diamond Special" of the Illinois Central Railroad, an all-Pullman car train that ran between Chicago and St. Louis. Just prior to its scheduled departure at 9:00 PM, George Pullman and several Illinois Central officials arrived at the 12th Street Station to witness the train's departure. When the train departed on time and without incident, Pullman and the other men were relieved to see that the boycott seemed "ineffective."[27]

Trouble, in fact, already had started just a few miles away where a gate-tender refused to open a gate for an Illinois Central train to pass. Less than ten minutes into its run, the Diamond Special slowed to a halt, joining several other Illinois Central trains. A large crowd of people sympathetic to the strikers gathered to support the stoppage. Eventually, after more than one hundred Chicago policemen arrived, the station agent opened the gate and trains began to move on to their destinations. The next morning, however, Central Illinois officials discovered that their switchmen were on site, but refusing to handle Pullman cars. When the railroad fired the men, some 4,000 employees walked off the job in protest, greatly hampering operations at the Illinois Central.[28]

These events played out precisely as Debs had hoped. A few days prior, Debs had described to the press how the boycott was likely to unfold. "The trouble will probably begin with the switchmen," he predicted. "We expect the first to refuse to switch a Pullman car will be either laid off or discharged." As soon as any attempt was made to replace the men, said Debs, "every member of the union employed on that road will quit." Similar versions of this scenario played out on the Chicago & North Western, Chicago Burlington & Quincy, and Atchison Topeka and Sante Fe railroads. By June 28 these lines had between 1,000 and 3,000 employees on strike. "If the railroad companies insist on handling Pullman cars," said ARU secretary Sylvester Keliher, "they will be tied up."[29]

These scenarios of the boycott leading to workers being fired and then many more workers striking out of sympathy explains why this event is known to history as the Pullman Strike, as opposed to the Pullman Boycott. While some initial accounts published in the immediate aftermath of the strike used the phrase Pullman Boycott, most participants at the time spoke of it as a strike. When asked about the competing terms by the U.S. Strike Commission, Debs said he preferred to call it a strike rather than a boycott because the latter had a more negative reputation among the general public.[30]

As the strike began to spread, rail traffic in and out of Chicago began to snarl. And because the American railway system formed an intricate web of rails that depended on precise scheduling and timely arrivals and departures, the effects of Chicago's disturbances soon were felt throughout the nation.

In response to the strike, the GMA moved quickly to enact a battle plan. On June 27 it named a special manager to head up the organization's campaign against the boycott and the ARU. John M. Egan was an experienced railroad executive, having served until recently as general manager of the Chicago Great Western railroad. No longer in that position, he was free to devote his time and attention to the task at hand.

At the Rookery building he quickly established a command center, bringing in telegraph and telephone lines and personnel to operate them twenty-four hours a day. "We mean business," Egan told the press. He wired member railroads instructing them to fire any men who defied orders. He later issued a follow-up directive declaring that these fired railroad workers would be permanently barred from employment in the industry and that their replacements would keep their jobs for life. To find such replacements, Egan set up hiring centers in eastern cities. "There are thousands of idle men now in the country," he said, "who know more or less about railroading." To entice workers, the GMA paid their transit, food, and housing costs until they were placed in a job. Some 2,500 replacement workers were hired through this initiative.[31]

Egan also established an intelligence-gathering network to record any episodes of violence or vandalism, stoppage of trains, intimidation of employees, or menacing crowds. He passed these reports on to the Chicago police, the Cook County sheriff, the U.S. Marshal posted in the city, and later the military. Egan also hired detectives and spies to infiltrate the ARU and send reports to GMA headquarters. To cultivate media coverage that was favorable to the GMA and critical of the ARU, Egan also established a press bureau.[32]

Just a few blocks away, Debs likewise hunkered down in the ARU headquarters. Chief among his efforts was responding to innumerable telegrams from sympathetic railroad unions and groups of unaffiliated railroad workers asking for instructions if and when they should strike. Debs laid out several conditions. Only a local could call a strike; the ARU had no power to order a walkout. A strike was called for if a railroad insisted on attaching Pullman cars to their trains and if it fired any workers for refusing to handle said cars. A local should only call a strike if its leadership was certain a majority of the membership would support it. But it was crucial, warned Debs, that strikers confine their protest to supporting the Pullman strikers and not use it as an opportunity to pursue redress of their particular grievances like wage cuts with their railroad management. "When it is won," he counseled, "restoration of wages will be an easy matter."[33]

Aware of the bad publicity produced by disruptions to passengers and halts in freight traffic, Debs also issued guidelines. Railroad workers should avoid stopping trains with passengers. And they should not interfere with trains already assembled, even if they included Pullmans.[34]

In the first few days of the boycott, despite the tough talk by Egan and GMA, as well as the relentlessly anti-labor coverage by the local and national papers, Debs and the ARU had reason to be optimistic. By June 28, the second full day of the boycott, some 18,000 railroad workers had struck or were fired and the numbers were growing by the hour.[35] Hundreds of these men also joined the ARU. Encouraging telegrams poured into the ARU headquarters from union leaders across the country. Debs was thrilled and more than a little surprised at how many railroad workers had joined the boycott or struck in sympathy. These included many who belonged to the conservative railroad brotherhoods, organizations that had declined Deb's request on June 26 to join the boycott.[36] For example, some four hundred brakemen, switchmen, and engineers on the Chicago Great Western railroad, the line run by the GMA's John Egan up until May, refused to handle trains carrying Pullman cars.[37] Offsetting the rejection by the brotherhoods was the enthusiastic endorsement by the Knights of Labor which, despite its greatly diminished membership from its peak in 1886, still wielded influence in the national labor movement. On June 27 its head, James Sovereign, issued a call to all Knights to lend assistance to the ARU in its "fight against plutocratic enslavement." A few days later he sent instructions to all Knights locals to convene meetings with members to discuss ways of assisting the boycott.[38]

By June 29, the number of strikers had soared to more than 100,000, on its way to an eventual total of 250,000. Most of the work stoppages occurred in the Midwest and West, where the ARU enjoyed far greater popularity as compared to the East where the conservative railroad brotherhoods still held sway. Of significance, scores of Pullman workers struck at two very profitable company shops in St. Louis and Ludlow. If they maintained their strike, it might put significant pressure on the company to agree to arbitration. In the West, an official of the Northern Pacific railroad reported that "not a wheel is turning" on the entire road, while another dispatch reported the Atchison Topeka and Sante Fe railroad likewise had ground to a halt. Debs also received word that striking engineers had halted all movement on the Southern Pacific line in Oakland, California and had refused an offer of a $1,000 bonus and lifetime employment as an inducement to return to work. In some locations strikers had convinced some replacement workers to quit, some of whom subsequently joined the ARU.[39]

Also joining the strike were 4,500 railroad workers of the Chicago, Rock Island, and Pacific Railroad, the line whose general manager was Everett St. John, the man serving as Chairman of the GMA. They had walked off the job on June 29 after Debs and other strike leaders spoke to them at Blue Island, a small town along the line just outside of Chicago. These workers represented one-third of the railroad's total workforce and their absence prompted the Rock Island to suspend service into Chicago.[40]

One development that concerned Debs was the rapid increase in the number of crowd actions in Chicago and surrounding towns and cities. On Friday June 29, a large crowd of men, women, and children stopped suburban commuter trains on the Illinois Central line at Chicago's Grand Crossing. They detached the locomotives and drove them into a nearby railyard. Others spiked switches to ensure the trains could not move. Likewise, the Diamond Special was unable to depart due to strikers tampering with switches and signals, as well as either persuading or intimidating towermen from taking up their positions. Crowds also shut down the movement of trains in and out of the city's massive Union Stock Yard, preventing the arrival of livestock and the departure of slaughtered meat. Several lines reported cars damaged by rocks thrown from overpasses.[41]

Outside Chicago, twenty-three miles away in Riverdale, a crowd stopped a train running on the Panhandle line and detached several Pullman cars. The train departed, but then was halted by a railroad official who insisted it would not leave without the Pullman cars. After several hours, the Pullmans were reattached and the train made its way to Chicago. A similar scene played out in nearby Hammond, Indiana, an industrial city on Chicago's southern border. But in this case the Pullmans were not reattached and the train was held in the station overnight.

Likewise, railroad workers and sympathizers in more distant localities such as Terre Haute, Indiana; Pueblo, Colorado; Albuquerque, New Mexico; Minneapolis, Minnesota; Jamestown, North Dakota; and Dubuque, Iowa managed to stop trains and tie up railroad traffic.[42]

These kinds of crowd actions that involved strikers, but also men, women, and children not employed by the railroads, were quite common in Gilded Age labor disputes. Whole communities often mobilized during strikes as an act of solidarity and support for those on strike. Many of the participants faced similar struggles with low wages and long hours, and so they turned out in force to support their friends, family members, and neighbors. Crowds were also often motivated by a shared sense of anger and resentment against powerful businesses and their exploitative policies. This was especially true of railroads, the largest corporations in the nation that were operated by stupendously wealthy men like Vanderbilt, Stanford, and Gould, who were frequently involved in corruption scandals involving public officials and Wall Street malfeasance.[43]

Some reports of crowds stopping trains included allegations that strikers had used threats of violence against workers who opposed the strike and boycott to convince them to leave their posts. Others claimed that some of these workers had been beaten by strikers. But overall, the amount of property damage and violence was minor. Both Mayor Hopkins and Police Superintendent Michael Brennan attested that most of the vandalism and violence was fairly minor and the situation was under control. The Sheriff of Cook County had dispatched several hundred deputies to areas experiencing unrest, but said the state militia was not needed at this point.[44]

While these incidents indicated widespread solidarity among railroad workers, including many not formally affiliated with the ARU, and their communities, Debs recognized that they also had the potential to undermine the ARU strike. He understood that victory over the Great Northern railroad back in May was due in large part to the peaceful behavior of the workers. If violence and vandalism escalated, the GMA and the anti-labor press would frame it in hysterical terms, castigating the ARU as a violent, radical organization bent on using force to achieve its diabolical ends.

To counter such claims—and to dissuade railroad workers from engaging in violence—Debs issued on June 29 a general appeal. "The struggle with the Pullman Company," he began, "has developed into a contest between the producing classes and the money power of the country." Pullman workers struck because the "heartless" Pullman corporation denied them "a just proportion of the proceeds of their labor." The ARU resolved to support them by refusing to handle any Pullman cars until the dispute was settled. Then the GMA "came to the rescue" of George Pullman to support him "in his devilish work of starving his employees to death." The nation's railroad workers, said Debs, must take a stand against these corporations that seek to reduce them "to a condition scarcely removed above chattel slavery . . . The great principle of American manhood and independence is involved."

Debs then shifted his focus to the conduct of the boycott and strikes:

> I appeal to the striking men everywhere to refrain from any act of violence. Let there be no interference with the affairs of the several [railroad] companies involved, and above all, let there be no act of depredation. A man who will destroy property or violate law is an enemy and not a friend of labor. The great public is with us and we need only to maintain a dignified, honest, straightforward policy to achieve victory.

This latter message was intended to show the general public that the ARU was a peaceful organization that sought justice for its members. Debs also wanted to convince railroad workers to remain peaceful and to act within the law. This was a message he would deliver many times over the course of the strike in public speeches, exchanges with journalists, and additional proclamations, as well as in countless telegrams to leaders of ARU locals.[45]

Despite Debs' consistent pleas for non-violence and assurances from city officials that the violence was in hand, newspapers in Chicago depicted the strike in sensational terms that wildly exaggerated the attendant incidents of vandalism and violence. The day following Debs' call for non-violence, Saturday June 30, the *Chicago Tribune* bristled with outrage and warnings of social upheaval. "LAW IS TRAMPLED ON" declared one headline on page one. "MOB IS IN CONTROL" read another.[46] The next day the paper's coverage was even more hysterical. Page one carried the headline "MOBS BENT ON RUIN—Debs' Strikers Begin a Work of Destruction," while on page three another proclaimed "MANY LIVES IN PERIL—Murderous Tactics of Debs' Strikers at Grand Crossing." Every article on the paper's first four pages offered breathless coverage of the "outrages" allegedly committed by strikers. It also referred to Debs as "Dictator Debs"—a name the *Tribune* had introduced several days earlier—fifty times in the single issue. Newspapers all across the country parroted the *Tribune*'s tone and phrasing, including the nickname "Dictator Debs."[47]

This characterization of Debs as a dictator was a well-established Gilded Age anti-labor trope. It allowed business leaders and pro-business politicians, editors, and clergy to invert the actual power dynamics involved in labor–capital disputes. In this framing capital, despite its tremendous wealth, political connections, favorable media coverage, and access to state power in the form of courts and force (police, militia, federal soldiers), was the aggrieved party. Labor, on the other hand, with its tiny or non-existent strike funds, minimal political power or legal protections, and almost universally hostile media coverage, was the aggressor. Leaders like Debs were not David-like defenders of powerless and oppressed workers against Goliath-like corporations. Rather, they were powerful, dangerous dictators who sought to seize control of others' private property and force the legitimate owners to bend to their autocratic will. "The American Railway Union," declared the *Inter-Ocean*, is determined to exterminate the [General] Managers' Association."[48] Framing labor–capital conflict in this manner legitimized as heroic business leaders' actions during strikes, everything from refusing to negotiate and hiring replacement workers, to calling upon local, state, or federal authorities to send police or soldiers. Keenly aware of the value of this depiction, John Egan told reporters, "we are determined to resist the dictation of the American Railway Union with all our resources."[49]

***Figure 4.1* "Revoked by the Present Ruler of the Land," *Chicago Tribune*, July 4, 1894, 1. This cartoon was one of many that depicted Eugene Debs as a dictator who cared little for the suffering of the American people brought on by the strike.**

One of the ways the GMA railroads endeavored to resist was by causing or exacerbating tie-ups along key freight and passenger lines in order to generate negative publicity for the ARU. For example, some railroads stopped carrying freight, falsely claiming that violent mobs of strikers controlled large sections of rail line. They did so knowing it would lead to newspaper stories about the strike causing shortages of medicine, undelivered mail, rotting food, spiking prices, business closures, and suffering passengers. The latter included a heart-rending story of a man unable to reach the sickbed of his gravely ill child and another about a woman prevented from attending her husband's funeral. Their goal was to depict Debs as a heartless seeker of personal power to turn public opinion against the strike and compel the federal government to intervene in the conflict. The ARU tried without success to make arrangements that would eliminate these kinds of incidents, but were rebuffed at every turn by the railroads. In one telling incident, the Grand Trunk Line announced that due to crowd disruptions it would no longer run funeral trains to Mount Olivet cemetery. ARU officials responded by notifying railroad officials that strikers would not interfere with funeral trains. The railroad then announced that it would run no funeral trains until strikers allowed Pullman cars on other trains.[50]

Egan and the managers of the GMA welcomed this negative and alarmist coverage of the *Tribune*, knowing it would undermine public support for the strike. Indeed, Egan as the frontman for the GMA did his best to stoke the public's fears. "The situation is becoming critical," he told reporters on June 30 after a day of unexceptional vandalism and interference with trains, "and in a few hours we will be in the midst of a reign of physical violence." Moments later, in a statement that revealed his desire to see state militia or federal troops sent in, Egan said darkly, "I do not see how the police will be able to battle such an extended evil."[51]

At the same time, members of the GMA and Egan presented a confident front. When he was asked about a rumor that the GMA was pressuring George Pullman to settle the strike, C. H. Chappel of the Chicago and Alton railroad said it was not true: "We have organized to resist this strike to the bitter end."[52] Egan said: "There will be no surrender or compromise on the part of the railroad companies." When asked about the financial hit to the railroads, Egan said rather blithely, in a manner that suggested it was no big deal, that the member railroads of the GMA were losing $250,000 a day.[53]

Not content to rely on the media to win the strike, the GMA developed a multifaceted strategy. At their daily meeting that morning a special committee delivered a report that outlined the organization's legal strategy. GMA member railroads must coordinate their legal efforts against the ARU. This would be accomplished by establishing a legal subcommittee to study all laws relevant to the strike and counsel the GMA's attorneys on the ones most likely to be advantageous to the organization. Members of the legal subcommittee would also endeavor to establish a "proper understanding" with government prosecutors that included recommending strikers and union officials for prosecution. In order to gain speedy resolutions to these cases, the subcommittee ought to recommend indictments and prosecutions under *federal*, rather than state or local laws. In particular, such prosecutions should focus on interference with the U.S. mail and interstate commerce. When advised by the subcommittee, individual railroads should seek federal court injunctions against strikers trespassing on railroad property or interfering with their employees. Finally, all legal costs accrued by individual member railroads would be paid for collectively by the GMA. The general managers unanimously approved the report.[54]

On the same day the GMA firmed up its war plan, the ARU worked to spread the strike across the nation and to gain much-needed support from local labor organizations. Accordingly, it welcomed to Uhlich Hall representatives of the several local labor organizations, including the Chicago Trades and Labor Assembly, a powerful labor federation representing 150,000 workers. The mood of the gathering was upbeat, reflecting the sense of many that the boycott was going well, perhaps even exceeding expectations. Speakers called for labor unity and denounced the railroads and the Pullman Company. One declared George Pullman "a Czar greater than the Emperor of Russia." Another characterized the struggle against the GMA as "the greatest battle for human rights in the history of the world." Still another read a resolution that said the source of labor discontent was rooted in the development of a "master and man" relationship between employers and employees that embodied "the essence of slavery" that kept workers "on the verge of starvation and pauperism." He also urged all workers to aid the railroad workers and "to prevent our municipal, county, State, and National Government from being used to subjugate labor." Fanny Kavanaugh, a woman prominent in city reform circles, stood and recommended a delegation call upon Governor John Altgeld to insist the railroads run their trains without Pullman cars or forfeit their state charters.[55]

Someone in the crowd nominated Debs for the presidency in 1896 and the crowd cheered enthusiastically and called for Debs to mount the stage and offer some remarks. He did so and presented an upbeat assessment of the strike and the chances for victory. "The railroads for once will feel the full power of organized labor." They never anticipated the remarkable unification of labor across the country. Victory in the strike would lead to the government takeover of the railroads and telegraphs. Debs also spoke harshly about the press for its decidedly biased coverage of the strike and boycott, noting that it revealed the newspapers were "subsidized and controlled by capital."[56]

Later that afternoon, leaders of the Chicago Trades and Labor Assembly returned to Uhlich Hall to offer that if the standoff persisted, they would declare a general strike in which "every union man in the city would go out on strike." Given Debs' belief that labor generally lost its battles due to its persistent failure to overcome shortsightedness and selfish interests, such a magnanimous pledge of solidarity doubtless boosted his spirits. Debs knew a general strike might be disruptive enough to force Pullman to the negotiating table, but it was also fraught with peril. He thanked the representatives, but said he preferred to wait a few more days before initiating that kind of action.[57]

> The "nomination" of Eugene Debs for president was made in jest as a way to convey the workers' appreciation for the ARU leader. But it turned out to be prescient, for Debs would indeed be nominated for president of the United States as the candidate of the Socialist Party in 1900, 1904, 1908, 1912, and 1920.

## A General Strike

In contrast to a traditional strike affecting a single business or industry, a general strike is a work stoppage engaged in by a large coalition of workers in different industries and often across many localities. Most often a general strike is called when striking workers at, say a factory or mine, come up against an owner who refuses to meet their demands, or even to negotiate. General strikes are sometimes called "sympathy strikes" because many of the workers join the strike to show support to the initial group of striking workers. The goal is to cause so much economic disruption in a city or region that political leaders and other business owners begin to pressure the company involved in the initial strike to negotiate a settlement with their employees. Although they can be effective, general or sympathy strikes are rare.

What gave Debs pause was that the GMA not only was comprised of railroads possessing a combined $818 million[58] in capitalization and that it could count on the press to present them as victims of union tyranny, but also that it had the political influence to compel intervention by the federal government. The railroads were the most powerful corporations in the nation and the Cleveland administration was decidedly pro-corporation and pro-railroad. In particular, Attorney General Richard Olney's ties to the railroad industry were widely known, as were his efforts on behalf of railroads a few months prior—in the form of federal court injunctions and dispatching regiments of the U.S. Army—against Coxeyites who commandeered trains.

By this point in the strike the GMA had in fact secured firm assurances from the Department of Justice that the federal government fully supported the railroads and that it was at that very moment laying the groundwork for a full-on legal and military assault on the ARU to end the strike and the union itself. Olney presently informed the media that he viewed the strike as a serious threat to law and order, not to mention property rights and the rights of businessmen to conduct their affairs without any outside interference.[59]

Olney did not want to leave the suppression of the ARU boycott to state or local officials who, in his view, likely would move too slowly and timidly. He believed the most effective way to end the strike and weaken if not destroy the ARU was through *federal* intervention. To transform this dispute that was centered in Chicago into a matter to be resolved by the Department of Justice in Washington, D.C., Olney planned to exploit a technicality regarding the United States mail. The U.S. Constitution required the federal government to create and maintain a postal service that delivered mail throughout the nation. And because many trains included mail cars, or simply carried sacks of mail in regular baggage cars, Onley realized he could charge Debs and the ARU with the federal crime of conspiring to interfere with the U.S. mail by tying up trains. He also intended to charge them with interfering with interstate commerce.

Olney officially launched his mail strategy on June 28, the second full day of the boycott. He sent a telegram to Thomas E. Milchrist, the U.S. Attorney at Chicago, instructing him to, "See that the passage of regular trains carrying the United States mails in the usual and ordinary way as contemplated by the act of Congress and directed by the Postmaster-General is not obstructed." The telegram also ordered Milchrist to procure warrants from federal courts against "any and all persons engaged in such obstruction." He also was to direct the U.S. Marshall for Northern Illinois to serve these warrants and make arrests—and to deputize as many citizens as needed to carry out the job. Olney subsequently sent the same telegram to U.S. district attorneys in other areas in the country affected by the strike.

Milchrist called in reporters and explained that this set of instructions was in line with Olney's decision a few months earlier in a strike against the Northern Pacific railroad in which the Attorney General had effectively declared, "a train which carries the mails is a mail train and that interference with any part of it is interference with the mails. So when a Pullman car which is part of the regular makeup of the train is cut off the act is an interference with the mails." This definition of what constituted a mail train was not based on any statute, nor was it stipulated in the contracts between railroads and the U.S. government. It was Olney's definition and by making it so capacious it allowed him to prosecute the ARU for simply decoupling Pullman cars from trains carrying mail. Those Pullman cars were, according to Olney, "part of the regular makeup of the train" and the mere removal of them—even if it did not involve the cars carrying the mail—constituted "interference" and violated federal law. To ensure the widest possible distribution of this unique definition, Milchrist provided the press with a copy of the telegram and it was printed in papers across the nation the next day.[60]

Milchrist's next move, likely at Olney's instruction, was to appear later that day at the daily meeting of the GMA, a move that eliminated any pretense of neutrality on the part of the Department of Justice. Milchrist assured the men that Attorney General Olney backed them in their fight with the ARU and then he read to them his telegram after which he asked them to provide names of men who had obstructed or attempted to obstruct the passage of trains carrying mail. He promised that the U.S. Marshal John W. Arnold would act on this information quickly and arrest the perpetrators.[61]

That same day another dimension of Olney's mail strategy appeared as various officials in the Railway Mail Service (RMS), the branch of the United States Postal Service that oversaw mail delivery by rail, began to lodge formal and very public complaints about interference with mail trains. In Chicago, the division superintendent of the Railway Mail Service, sent a message to Debs demanding that a Pittsburgh-bound train be allowed to leave the city. Because the train loaded with mail also included several Pullman cars, striking trainmen had refused to handle it. After an hour the train departed. But when the superintendent subsequently received a telegram from nearby Cairo, Illinois about another mail train being held up, he personally called upon Debs at ARU headquarters to lodge a formal complaint. Debs explained that he had sent orders hours ago that the train be allowed to depart. To demonstrate his sincerity, Debs composed and sent with the superintendent watching a telegram to strikers in Cairo instructing them to release the train.[62] When the trains did not move, another superintendent warned Debs that the ARU had better allow the mail to move or "the whole power of the government will be summoned . . . to set them in motion"[63]

The next day, June 29, Olney informed the press that he had met with acting Postmaster-General Frank Jones and that they had decided "to rigidly insist upon carriage of all mails and to prosecute all who interfere with postal transportation."[64] Later that same day at Hammond, Indiana, the industrial town that bordered Chicago, the U.S. Marshal and two deputies arrested the president of the local ARU chapter, Alexander Shields, and two others. All were charged with "obstructing and retarding the passage of the United States mail."[65]

The GMA played a key role in Olney's mail strategy. To increase the number of mail trains being tied up in the strike, the railroad managers rejected offers by the ARU to allow trains carrying the U.S. mail that did not include Pullman cars to move freely. Instead, they adopted a policy of attaching mail cars to trains that included Pullman cars which they knew ARU workers would refuse to handle. They also placed bags of mail on trains with Pullman cars that ordinarily did not carry mail, thereby increasing the number of train stoppages that could be classified as interfering with the mail.[66]

Debs knew that the mail issue was fraught with danger. Olney's broad definition of what constituted a mail train exposed the ARU to potential prosecution. Accusations against the ARU for delaying the mail also risked alienating the general public and turning them against the union men. Already the anti-labor press had begun to emphasize the issue. The *Chicago Tribune*'s June 29 issue mentioned mail cars fifty times. The next day it did so more than seventy-five times. This drumbeat would continue for weeks, even though overall delays in mail delivery were minimal.[67]

As the mail issue put greater pressure on the ARU, so too did continuing incidents of vandalism, violence, and intimidation by striking railroad workers and their sympathizers. One public official especially concerned about these incidents was the governor of Illinois, John Peter Altgeld. Born in Germany, he emigrated with his family to the United States when he was just a baby. As a youth he labored on the family's struggling farm in Ohio and later served in the Union Army during the Civil War. Following the war he took jobs as a farm laborer, teacher, and railroad worker, reading law in his spare time until admitted to the Missouri bar in 1871. Altgeld moved to Chicago in 1875 where he established a lucrative law practice focused on the city's booming real-estate sector. Deeply interested in social reform causes, he joined the Democratic Party. After a failed run for Congress in 1884, he won election in 1886 to serve as a judge on the Superior Court of Cook County. In 1892, after an unsuccessful bid for the Senate the year before, Altgeld won election as governor.[68]

His reputation as a public official sympathetic to workers and immigrants was soon put to the test. Pressure from labor activists and civil rights advocates had been building in recent years to pardon the anarchists convicted of carrying out the 1886 Haymarket bombing. They argued—and Altgeld agreed—that the men had not received a fair trial. The anarchists had been convicted for their radical beliefs, rather than any hard evidence of their involvement in the bombing. Justice demanded that Altgeld right this judicial wrong by pardoning the three anarchists still in prison (four had already been hanged and one had died by suicide). Fully aware of the political firestorm that his decision would unleash, Altgeld announced the pardons in June 1893, arguing the men had been victims of "hysteria, packed juries, and a biased judge." He was denounced by politicians and editors across the country as an advocate of anarchism and lawlessness.

Now one year later, Altgeld faced another crisis involving labor. In his initial statements on the Pullman strike, he upheld the rights of workers to join unions and stage strikes, but he also insisted workers remain peaceful. As incidents of vandalism and stopping of rail traffic mounted, he faced pressure to deploy the state militia to restore order. Altgeld understood the perils of such a move. He believed it necessary to prevent the violence and vandalism from escalating, but that it also fed the narrative of the GMA that the strike was spiraling out of control. He was also keenly aware that in recent years militia in other states had been involved in deadly clashes with strikers. As a consequence, he sent only small detachments of soldiers to specific hot spots. On June 30, at the request of Illinois Central railroad officials who complained of crowds stopping trains, he dispatched 300 soldiers to Cairo, Illinois. The following day, July 1, he sent 265 soldiers to Decatur, Illinois to assist the sheriff who had indicated he could not maintain order and another 220 to Danville, Illinois in response to the sheriff who had requested rifles.[69]

What Altgeld did not know was that even as he was trying to contain the conflict, officials in Washington, D.C. led by Olney were laying the groundwork for federal intervention, including the eventual introduction of federal troops. As a prelude to this decision, Olney instructed the U.S. Marshal in Chicago to deputize hundreds of deputy marshals. This longstanding practice allowed a U.S. marshal to recruit ordinary civilians to serve as temporary law-enforcement officers with powers to arrest alleged lawbreakers. Once the crisis passed, the men returned to civilian status. Initially, Marshal John Arnold deputized four hundred men. But as the strike grew in size and intensity, that number soared to 5,000 in Chicago alone, with thousands more in the West. In yet another sign of collusion between the GMA and the federal government, two-thirds of these deputies were recruited and paid by the GMA railroads. Many of them were actually railroad employees. The Rock Island railroad, for example, enjoyed the protection of 500 deputy marshals, half of whom were their own employees. The GMA not only paid thousands to work as deputy marshals, but also covered the costs of their food, lodging, clothing, and guns. This policy of granting the railroads the power to deputize and pay more than 3,300 men to act as agents of the U.S. government was one of many singled out in the aftermath of the strike by the United States Strike Commission as dangerous and "a bad precedent."[70]

In Washington, Olney moved the Cleveland administration ever closer to military intervention. On Saturday June 30, at the urging of the GMA, he appointed Edwin Walker as special attorney for the federal government in Chicago to oversee the federal response to the strike. Like Olney, Walker was a longtime railroad lawyer with strong ties to the industry. Indeed, at the outset of the boycott he had been hired by the GMA as legal counsel. Walker's appointment was yet another sign that the Department of Justice was doing everything in its power to defeat the strike and did not care to hide it.[71]

The next day, Sunday July 1, Olney sent word to Milchrist instructing him to write up a petition seeking an injunction against the ARU that would prohibit any action that contributed to the interference with the operation of a railroad engaged in interstate commerce and transporting the mail. In this task on behalf of an ostensibly neutral Department of Justice, Milchrist received assistance on how best to word and frame the petition from Walker, several GMA lawyers, and the two federal judges who received the petition. The next morning, Monday July 2, those same judges, Peter S. Grosscup and William A. Woods, granted the injunction.[72]

The use of injunctions to stymie strikes and protests was relatively new in American history. Federal judges at Olney's urging had used them recently against Coxeyites who commandeered trains and against striking Northern Pacific railroad workers. In both cases the justification for the injunctions centered on the fact that the affected railroads were bankrupt and their operations were under the oversight of a federal receiver. But this new injunction against the ARU was framed so broadly as to apply to *any* railroad, regardless of financial status. And it was based on several novel legal claims. First, it asserted the ARU boycott violated federal law by interfering with interstate commerce and the delivery of the mail. The union and its members were, therefore, guilty of a criminal conspiracy facilitated by violence and intimidation against replacement workers and destruction of railroad property. Second, it argued the boycott violated the Sherman Antitrust Act of 1890. Congress had passed this law to curtail monopolistic practices by large corporations by outlawing combinations or trusts that conspired to diminish or eliminate competition. In its first four years of existence, the Sherman Antitrust Act was rarely invoked by the Department of Justice, especially under the tenure of Olney. But in 1894, Olney saw in the law a powerful weapon that could be deployed not against rogue corporations, but rather against unions deemed to be conspiring—by strike or boycott—against the free flow of commerce. This was an interpretation of the statute never intended by the lawmakers who wrote it.[73]

## The Sherman Anti-Trust Act

As corporations grew larger and more powerful in the 1880s, more and more Americans began to call for Congress to impose some regulations on their behavior. In particular, many were concerned that big industrial enterprises were using their power and influence in the economy to diminish competition to become monopolies, or something close to it. Some conspired to weaken or drive into bankruptcy rival businesses by striking secret deals with railroads that gave them discount shipping rates while their competitors suffered under much higher rates. Some big businesses joined combinations with similar businesses (trusts or pools) that allowed the members to collude to set prices that were immune to competition. In 1888 Senator John Sherman of Ohio put forth a bill that empowered the government to prosecute companies who engaged in uncompetitive practices. "The popular mind is agitated with problems that may disturb social order," he told his colleagues, "and among them all none is more threatening than . . . the concentration of capital into vast combinations. . . . Congress alone can deal with them and if we are unwilling or unable there will soon be a trust for every product and a master to fix the price for every necessity of life." The bill became law in 1890.

The injunction prohibited ARU officials from "compelling or inducing" any railroad employees "to refuse or fail to perform any of their duties." This included all forms of communication between the union leadership and its members that could be construed as "ordering, directing, aiding, assisting, or abetting" the boycott and sympathy strikes. To send a letter or telegram, or to make a speech or issue a public statement concerning the strike, violated the injunction and was grounds for arrest. The injunction likewise imposed broad and draconian restrictions on railroad workers. They must cease any activity that interfered with the operation of the railroads. This included not only violence and intimidation employed to dissuade replacement workers from taking their jobs, but also "persuasion," that is peaceful verbal engagement. Mere conversations with replacement workers were illegal. Additionally, unlike traditional court orders or injunctions, this one, said Milchrist, need not be served directly to specific individuals to compel them to cease their activities. Rather, it was sufficient to place the announcement in local newspapers, post it in public spaces around the city, and to read it to crowds of strikers, thereby placing every member of the ARU and the railroad workers who supported them subject to indictment for strike-related activity.[74] Tellingly, the injunction placed no restrictions on the actions of the GMA. It was free to communicate with its member railroads to develop a collective strategy for breaking the boycott and the ARU.

Debs and other ARU officials were stunned by sweeping restrictions imposed upon them by the injunction, which because of its unprecedented reach many called an "omnibus injunction." Debs quickly convened a meeting of the ARU's executive board to determine the union's response. If they defied the injunction, they faced arrest and prosecution. But if they obeyed it the strike would collapse. Ultimately, the board decided to ignore the injunction and take their chances with the courts. In anticipation of legal action against them, the board subsequently hired a lawyer who worked for a large railroad, but also moved in reform circles and supported workers' rights, Clarence Darrow.[75]

The public response to the injunction was mixed. Locally, all the Chicago newspapers with the exception of the *Chicago Times*, praised the injunction as fully justified. The *Tribune* ran the headline "To Kill the Strike—Uncle Sam Will Use the Law Backed by Riot Guns."[76] But outside of Chicago, some editors expressed concern over the injunction's unprecedented scope. The *New York Times* had been very critical of the ARU boycott, but its editors now reported with some alarm that the judges behind the "sweeping" and "extraordinary" inunction had characterized it as a "Gatling gun on paper." It was "a veritable dragnet in the matter of legal verbiage" that would allow for the arrest of nearly anyone involved in or supportive of the strike.[77] The *New York World* condemned the injunction as an "outrageous . . . stretch of federal power" that "placed at the disposal of railroad managers" all the powers of the federal government against their employees.[78]

Injunctions offered many advantages to big business. For one, they were granted by a judge and not a grand jury that might include citizens sympathetic to labor. Additionally, injunctions prohibited actions that under normal circumstances were perfectly legal, such as holding meetings and sending telegrams. And finally, they could be worded so broadly as to render a union utterly powerless to maintain a strike. The injunction issued against the ARU did just that. It ordered the union's members and officers to cease all action related to the strike.

Initially the injunction applied to only Illinois, Indiana, and Wisconsin, but it was soon utilized by federal judges throughout the Midwest and West. As soon as word of a disturbance somewhere reached the Department of Justice, Olney sent word urging local US attorneys to apply to a federal court for an injunction. In every case, federal judges acquiesced and within days of the original injunction ARU locals throughout many parts of the Midwest and West found themselves under the threat of indictment by federal authorities. "From Michigan to California," Debs later recounted, "there seemed to be concerted action on the part of the courts in restraining us from exercising any of the functions of our offices."[79]

Ever the optimist, Debs saw a potential silver lining in the injunction: it was so extreme that it might stoke the outrage of countless thousands of railroad workers to join the strike and increase the pressure on the GMA to settle. Accordingly, he sent a telegram on Monday July 2 to ARU locals declaring "if strike not settled in forty-eight hours, complete paralysis will follow."[80]

During the day on July 2, Chicago was relatively quiet, with only a few minor incidents involving crowds and police. But just outside the city at Blue Island a minor confrontation unfolded that federal authorities would seize upon as the pretext for sending in the U.S. Army. In the morning at Blue Island a modest contingent of deputy marshals tried and failed to disperse a much larger crowd. That afternoon a crowd of about 2,000 was still on hand when a train carrying U.S. Marshal John Arnold and Cook County Sheriff James H. Gilbert, along with a contingent of police and deputy marshals and some railroad officials, pulled slowly into the yards at Blue Island and came to a stop. Arnold stood on a car and ordered the crowd to leave the tracks so that the men under his command could clear obstructions to allow stranded trains to leave for Chicago. A man in the crowd said they would only allow mail trains to depart. When Arnold responded by placing armed deputies in front of a train he intended to move, a melee ensued. Scuffles and fist fights broke out between deputies and members of the crowd. Rocks thrown from the crowd rained down on the train and people on board. Some deputies drew their pistols, but none dared open fire. After men in the crowd pulled the train's coupling pins causing the cars to separate, Arnold temporarily gave up the effort.

When the situation had calmed down by 4:00 PM, Arnold decided the best way to disperse the crowd was to read the injunction to them. As soon as he commenced the crowd nearly drowned out his words with derisive shouts, jeers, and groans. "To hell with the courts!" shouted one onlooker, to which another added, "We are the government!" Arnold concluded the reading by demanding, in the name of the President of the United States, that they disperse and cease their interference with rail traffic. If they refused to comply, he warned, the federal government would send more men—"even if bloodshed were necessary"—to enforce the injunction. No one moved. Arnold then ordered a second reading of the injunction that elicited the same response. He again spoke to the crowd, demanding their dispersal and threatening "bloodshed" if they refused. Speeches by two local figures, the local deputy sheriff and a prominent local saloon keeper, finally convinced the people to disperse. The tracks were then cleared of a derailed car, allowing a passenger train to depart the station unmolested. With the exception of two box cars overturned across some tracks later that evening, Blue Island remained quiet until the next morning.[81]

Nonetheless, as these events unfolded at Blue Island, in Chicago the GMA's Egan called upon the federal government to send in the military. "There is no other recourse left," he said to reporters, painting a dire picture of violence and anarchy at odds with the reality on the ground. U.S. marshals, sheriffs' deputies, and police, said, were no match for the riotous mobs. "It is the government's duty to take this business in hand," said Egan, "restore law, suppress the riots, and restore to the public the service which it is now deprived of by conspirators and lawless men." Doubtless aware of Olney's desire to deploy federal troops to crush the strike, he urged the federal government to dispatch U.S. Army soldiers from Fort Sheridan to Chicago, a step he insisted would cause the strike "to collapse like a punctured balloon."[82] As if on cue, that evening as relative calm prevailed in Blue Island, Arnold telegraphed Olney that the situation there was beyond his control. "Our force is inadequate," and the only way to get trains moving again was with federal troops of the Fifteenth Regiment from nearby Fort Sheridan.[83] Olney then wired Milchrist in Chicago to say that if he believed federal troops were necessary, he should wire a request cosigned by Walker, Arnold, and judges Grosscup and Woods.

Olney had for days been making the case to President Cleveland that the time had arrived to deploy federal troops to break the strike.[84] Cleveland had a lot riding on this decision. On the one hand, he was a fiscal conservative with strong pro-business sentiments that led him to sympathize with the position of the GMA. On the other, he feared the political fire storm he would ignite if he turned the U.S. military against American citizens. But exaggerated accounts of the vandalism and violence at Blue Island on July 2 by federal officials and their explicit calls for federal troops provided Onley with the leverage to gain Cleveland's support.

The president convened a meeting at the White House that lasted well past midnight. Olney's dire description of the situation, supplemented with alarming dispatches from U.S. attorneys and U.S. marshals in the West and Midwest, moved the administration to the precipice of calling out the military. A secret dispatch was sent to the commanding officer at Fort Sheridan to prepare his entire force to depart for Chicago via a special train that was on its way to his location.[85]

The next day, July 3, Olney received the message he wanted: a request wired from Arnold cosigned by Walker, Milchrist, and Judge Grosscup that federal troops be sent to Chicago. In justifying the request, Arnold presented a dire description of the situation in Chicago that was both inaccurate and exaggerated. He cited the violence that had occurred on July 2 in the suburb of Blue Island as having taken place in Chicago and did not point out that it had since abated. Further, Arnold asserted—without providing any evidence or mentioning the availability of Chicago police and Illinois state militia—"that no force less than the regular troops of the United States can procure passage of the mail trains or enforce orders of the court." Finally, he suggested an impending escalation of chaos by citing a rumor that Chicago's unionized workers were about to stage a massive general strike that would paralyze the city. They "are quitting employment today," wrote Arnold, "and in my opinion will be joining the mob tonight, and especially tomorrow." Federal troops are needed "at the earliest possible moment."[86]

When Olney presented Cleveland with this telegram, the president gave his authorization for military intervention. At 3:30 PM Secretary of War Lamont sent orders to Colonel Robert E. Crofton at Fort Sheridan to move his entire force to the city of Chicago "to prevent the obstruction of the United States mails, and generally to enforce the faithful execution of the laws of the United States." This move fulfilled a prediction made that same day by the editor at the *Chicago Times* who wrote of Olney's legal maneuvers, "the object of the injunction is not so much to prevent interference with trains as to lay a foundation for calling out the United States troops."[87]

Having achieved his goal of federal military intervention, a delighted Olney told the press, "The subject has now passed out of my hands . . . it is for other branches to execute such action as the courts take." By "other branches," the Attorney General meant the U.S. Army. Hours later, at 12:30 AM, July 4, the train carrying Crofton and 587 men and officers—eight companies of soldiers of the Fifteenth Regiment, two troops of Seventh Cavalry of the U.S. Army, and one light artillery battery—arrived in Chicago.[88]

## NOTES

1 Eugene V. Debs, "President's Keynote Address to the 1st National Convention of the American Railway Union," 3.
2 *Chicago Tribune*, June 14, 1894, 2 and June 15, 1894, 5.
3 *Chicago Tribune*, June 16, 1894, 3.
4 USSC, 87.
5 USSC, 88.
6 USSC, 87.
7 USSC, 91.
8 Ray Ginger, *The Bending Cross: A Biography of Eugene Victor Debs* (New York: Russell & Russell, 1949), 110, 113.
9 Janice L. Reiff, "A Modern Lear and His Daughters: Gender in the Model Town of Pullman," in Richard Schneirov, Shelton Stromquist, and Nick Salvatore, eds., *The Pullman Strike and the Crisis of the 1890s: Essays on Labor and Politics* (Urbana, IL: University of Illinois Press, 1999), 75–77; Almont Lindsey, *The Pullman Strike: The Story of a Unique Experiment and of a Great Labor Upheaval* (Chicago: University of Chicago Press, 1942), 128–129; *Chicago Times*, June 16, 1894, 1; USSC, 434.
10 *Chicago Tribune*, June 16, 1894, 3; USSC, 92, 590.
11 *Chicago Tribune*, June 17, 1894, 5; Chicago *Inter-Ocean*, June 17, 1894, 7; USSC, 92–93.
12 *Chicago Inter-Ocean*, June 17, 1894, 7.
13 *Chicago Tribune*, June 19, 1894, 12; Chicago *Inter-Ocean*, June 19, 1894, 7.
14 *Chicago Inter-Ocean*, June 20, 1894, 4
15 USSC, 93.
16 USSC, 93; Lindsey, 131–132.
17 USSC, 93–94.
18 USSC, 94; *Chicago Tribune*, June 22, 1894, 4; *Chicago Inter-Ocean*, June 22, 1894, 1, 7.
19 Chicago *Inter-Ocean*, June 23, 1994, 1; Lindsey, 130; USSC, 94, 590.
20 *Chicago Tribune*, June 23, 1894, 3 and June 24, 1894, 11.
21 *Chicago Tribune*, June 23, 1894, 3
22 *Chicago Tribune*, June 24, 1894, 11.
23 Jack Kelly, *The Edge of Anarchy: The Railroad Barons, the Gilded Age, and the Greatest Labor Uprising in America* (New York: St. Martin's Press, 2019), 117–118; Lindsey, 114–115.
24 USSC, 250; *Chicago Tribune*, June 26, 1894, 8.
25 USSC, 252, 253, 590, 625–626; *New York Times*, July 3, 1894, 2.
26 *Chicago Tribune*, June 27, 1894, 8; *Chicago Inter-Ocean*, June 27, 1894, 1.
27 Kelly, 107.
28 USSC, 325–326. *Chicago Inter-Ocean*, June 27, 1894, 1.
29 *Chicago Tribune* June 23, 1894, 3 and June 27, 1894, 2; Lindsey, 134.
30 USSC, 144.
31 USSC, 252; *Proceedings of the General Managers Association of Chicago*, no. 22; Chicago, June 25, 1894 to July 14, 1894, 102, 106–107, 115, 145, 156, 171; Kelly, 119; Lindsey, 138; *Chicago Tribune*, June 30, 1894, 1; *Chicago Inter-Ocean*, June 30, 1894, 1.

32 USSC, xiii–xiiii, 252, 269–270; Report of John M. Egan, *Proceedings of the General Managers Association of Chicago*, no. 22; Chicago, June 25, 1894 to July 14, 1894, 221–227, 92–219; Lindsey, 138–139.
33 *Chicago Tribune*, June 29, 1894, 8; Kelly, 109, 111.
34 Kelly, 109.
35 *Chicago Tribune*, June 29, 1894, 1; USSC, 325–26.
36 *Chicago Tribune*, June 30, 1894, 1; *Chicago Inter-Ocean*, June 27, 1894, 3.
37 *Chicago Tribune*, June 29, 1894, 8;
38 *New York Times*, June 28, 1894, 1 and July 1, 1894, 2.
39 *Chicago Tribune*, June 29, 1894, 2, 8; Kelly, 124.
40 *Chicago Tribune*, July 1, 1894, 2; USSC, 212–226.
41 *Chicago Tribune*, June 30, 1894, 1–2; *Chicago Inter-Ocean*, June 30, 1894, 2.
42 *Chicago Tribune*, June 30, 1894, 1–2.
43 Edward T. O'Donnell, *Henry George and the Crisis of Inequality: Progress and Poverty in the Gilded Age* (New York: Columbia University Press, 2015), 173–182; USSC, xliii, 339–408, 385, 389, 390, 392.
44 *Chicago Tribune*, July 1, 1894, 5.
45 *Chicago Inter-Ocean*, June 30, 1894, 2.
46 *Chicago Tribune*, June 30, 1894, 1–4; *Chicago Inter-Ocean* June 30, 1894, 1, 12.
47 *Chicago Tribune*, July 1, 1894, 1–4.
48 *Chicago Inter-Ocean*, July 1, 1894, 1.
49 *Chicago Tribune*, June 29, 1894, 1; *Chicago Inter-Ocean*, June 30, 1894, 1.
50 *Chicago Tribune*, June 30, 1894, 1, 2, 3 and July 2, 1894, 1, 2; *New York Times*, July 3, 1894, 1; Kelly 109, 127–128.
51 *Chicago Tribune*, July 1, 1894, 5
52 *New York Times*, June 29, 1894, 1.
53 *Chicago Inter-Ocean*, June 30, 1894, 1.
54 *Proceedings of the General Managers Association of Chicago*, no. 22; Chicago, June 25, 1894 to July 14, 1894, 123–126; Lindsey, 141–142.
55 *Chicago Tribune*, July 1, 1894, 10; *Chicago Inter-Ocean*, July 1, 1894, 2.
56 *Chicago Tribune*, July 1, 1894, 10; *Chicago Inter-Ocean*, July 1, 1894, 2.
57 *New York Times*, July 1, 1894, 1.
58 Kelly, 118.
59 Lindsey, 169–170.
60 *Chicago Tribune*, June 29, 1894, 8; Lindsey, 151, 156–157.
61 Lindsey, 152; *Proceedings of the General Managers Association of Chicago*, no. 22; Chicago, June 25, 1894 to July 14, 1894, 113.
62 *Chicago Tribune*, June 29, 1894, 8; *Chicago Inter-Ocean*, June 29, 1894, 1.
63 *Chicago Tribune*, June 30, 1894, 3; *Chicago Inter-Ocean*, June 30, 1894, 2.
64 *Chicago Inter-Ocean*, June 30, 1894, 1.
65 *Chicago Tribune*, June 30, 1894, 1.
66 USSC, 159, 255; Lindsey, 150; *Washington Post*, July 4, 1894, 2; *Chicago Tribune*, June 30, 1894, 2, 3.
67 Kelly, 138.
68 Harry Barnard, *Eagle Forgotten: The Life of John Peter Altgeld* (Duell, Sloan and Pearce, 1938), 15–151.
69 Kelly, 157–158; Barnard, 291; *Chicago Tribune*, June 30, 1894, 2.

70 Lindsey, 165–166; *New York Times*, July 3, 1894, 1; USSC, xlv.
71 Nick Salvatore, *Eugene V. Debs: Citizen and Socialist* (Urbana, IL: University of Illinois Press, 1982), 131; Lindsey, 154–155.
72 *Chicago Tribune*, July 2, 1894, 1; Kelly, 151; Lindsey, 160–161.
73 Lindsey, 156–157. For a broader examination of the anti-labor position of the American judiciary, see Melvin, "Dubofsky, The Federal Judiciary, Free Labor, and Equal Rights," in Schneirov, et al., 159–178.
74 *New York Times*, July 3, 1894, 1.
75 Ginger, 132–133.
76 *Chicago Tribune*, July 2, 1894, 1
77 *New York Times*, July 3, 1894, 1
78 Lindsey, 163.
79 USSC, 143.
80 A. P. Winston, "The Significance of the Pullman Strike," *Journal of Political Economy*, vol. 9, no. 4 (September 1901), 554.
81 *Chicago Inter-Ocean*, July 3, 1894, 1, 4; *Chicago Tribune*, July 3, 1894, 1
82 *Chicago Inter-Ocean*, July 3, 1894, 3.
83 Lindsey, 164; *Appendix to the Report of the Attorney General 1896* (Washington, D.C.: U.S. Government Printing Office, 1896), 62.
84 *Chicago Inter-Ocean*, July 3, 1894, 4; *Chicago Tribune*, July 3, 1894, 1.
85 Grover Cleveland, *The Government in the Chicago Strike of 1894* (Princeton, N.J.: Princeton University Press, 1913), 234; Lindsey, 170–171; *New York Times*, July 2, 1894, 2; *Chicago Inter-Ocean*, July 4, 1894, 1.
86 Barnard, 289–290; Ginger, 135.
87 *Chicago Times*, July 3, 1894, 1
88 *New York World*, July 4, 1894, 7; *Chicago Tribune*, July 4, 1894, 1.

CHAPTER 5

# Rioters Will Be Fired Upon

## JULY 4, 1894

As the sun rose over Chicago on Independence Day, July 4, 1894, its residents awoke to news that federal troops had arrived overnight. Many experienced a sense of both expectation and anxiety. On the one hand, they looked forward to a holiday that ordinarily featured parades, picnics, and fireworks. But on this particular day marking the nation's 118th birthday, people also feared that the arrival of federal troops might mean an escalation of violence. That had been the case seventeen years earlier when President Rutherford B. Hayes sent in the military to crush a massive railroad strike known as the Great Uprising. These federal soldiers, along with state militia units, killed some one hundred strikers and their supporters in several violent clashes.

The people most shocked—and infuriated—by the arrival of federal troops were the city's mayor, John Hopkins, and state's governor, John P. Altgeld. According to Article 4, Section 4 of the U.S. Constitution, the federal government may send the U.S. army into a state to suppress an uprising only upon request by the state legislature or governor of that state. Neither Altgeld nor the Illinois state legislature made any such request. In fact, Altgeld had the situation in hand. Over the past few days, through judicious deployment of the state militia to areas of unrest and railroad tie-ups like Decatur and Danville, Altgeld had restored order and the free flow of trains without any violence. On several occasions these deployments had come in response to requests for state militia troops by the U.S. marshal for the Southern District of Illinois, a clear indication of his willingness to work with federal authorities. And yet the Cleveland administration, without alerting Altgeld, had just deployed nearly 600

DOI: 10.4324/9781003388784-6

troops to Chicago, a city experiencing some disturbances that police and federal marshals had managed to contain. The report of the Strike Commission that later investigated the Pullman Strike was especially critical of this unprecedented and constitutionally dubious decision.

Likewise stunned was Mayor Hopkins.[1] Under his direction the Chicago Police Department, comprised of some 3,000 regulars and 500 reserves, had successfully met and contained any disturbances related to the strike. Police Superintendent Michael Brennan conferred regularly with John Egan and the GMA to hear their concerns and when requested to dispatch patrolmen to quell violence or disruption of train service.[2] Brennan later expressed criticism of deployment of soldiers, saying the police had been successful in breaking up the disturbances and imposing order.[3]

Cleveland's decision reflected the view of Olney and the GMA that federal troops were preferable to state militia and local police. The latter were aware of the pro-labor sentiments of Altgeld and Hopkins and did not trust them to use the force they desired to end the strike and destroy the ARU. Egan and the GMA also worried, based on previous significant labor–capital conflicts, that militia soldiers and local police might hold back out of sympathy for the strikers and their families. Indeed, on several occasions in recent days in California state militia forces refused to fire upon or attack crowds of strikers and sympathizers.[4]

Olney had revealed his preference for focusing on Chicago and the use of federal troops over state militia back on June 30 in a letter to Edwin Walker as the latter took up his new position. "It has seemed to me that if the rights of the United States were vigorously asserted in Chicago," wrote Olney, "the origin and center of the demonstration, the result would be to make it a failure everywhere else and to prevent it spread over the entire country." Then after discussing the utility of injunctions and federal deputies in suppressing the strike, he offered a thinly veiled assertion that the situation called for the U.S. military: "I feel that the true way of dealing with the matter is by a force which is overwhelming and prevents any attempt at resistance."[5]

This first contingent of "a force which is overwhelming" had arrived by train in the early morning hours of July 4. From the train station they marched through the streets to Lake Front Park where they established a camp. Across Michigan Avenue which bordered the park stood a row office buildings and hotels, including the one where Debs was staying. He first became aware of the presence of federal troops in the city when he looked out the window from his hotel room to see soldiers stacking rifles. Stunned, he called his brother Theodore over. "They're regulars, Theodore, they're regulars. Do you get that? Cleveland has sent the troops in." For the moment, Debs hoped that federal troops might actually benefit the ARU by establishing order and minimizing violence and vandalism on the part of the crowds, thereby lifting "the stigma of which is placed by capital on labor."[6] He would soon come to realize that the arrival of federal troops signaled the final phase of the government's effort to crush the strike and destroy his union.

General Nelson A. Miles was still en route to Chicago, so the federal soldiers remained under the command of Colonel Crofton. He made no effort to confer with Mayor Hopkins or Police Chief Brennan and instead huddled for a strategy session with U.S. Marshal John Arnold, special U.S. attorney Edwin Walker, and the GMA strike director, John Egan. They convinced Crofton to deploy contingents of soldiers to locations in and near the city that had experienced disturbances on July 2. He sent four companies (approximately 250 men) to Blue Island, two companies (approximately 125 soldiers) to both the Union Stock Yard and two more to the neighborhood of Grand Crossing. All three set up camps and set watches.[7]

Many soldiers were likely surprised by how calm the city was. Newspaper accounts from the previous few days had, as Debs put it, given the nation "the impression that Chicago is at the mercy of a mob of dangerous man, razing and sacking buildings and destroying railroad property."[8] But the soldiers encountered only curious onlookers. Blue Island, wrote one journalist, was "quieter than a blue law Sunday." Soldiers there stood watch as railroad workers removed cars derailed and overturned during previous days of unrest. In Grand Crossing soldiers passed the time by playing baseball. Matters were a little more tense at the Union Stock Yard, located in the middle of a densely packed working-class neighborhood. Ordered to escort a freight train loaded with meat out of the yard, soldiers fixed bayonets and lined the tracks to hold back the crowd, while another group of soldiers on foot ran alongside the engine for more than a mile until it was judged to be safely on its way.[9]

Miles arrived in the city at 11:30 AM. He was one of the most decorated and celebrated soldiers in the nation. Born in rural Massachusetts, he joined the Union Army as a volunteer at the outset of the Civil War. Four years later, after participating in many of the war's most famous battles, he had risen to the rank of brigadier-general. After the war he spent much of the next twenty-five years playing a key role in the Army's many campaigns to defeat Native American resistance and force tribes onto reservations. In 1890 he was promoted to Major General and named the Commander of the Military Division of the Missouri, a large territory comprising Colorado, Kansas, New Mexico, and the so-called Indian Territory. In October 1892 the organizers of Chicago's World's Columbian Exposition selected him as Grand Marshal for the massive parade that kicked off the city's yearlong celebration. Miles' success fed his ambition and he longed for the top military post, Commanding General of the United States Army. Many believed his ultimate goal was the presidency. Miles knew that a strong performance in quelling the strike in Chicago would boost his fortunes.

> General Nelson A. Miles never did become president. In 1895 he was named Commanding General of the United States Army. Three years later he commanded a force in the Spanish–American War in Cuba and then led the invasion of Puerto Rico. Miles was later named the first head of the military government established on the island. He earned promotion to the rank of lieutenant general in 1900 and retired in 1903. One year later at the Democratic National Convention a few delegates cast votes for him for the presidential nomination.

As soon as he detrained, Miles headed for the Pullman Building to meet with Crofton, Milchrist, Walker, and the heads of several GMA railroads. That this meeting took place in the corporate headquarters of the company at the heart of the strike indicated there was little concern on the part of the government officials to appear neutral. In the days leading up to the deployment of federal troops, Miles had expressed concern in White House meetings about the dangers of such a move, especially the idea that the soldiers might fire upon American citizens. But now when he spoke to the press in the later afternoon, Miles used aggressive, threatening language. The Army regulars were not in Chicago "for display or picnic purposes." Chicago residents should be aware, he warned, that these men carried deadly weapons and were not afraid to use them. "[G]reat loss of life will follow if the troops fire." One officer on hand added that, "they will take aim and will shoot to kill, and will keep on shooting as long as it is necessary."[10]

Then Miles stepped far outside of his role as commander of military forces to offer a forceful political condemnation of Debs and the ARU. The strike "is revolutionary and wholly unwarranted by the Constitution of the United States and the laws of the country." Debs and his union, continued Miles, are on the side of "usurpation, mob violence, and illegal possession or destruction of property." They threaten the well-being of the railroads which are "great public highways, the arteries of commerce and the life of the Nation." The federal government has the authority to intervene if local and state officials prove unable to maintain the free flow of interstate commerce and the mail.[11]

The surprise arrival of federal troops, along with the bellicose comments by Miles that suggested his troops would be used to restore order and subdue crowds, necessitated a response from city officials to clarify the role of the Chicago police. Superintendent Brennan issued an order that noted the "unusual" presence of federal troops, but asserted the supremacy of police authority when it came to "maintaining the public peace and the protection of life and property within the limits of the city." The only exception was the protection of property owned by bankrupt railroads that were under federal receivership, a legal status that placed them under the management and oversight of the federal government.[12]

For his part, Debs spent much of July 4 at ARU headquarters while union representatives moved throughout the city, speaking at gatherings and urging strikers and their sympathizers to stay away from the railyards and refrain from vandalism or violence. Towards midday a representative of Mayor Hopkins paid a visit to see if Debs would be willing to attend a meeting the next day involving representatives of the ARU, the GMA, and city officials about resolving the strike. Debs consented and the meeting was set for 11:00 AM on July 5. He later received word that Egan of the GMA had rejected outright attending any such meeting if Debs was present. "The General Managers are in thorough harmony," said Egan, "and are firmly agreed to fight this strike shoulder to shoulder to the finish. There is no chance for arbitration." Rumors that the wealthy carriage manufacturer Peter Studebaker, who was also a Pullman shareholder, was working to bring about a resolution to the strike likewise came to nothing.[13]

With Chicago residents enjoying the holiday and calm prevailing throughout the city, journalists sought interviews with the figures at the center of the conflict. Special U.S. Attorney Edwin Walker told the press that even if a settlement was reached in the strike, he would not let up in his pursuit of Debs. "Every man who has trampled on the law will be punished." Tomorrow, July 5, he would begin assembling a grand jury that would hear evidence against Debs and other ARU leaders. "A charge of criminal conspiracy will be brought against all of the officers of the American Railway Union," said Walker. And lest anyone misapprehend his determination and singular focus, he concluded, "We shall have Debs." District Attorney Thomas Milchrist added that not only Debs and Howard faced prosecution, but also the entire executive board of the ARU. "Under the Federal statues they all have been guilty of a conspiracy" to impede interstate commerce and the free movement of the mail.[14]

When asked for his view of the strike, the GMA's John Egan seized the opportunity to reframe the nature of the conflict in light of the arrival of federal troops and the tough talk of Department of Justice officials and Miles. In the same way that George Pullman, at the outset of the boycott, declared that the fight was no longer between his company and his employees, but rather one between the ARU and the GMA, Egan asserted that it had now evolved to a new stage that no longer involved the GMA. "So far as the railroads are concerned with this fight," said Egan, "they are out of it. It has now become a fight between the United States Government and the American Railway Union, and we shall leave them to fight it out." Egan intended this new depiction of the strike, which echoed that of Miles, to present Debs and the ARU as enemies of the people who sought to defy, even overthrow, the national government. [15]

In New Jersey, reporters found George Pullman at his summer home and pressed him for an assessment of the situation. Speaking in a calm and reserved tone, Pullman repeated his mantra that there was "nothing to arbitrate" and then proceeded to offer his familiar summary of the company's benevolent efforts to keep men and women employed during the economic downturn. He also reiterated the impossibility of either raising wages or lowering rents for Pullman properties, steps that would violate "the inexorable laws of trade." For Pullman and his fellow industrialists, the conflict represented a dangerous challenge to their conception of American liberty as defined as the rights of individuals to possess, utilize, and dispose of private property as they saw fit, without interference from others. "Shall the railroads be permitted to manage their own business," asked Pullman, "or shall they turn it over into the hands of Debs, Howard, and the American Railway Union?"[16]

When Debs was approached by a United Press reporter in the afternoon, he had had several hours to reassess his initial hope that federal soldiers might act as a neutral force to keep order and prevent vandalism. Perhaps it was the use of federal troops earlier in the day to run a freight train out of the Union Stock Yard. Or Miles' condemnation of the strike as "revolutionary and wholly unwarranted." Or the bloody rhetoric of Miles and his officers talking about mowing down the crowds with rifle and artillery fire that convinced him the troops posed not merely a threat to the vitality of the strike, but to the fate of the republic. The crisis at hand was not the strike, said Debs, but rather the extraordinary, undemocratic power wielded by big business. Public officials in Washington, D.C., elected by the people to serve the people, were guilty of "yielding to the wishes of the [railroad] managers" who called for federal troops when state and local officials in Chicago were in full control of the situation. "[I]t is corporation greed and avarice alone that have brought us to the verge of a revolution." [17]

Like Pullman, Debs argued the conflict exposed a crisis of American liberty. But where Pullman defined liberty as the rights of employers and property owners to run their affairs free of any interference by employees, unions, or government officials, Debs saw a system that was leading to "the absolute enslavement of the American working man and his complete and utter degradation for all time to come" by corporate power. Laissez-faire capitalism had "force[d] the laboring people into active resistance to the encroachment upon their personal rights" which Debs had long defined as earning a living wage that allowed one to thrive as a respected, independent citizen living in decent conditions with opportunities for advancement. Victory in this "desperate struggle," said Debs, would restore the American laborer to "his just and rightful throne as a free man." Which version of American liberty would prevail—Pullman's or Debs'—remained to be seen. But it was increasingly clear that Pullman's had the backing of the Cleveland administration, the Department of Justice, and the U.S. Army.

Chicago remained relatively quiet until early afternoon. Previous trouble spots like the Union Depot saw trains come and go in an "almost Sunday quiet." Some railroads ran passenger and freight trains more or less on time without incident. The Baltimore & Ohio reported "Passenger trains on fairly good time. No delays due to strikers," while the Chicago and Northwestern declared, "We are practically operating all our passenger trains in and out of Chicago . . . We are rapidly resuming the handling of freight." Others, like the Chicago and Alton, reported a more uneven status with some passenger service restored, but "No freight trains moving anywhere." The mixed nature of these reports allowed both the GMA and ARU to express confidence in their ability to win the strike.[18]

But in the afternoon large crowds began to interfere with the movement of trains and clash with police, deputy marshals, and soldiers. A reporter for the *Tribune* noted that "It was hoped the presence of the troops would have a quieting effect. Their presence only enflamed the mob." In some places crowds impeded rail traffic by overturning boxcars onto tracks or derailing trains or diverting them onto side tracks by forcing open switches. Another tactic was to separate cars from the engine by pulling their coupling pins. When railroad crews arrived to clear tracks, right overturned cars, and reattach cars, the crowds drove them away. On several occasions they swarmed trains and compelled the engineers and firemen to abandon their posts. As evening set in, crowds overturned and derailed more cars and in several locations set fire to rows of boxcars. Elsewhere people on bridges and overpasses hurled stones and bricks at passing trains, smashing windows and injuring passengers and crew members. These disturbances eventually petered out in the early morning hours.[19]

Strikers in the West likewise remained active. A few days prior in Trinidad, Colorado, striking railroad workers had taken control of the railyards and stopped most rail traffic. When forty-two deputy marshals arrived to arrest the strike leaders, workers seized them, prompting President Cleveland to dispatch five companies of U.S. Army soldiers from Fort Logan. They took control of the town and railyards and freed the marshals who proceeded to arrest forty-eight "ringleaders" and threaten local officials with arrest if they tried to interfere.[20]

On July 4 federal troops also arrived in Los Angeles to wrest control of the city's railyards from strikers. Soon trains begin departing the city with contingents of soldiers on board. Also, on July 4, a force of California militia arrived in Sacramento, but they encountered significant resistance from strikers and a sympathetic community. The day before, crowds had detached Pullman cars from trains and then roughed up the U.S. Marshal and his deputies who tried to intervene. But to the dismay of the U.S. Marshal, the militia soldiers proved sympathetic to the strikers and refused to attack or shoot them. He subsequently wired Washington to request federal troops. Strong resistance by strikers and their sympathizers in Oakland, as well as Ogden, Utah, likewise led to the dispatch of federal troops.

## THURSDAY JULY 5, 1894

The next morning, July 5, Chicago residents shook off their holiday revelries and prepared for a regular work day. The daily papers brimmed with alarmist details of the previous day's crowd actions. They also proclaimed, falsely as it turned out, that the U.S. military would henceforth be acting under new rules of engagement. "Today there will be no more passive tolerance of stones and jeers," noted the *Inter-Ocean*. As ever, the *Tribune* offered an even more sanguinary prediction. "[R]ioters will be fired upon, they will be bayoneted, will be trampled under foot by cavalry, and mowed down by artillery."[21] Adding to the ominous atmosphere that morning was news that Miles had called in reinforcements—four companies of soldiers from Fort Leavenworth in Kansas and three companies from Fort Brady in Michigan—that would bring the number of troops in the city to 1,936.[22] By noon several hundred had arrived and were setting up camp in Lake Front Park.[23] Likewise augmenting federal authority in the city was a surging number of deputy marshals which now topped 1,000.[24]

Governor Altgeld spent the early morning hours finalizing and then wiring a letter to President Cleveland protesting the deployment of federal troops. Seething with indignation, Altgeld did not mince words. In his second sentence the governor accused the president of being led astray by his advisors. "Surely the facts have not been presented correctly to you in this case or you would not have taken this step," which is "entirely unnecessary" and "unjustifiable." A president was only justified in sending federal troops into a state when state and local officials were unable to maintain order and enforce the law. Such was not the case in Illinois. It possessed an excellent state militia that stood at the ready to be deployed by the governor wherever needed. Altgeld reminded Cleveland that he had successfully deployed the militia to keep order during a recent coal strike in the state. He further pointed out that when the U.S. Marshal for the Southern District of Illinois requested help in quelling disturbances related to the Pullman Strike "troops were promptly furnished him." Had his counterpart in the state's Northern District (which included Chicago) requested similar assistance, wrote Altgeld, he would have received it.[25]

Altgeld then shifted his focus to the claims of the railroads that their paralysis stemmed from interference from strikers and their sympathizers. Rejecting this claim as representing a campaign of misinformation by the railroads, the governor said the real reason stemmed from the inability of the railroads to find enough men to run their trains. The railroads, he noted, "are anxious to keep this fact from the public, and for this purpose are making an outcry about obstructions in order to divert attention." To prove his point, Altgeld cited two recent examples where railroads requested he send state troops to suppress interference from strikers who were in "a condition bordering on anarchy." But in both cases, militia commanders reported that there were no disturbances and that the railroads were tied up due to a lack of men.

The governor did acknowledge there were actual cases of trains being stopped by crowds of strikers and sympathizers, but said "all these troubles were local in character and could easily be handled by the State authorities." Despite the newspapers publishing "pure falsifications" and "wild exaggerations" about the strike, "so very little actual violence has been committed." And of it, only a small percentage has been committed by striking railroad workers.

Altgeld closed by arguing that Cleveland's decision to send federal troops to Chicago violated not just federal statutes, but also "local self-government . . . a fundamental principle of our Constitution." To exhibit such disregard for this principle "is to do violence to the Constitution."

Twice in his final paragraph he called for "the immediate withdrawal" of federal troops from Illinois.[26]

Cleveland's reply was as brief—two sentences—as it was dismissive. The president ignored all the key points raised by Altgeld and instead simply asserted that his actions were "in strict accordance with the Constitution and the laws of the United States." Troops had been sent at the demand of the Post Office for the removal of obstructions to the movement of mail and at the request of officers of the federal courts who claimed court orders "could not be executed through the ordinary means." Additionally, the decision was in response to "abundant proof that conspiracies existed against" interstate commerce.[27] Several other governors like David A. Waite of Colorado and William Stone of Missouri who sent messages to the president protesting the introduction of federal troops into their states received similar replies.

Altgeld received savage treatment in the local and national press which called him impudent and disrespectful. Some, including the *Tribune*, even called him an anarchist who sympathized with those perpetrating violence and destruction of property. Nonetheless, the following day he responded to Cleveland with a lengthy, point-by-point refutation of the president's claims about his authority to send federal troops wherever he deemed necessary. He also reiterated his demand that federal troops be withdrawn from Illinois. Cleveland responded with a single sentence that brushed aside Altgeld's argument and said the dangerous situation called for public authorities to stop talking and instead take action to restore order.[28] Olney later reiterated Cleveland's assertion of federal supremacy over state sovereignty, prompting Altgeld to say of the Attorney General, "He is the especial representative of the great trusts and monopolies of the country that have been plundering the public and are trying to use the government as a convenience."[29]

While Altgeld waged his futile battle with Cleveland, Debs spent a busy morning at ARU headquarters conferring with advisors, sending telegrams, and speaking with reporters. At 11:00 AM he attended the conference organized by Mayor Hopkins and the City Council that aspired to arrange some sort of resolution to the strike. But it turned out to be a waste of time as Egan made good on his vow the previous day that the GMA would send no representatives. Hopkins also revealed that he had wired George Pullman asking him to return to Chicago to take part in negotiations to end the strike but that he had refused.[30]

When he returned to the ARU offices, Debs composed a lengthy statement that he subsequently released to the media. Hoping to combat the wildly inaccurate depictions in the newspapers of him, the ARU, the cause of the strike, and the strikers' demands, Debs said he was issuing "an honest, impartial statement of the issues involved and the facts as they actually exist" so that the American people could judge the situation for themselves. He began by stating that the Pullman employees struck not at the behest of the ARU, but rather "entirely of their own accord." The ARU actually advised against the strike, said Debs, but their grievances against Pullman had become "so aggravated, so galling, that patience deserted them and . . . their very souls rebelled."[31]

After summarizing their struggle against low wages and high rents, Debs castigated Pullman for refusing to submit the matter to arbitration. If the tables had been turned and his employees had refused to arbitrate and demanded his "unconditional surrender" to their demands, the public would have rightly condemned them as unreasonable. "The American people," said Debs, "are a peace-loving people—they want neither anarchy nor revolution . . . they believe in law and order . . .but they also believe in fair play." They will not tolerate the GMA's "arbitrary and dictatorial defiance" of the Pullman employees' reasonable demands. The ARU is not looking for recognition by Pullman or the railroads. It only insists the Pullman Company "meet its employees and do them justice." They will accept the outcome of any arbitration process. "Let the spirit of conciliation, mutual confession, and compromise animate and govern both sides, and there will be no trouble in reaching a settlement that will be satisfactory to all concerned." Debs cautioned people not to interpret his statement as a sign that the strike was weakening. "We firmly believe our cause is just, and while we hold that belief we will not recede."

Recognizing that rumors abounded of a general or sympathy strike being called in Chicago, with the goal of spreading it across the nation, Debs addressed the critics who claimed such tactics were wrongheaded and illegitimate. The leading practitioners of sympathy strikes, he said, are *corporations*. Taking aim at the GMA, Debs explained that when one member railroad was hit by a strike, "all go to the rescue. They stand together, they supply each other with men, money, and equipment." Labor in uniting to defend its interests is merely following their example. If corporations believe the sympathy strike is "vicious and indefensible," they must be the first to stop engaging in them. "In this contest labor will stand by labor," said Debs, especially as workers witness "the spectacle of Mr. Pullman fanned by the breezes of the seashore while his employees are starving."

One matter not addressed by Debs in his statement was his response to the arrival of federal troops in Chicago. When reporters asked him, he said the situation in the city did not justify the sending of troops. But he admitted he was not surprised as Cleveland was under the sway of Attorney

General Richard Olney, a man with strong and ongoing ties to the railroad industry. "Olney is the paid attorney of the [railroad] corporations," said Debs, "and the President seems to be the pliant tool of his Attorney-General." Workers have no quarrel with the military, he continued, but they are under no illusion regarding its role in the strike. "The soldier has never been the friend of labor," said Debs. "He has been the tool of capital in crushing labor."[32]

Despite this dark assessment of the threat posed by the military, Debs and other labor leaders projected confidence about the status of the strike. Victor Williams, a district organizer of the International Typographers Union, predicted that the introduction of troops would unify labor and cause more workers to join in support of the strike. James Sovereign, Grand Master Workman of the Knights of Labor, wired Debs to let him know his membership remained staunchly in support of the strike. "Neither make nor accept any compromise," wrote Sovereign. "Nothing but complete victory would satisfy our people." Sovereign also told reporters that his organization stood poised to join a general strike in support of the ARU and Pullman workers.[33]

One key source of optimism for Debs were the telegrams he was receiving from all over the country reporting that the strike was spreading. The GMA roads may get a train or two out of the city, Debs told the press, but they will not get very far when they encounter railroad workers who refuse to handle them. The railroads will find that "there are not enough men and soldiers to go around." Some of the headlines from the papers supported his contention. "Trains Lie Dead at Joliet," read one in the *Tribune*, while one in the *Inter-Ocean* declared, "Tie-Up on Big Four." Reports from California said strikers were in control of the railroads in Los Angeles, San Francisco, and the state capital, Sacramento. Another from Wyoming said strikers were in possession of the railyards at Cheyenne. And from Utah came word that strikers had halted the Rio Grande Western railroad.[34]

Equally inspiring was the looming prospect of a general strike in Chicago, supported by large sympathy walkouts in other cities. "[S]trike fever," reported the *Tribune*, "is spreading." In Milwaukee, the Federated Trades Council, an umbrella labor organization with fifty member unions, held a mass meeting that expressed strong support for a sympathy strike. Organizers in New York and New Jersey likewise reported growing support for a sympathy strike. The military might be able to suppress the strike in Chicago and a few other locales, but Debs believed a growing railroad strike across the country, supported by sympathy strikes in major industrial centers, would force the GMA and Pullman to the negotiating table.[35]

But expressions of optimism that morning were also found at the GMA headquarters. Egan and other railroad managers told reporters that the strike was faltering. Indeed, the same papers that contained stories suggesting growing success for the ARU also offered others that gave heart to the GMA. "Trains on the Move," proclaimed a *Tribune* headline on a page featuring several stories about locales where peace had been restored and passenger and freight trains began to move. Another story related that federal troops had wrested control of the town of Raton, New Mexico from strikers.[36]

Equally important were the ongoing stories of shortages—or in the parlance of the time, "famines" —of food, medicine, food, and other essentials caused by the strike which GMA officials believed would erode the public's support for Debs and the ARU. "Milk Famine Said to Be Imminent," reported the *Tribune* which also declared drugs and patent medicines to be in short supply. An editorial castigated Debs for causing the price of food, especially meat, to soar. Elsewhere the paper ran snippets of commentary on the strike, most of it anti-Debs and anti-ARU, from papers around the nation. "Debs and his mischief-makers have already taken the meat from the poor man's mouth," opined the *Elgin News*. "Bread will go next. What is to be gained by his senseless methods?" Many of these denunciations borrowed the *Tribune*'s now familiar terminology to describe Debs as a dictator and tyrant, and to characterize the strike as misguided and doomed to fail. "This warfare upon society," said the *New York World*, "seems to have been dictated mainly by the desire of a new labor organization to show its power . . . They have blundered to the lasting hurt of organized labor."[37]

Above all, the GMA leadership understood that what was of greatest value to their cause was sensational media coverage of continued episodes of violence and vandalism against the railroads because they could use it to justify ever more harsh repression by the courts, U.S. marshals and deputies, and federal troops. Trouble began towards midday in the Stock Yard when two companies of federal soldiers of the 15th Regiment took up formation around a freight train filled with livestock. A huge crowd gathered and began to denounce and jeer the soldiers. As before, the crowd included mostly men, but also many women and children. Soon the crowd closed in and scuffles broke out. The soldiers held their fire and battled the crowd with bayonets and rifle butts, until a contingent of 7th Cavalry showed up and sent the crowd flying. Quickly, the soldiers created a corridor along the tracks to allow the train to move and protect railroad workers as they fixed spiked switches. The train did not get very far before it encountered two dozen overturned boxcars. As the train waited for the arrival of a wrecking crew to remove the obstacles, an even larger crowd gathered and began harassing the soldiers. "Every roof and fence within sight," noted a *Tribune* reporter, "was literally black with people" eager to catch a glimpse of the action. When it became clear that no wrecking crew was forthcoming, the engineer commenced driving the train back to the Stock Yard, according to a *New York Times* reporter, "amid the wildest enthusiasm on the part of the strikers."[38]

At nearly the same time, a second confrontation was unfolding on the Rock Island railroad tracks leading into downtown Chicago. Three trains, the lead of which consisted of an engine and three coaches filled with soldiers of the 15th Regiment, made their way into the city until 51st St. where they encountered a derailed boxcar. A large crowd quickly gathered on the tracks in front of the trains, but they were subsequently driven off by the soldiers. When the boxcar obstruction had been removed, the trains resumed their journey but without soldiers who remained at 51st St. But the train only got as far as 40th St. where it encountered a large crowd and ten overturned boxcars blocking the tracks. The engineers then reversed direction and returned the trains to 51st St. A second attempt was made to bring the trains to their destination, this time with federal soldiers and US marshals on the ground clashing with members of the crowd and driving them away. Arriving once again at 40th St. they could see that an additional twenty or so boxcars had been overturned on the tracks ahead of them.[39]

Not long thereafter, a locomotive approached on a different track carrying Mayor Hopkins, Police Chief Brennan, and the city's Corporation Counsel. Their excursion was a fact-finding mission to determine the size and nature of the crowds and the most effective tactics for preventing them from menacing trains and placing obstructions on the tracks. With a large contingent of soldiers and policemen taking up positions along the right of way, keeping the crowd several hundred feet away from the tracks, the trains resumed their journey. It was slow going, as railroad workers, protected by police, soldiers, and deputy marshals, removed the many overturned cars on the tracks.[40]

This first direct exposure to an angry crowd of strikers and sympathizers, many of them women and children, confronting heavily armed U.S. Army regulars, seems to have impressed upon the mayor the volatility of the situation and the likelihood of significant bloodshed unless he took action. After staying aboard the locomotive for four or five blocks, Hopkins departed and headed straight for City Hall where he wrote and released a proclamation to the people of the city of Chicago. The disturbances of the last twenty-four hours, it read, "render it necessary that extraordinary measures be taken to preserve public peace and order." He threatened to exercise his legal right to call out the militia and to deputize unlimited numbers of civilians "for the protection of property and the preservation of the public peace." Hopkins then appealed to citizens to assist him in restoring order by avoiding places where crowds were gathered. He closed by announcing that the police were now directed to "disperse every assemblage of persons in the public streets or on or near railway tracks, and to promptly arrest all persons who refuse to disperse on demand."[41]

Notably missing from the proclamation was any mention of federal troops. Hopkins, it seems, was endeavoring to convince the public, either by appealing to their good nature or fear of arrest, to de-escalate the situation on the streets and railroad tracks, while at the same time demonstrating to the Cleveland administration, the Department of Justice, and U.S. military that he could handle the disturbances without federal troops. Part of this effort required that he counter the narrative being put forth by Egan and other GMA members that the Chicago police were not up to the task and this was the reason—not a lack of workers—why they could not run their trains and that therefore only federal troops could restore order. Accordingly, Hopkins wrote and released to the press a letter to Brennan ordering him to suspend any policemen who had been stationed that day on the Lake Shore and Michigan tracks where some railroad officials alleged the police had allowed rioters to overturn cars. Brennan complied and announced that he would swear in that evening hundreds of additional reserve policemen. There would be more than enough police protection tomorrow, he said, for any railroad to run its trains. If a line does not run, said Brennan, "it will be because it does not want to or because it cannot get the men to man the engines."[42]

In the late afternoon, while Hopkins and Brennan issued their missives and spoke with journalists, the police, soldiers, and deputy marshals engaged in periodic hit-and-run clashes with crowds along railroad tracks. These were minor engagements spurred along by the tendency of the crowds to disperse when confronted and then reassemble soon thereafter a few blocks away. During this time, General Miles was in a closed-door meeting with Colonel Crofton to confer about that day's clashes in the Stock Yards.

At 5:00 PM Miles emerged from the meeting and spoke with journalists in feverish, alarmist terms about the situation. "This thing has gone beyond a strike," said Miles. "It has become a dangerous riot. The crowd at the Stock-Yards is naturally gathering within itself the vicious and criminal classes. If it is not dispersed a grave crisis is before Chicago." If unchecked, these frenzied mobs would soon fan out across the city to wreak havoc and destruction in residential and business districts. When a journalist asked why his soldiers had not dispersed the crowds, Miles said their current orders were to protect federal property and not "to perform police duty." The latter was a calculated dig at the Chicago police department that echoed the allegations of railroad officials that the police were failing to disperse the rioters. Miles then noted ominously that his soldiers had exhibited extraordinary restraint in not firing on the crowds that jeered and insulted them. "They do not seem to realize what a terrible engine of destruction they are going against when they fool with the soldiers," said Miles. "Fifty of these soldiers could mow down 2,000 people in a few minutes." And then he arrived at what appeared to be the goal of his menacing remarks: instigating a federal declaration of martial law. "Conditions like these existing today cannot last many hours without ending in a declaration of martial law. Then the military will be supreme."[43]

## Martial Law

A declaration of martial law means a suspension of civil government, including courts, in a designated area (city, country, state, or region) and placing authority in the hands of military officials. It is intended as a temporary measure to bring order to a region beset by foreign invasion, natural disaster, or civil unrest. Declarations of martial law, either by state or federal officials, have occurred in U. S. history in crises ranging from the British attack on New Orleans during the War of 1812 and in the aftermath of the Great Chicago Fire of 1871, to the 1934 West Coast Longshoremen's Strike and the arrival of civil rights Freedom Riders in Alabama in 1963. Because it involves the suspension of democratically elected authority, martial law has been declared only rarely in U.S. history, often triggering significant opposition and protest.

It may have seemed odd to some that a man who fought in many of the Civil War's bloodiest battles, and who spent several decades leading military assaults against Native American warriors in the so-called Indian Wars of the 1870s and 1880s, appeared unnerved by what up to that point amounted to some isolated incidents of rioting and property damage, all of which had been suppressed with relative ease. But Miles was aware of the hysterical media coverage of the disturbances in Chicago that painted a picture of a city in flames being overrun by anarchists. As a man with ambitions to rise to the nation's top military post and even the White House, he understood the value of playing up the danger posed by the crowds. The more sinister the foe, the greater the glory that would be accorded him when he vanquished it. Olney viewed his remarks as pompous grandstanding and said, "if Miles would do less talking to newspapers and more shooting at strikers he'd come nearer fulfilling his mission on earth and earning his pay."[44]

As Miles was holding forth before reporters, another clash was taking shape at the Stock Yard. Police and soldiers had been sent a few blocks away to contend with another train stopped by a crowd. Their absence emboldened a group of men and boys to begin overturning cars onto the Western Indiana and Fort Wayne Railroad tracks. At 5:30 PM a Western Indiana passenger train arrived and came to a halt. With the tracks ahead blocked by countless cars and a large crowd gathering, the engineer began to back the train down the tracks toward its point of origin. But the crowd swarmed the tracks to force the train to stop. E. J. Gregory, an agent of the Western Indiana railroad, pulled his pistol and fired twice into the crowd, striking two men, both in the leg. The wounds were not fatal, but the gunfire enraged the crowd which threatened to stop the train and seize Gregory. But the engineer opened the throttle and the train left the area.[45]

Not long after that, at 6:00 PM a fire broke out in one of the remaining buildings of what was left of the White City on the Columbian Exposition grounds. Homeless people living there had made a cooking fire in the Terminal Station where the previous year several million Americans had stepped off Pullman cars to visit the world's fair. The fire quickly spread to the Court of Honor, and then to the Administration Building where President Cleveland had delivered his address at the grand opening of the fair. Fanned by a warm breeze the flames then began to consume the Manufacturing and Liberal Arts buildings. As the flames grew to more than one hundred feet in height and the peel of fire bells filled the air, the inferno attracted a huge crowd of onlookers. Standing on side streets and rooftops of buildings, they watched as one by one the grand structures collapsed, sending columns of sparks into the night sky.[46]

At 10:00 PM a large crowd gathered at Kensington, allegedly intent upon stopping the Diamond Special bound for St. Louis. That train, however, possibly tipped off by the station master, rocketed past the station without stopping. But a "police train" filled with policemen and railroad workers that was escorting the Diamond Special was forced to stop. Immediately the crowd began to pelt the train with rocks and other projectiles. Some of the policemen fired their revolvers into the crowd, but to no effect. The crowd swarmed the train, drove off the engineer and fireman, and then proceeded to detach the locomotive, open its throttle, and send it flying down the track with no one at the controls. It was later safely stopped before it crashed.[47]

By then more fires could be seen throughout the city, far from the smoldering ruins of the White City. These were burning boxcars, signal towers, and sheds set ablaze by crowds roaming freely along tracks and in railyards. The fires unnerved many Chicago residents, conjuring up memories of the great fire of 1871.

It had been another day of unrest in Chicago, but despite the feverish rhetoric of Miles and frenzied headlines of the local papers, no more so than in previous days. The clashes between the crowds and police, soldiers, and deputy marshals had occurred in several locations, but by no means was the city consumed by such incidents. Railroad property had been vandalized and some destroyed, but these incidents also occurred in specific locations and often involved the overturning and occasionally burning of what amounted to a small number of old boxcars. According to Miles the next day, "very little property" was destroyed, the most significant being about 100 burned boxcars.[48]

## FRIDAY JULY 6, 1894

In New Jersey the next morning, Friday July 6, George Pullman brushed off reporters who asked for his response to Mayor Hopkins' request that he return to Chicago immediately to join efforts to bring about a settlement in the strike. "I am so worn out and tired," he explained to a reporter. And besides, "the strike has gone beyond me, and I could say little of interest." He then boarded a train that took him from his seaside retreat to his other summer home, in the Thousand Oaks region of upstate New York.[49]

In Chicago, much of the city proper was quiet for the whole day, with the exception of some isolated incidents of trains being pelted by rocks.[50] But on the southern periphery near the town of Pullman in Kensington, Burnside, Wildwood, and Riverdale, large crowds interfered with trains and vandalized some railroad property. At about 9:00 AM on the Illinois Central tracks just south of Burnside, crowds set fire to forty-seven empty boxcars and a loaded coal car, and overturned two freight cars. When a force of policeman and deputy marshals arrived, the crowd drove them off. At roughly the same time in nearby Kensington, a crowd swarmed the tracks to stop an incoming Michigan Central train. The chief detective of the Michigan Central on the train, George Stark, who was also an acting deputy marshal, pulled his revolver and fired into the crowd, wounding one man just above his eye and killing another with shots to the forehead and back. Stark narrowly escaped the clutches of an incensed crowd due to the timely intervention of a squad of policeman and deputy marshals. They would clash with the crowds several times that morning and early afternoon until federal troops arrived.[51]

Mayor Hopkins' morning began with a visit from representatives of the GMA who requested greater police protection of their trains. According to the mayor, this was the first time they had expressed dissatisfaction with the level of police protection. Up to the previous day, he later recounted, they had assured him police protection had been "the most efficient protection they had ever received during similar [labor] troubles."[52] Two additional developments that morning strongly suggested an intensified campaign by the GMA to discredit the police department and, thereby, justify the presence of federal soldiers. First, the GMA issued a statement denying the claims made by Debs and other ARU officials that it was having trouble running its trains due to inadequate number of workers, not on account of inadequate police protection from crowd actions. As many as 90 percent of their employees, declared the GMA, along with large numbers of replacement workers, stood ready to carry out their duties, if only they could receive protection from "the lawlessness of mobs not as yet suppressed."[53] Next, several GMA member railroads issued statements that they intended to sue the city for damages done to railroad property on account of inadequate police protection.[54]

Despite his firm belief that the Chicago Police Department was handling the disturbances effectively, Mayor Hopkins consulted with his advisers and decided to request that Governor Altgeld send state militia troops to Chicago. He had in recent days sent small detachments to several hot spots outside Chicago. Their presence would increase the chances that the violence and vandalism could be quelled without resorting to federal troops. Accordingly, Hopkins wired the governor who concurred and immediately dispatched five regiments totaling 3,000 soldiers. Seeking to minimize the chances of bloodshed, Altgeld directed his militia commander to be very careful. Soldiers were to keep their rifles unloaded and only fire their weapons when ordered to do so. "There is no glory," wrote the governor, "in shooting at a ragged and hungry man. There is glory in being able to disperse a mob without bloodshed because it requires ability to do it." He emphasized that the militia soldiers were not "guards or custodians of private property"—meaning railroad property. Their charge was to "keep the peace, quell riots and enforce the law." When these 3,000 militia soldiers arrived later that day they joined 3,300 policemen, 1,000 federal soldiers, 1,000 deputy marshals, and 500 deputy sheriff's marshals.[55]

As a goodwill gesture, Hopkins gave his City Hall office over to the militia commander to use as his headquarters. Throughout the day as more militia arrived, contingents were dispatched to fifty train stations and crossings throughout the city, as well as the Stock Yards.[56]

News of the order to send in the militia, along with the Mayor's declaration the night before that the police would disperse crowds, appeared to greatly please General Miles who adopted a more measured tone. "The action of the Mayor and Governor in calling out the State troops is an excellent one," he said. "The police seem to be active and the effect of the action of the city authorities appears to be salutary." In contrast to his dire and apocalyptic description of the situation in Chicago the day before, he now told reporters that his force of 1,000 soldiers was more than adequate and that he would not be requesting reinforcements. He also opined that it would not be necessary to declare martial law because—even though incidents of violence, vandalism, and interference with trains had occurred that morning—he believed the situation had improved greatly over the last twenty-four hours. He also offered that "The lawbreakers" engaged in vandalism "constitute a very small percentage of the people" of Chicago. Miles then wired a formal report that said much the same thing to the White House where it was received during a cabinet meeting convened to discuss the strike.[57]

Miles' report convinced the administration to hold off on sending more troops at the present time and to continue to focus primarily on Chicago. However, they did discuss the situation elsewhere around the country. As before, the news was mixed. The arrival of federal troops in Raton and Trinidad, New Mexico had restored order, but disturbances in Las Vegas, New Mexico prompted the dispatch of federal troops to that location. In Montana an ongoing blockade of railroad tracks raised the likelihood that federal troops would soon be sent. The same was true for Utah as the state's governor formally requested military assistance. Offsetting these concerns was news that federal troops had assisted in ending a tie-up in Little Rock, Arkansas and trains were moving without delays through Sioux City, Iowa. The Post Office reported that overall the movement of the mail was improving in most locations.[58]

That afternoon in Chicago, despite the arrival of the militia, more disturbances erupted. In one high-profile incident, a railroad worker who had taken the job of a striking fireman was accosted on his way to work by a striker who tried to convince him to join the strike. When he refused, a scuffle ensued. His wife, who had accompanied him, called for help and when none appeared forthcoming pulled out a revolver and shot dead her husband's assailant.[59]

In Burnside and Wildwood, crowds that had settled down after disturbances in the morning resumed acts of vandalism, burning two hundred freight cars. At the same time, unrest exploded in the Stock

Yards as outnumbered groups of policemen tried unsuccessfully to stop crowds from overturning cars. A contingent of U.S. soldiers fixed bayonets, charged the crowd three times, and sent them scattering. But the latter reassembled elsewhere in the Stock Yards and by midafternoon began to set fire to boxcars, signal towers, and sheds. Soon, according to a *Tribune* reporter, "they had a roaring wall of fire down the tracks" from 55th to 61st streets that consumed scores of cars. When Chicago firemen arrived, noted one observer, they were "as helpless as so many children," as people in the crowd pelted them with rocks and bricks and cut their hoses.[60]

At roughly the same time that afternoon, about two hundred men surprised and pushed past the guards at the Pullman factory and entered the works. Given the many incidents of vandalism since the boycott began, many had been surprised that no disturbances had occurred at the facility. This was most likely due to Debs' incessant urging that ARU members stay away from the factory, and the fact that striking Pullman workers had voluntarily maintained a round the clock guard around the factory to prevent any vandalism or sabotage.

The intruders did no damage. They walked around the works and allegedly convinced or intimidated some workers to leave their posts, and then scattered when some heavily armed security guards arrived. Rumors abounded, reported the *Tribune*, that this incident was the first foray of a coordinated plan to attack the factory and destroy the four hundred Pullman cars sitting idle in the yard, as well as to burn the Hotel Florence. The arrival of two companies of the state militia in Pullman elicited "taunts, epithets, jeers, and disparaging remarks" from towns people as they set up camp on the lawn in front of the Hotel Florence, but the rest of the day and evening the situation remained quiet. The arrival of similar detachments of the militia to nearby Fordham, Kensington, and Riverdale had the same effect.[61]

Such was not the case near the Stock Yards where later that evening crowds gathered on the Panhandle tracks to set fire to more cars. "Soon from all parts of the yard flames shot up and billows of fire rolled over the cars," wrote an *Inter-Ocean* reporter, "covering them with the red glow of destruction . . . It was pandemonium let loose, the fire leaping along from miles." In all, some seven hundred cars were reduced to ash and molten metal.[62]

This sudden turn to arson on July 5 and 6 prompted Debs and others to accuse the GMA of hiring men to foment violence and vandalism, including arson, to turn the public against the strike. In fact, Debs had predicted more than a week prior that the GMA would hire arsonists. Many observers close to the action, including Miles, had acknowledged frequently that the overwhelming majority of the crowds were comprised of non-strikers. Indeed, they frequently commented on the large numbers of women, young boys, and children in the crowds. These descriptions suggested whole communities of working-class people were venting their anger against powerful industrial interests. But Debs and other ARU officials believed the crowds included hired agents of chaos. "We have it upon reliable authority," Debs told the press, "that thugs and toughs have been employed to create trouble so as to prejudice the public against our cause." Those who suspected the railroads of fomenting arson noted that the fires seemed to be set in a systematic manner, and that they mostly destroyed old railroad stock and only a few costly Pullmans. Most damning was the revelation by the Fire Department that several of the men arrested in the stockyards on the night of July 6 for cutting fire hoses wore deputy marshal badges. Most of the 1,000 men sworn in as deputy marshals in the past week were loyal railroad employees still on the payroll who were put forth by the GMA railroads.[63]

As the evening sky over Chicago filled with the scent of burning boxcars, hundreds of representatives of the city's many trade unions gathered for a conference at ARU headquarters in Uhlich's Hall. The question on the table, one that many believed would determine victory or defeat for the Pullman Strike, was whether they should declare a general strike and completely shut down the city. After considerable debate behind closed doors without journalists present, they emerged to say that sentiment favored a general strike if it was deemed necessary to achieving victory for the Pullman strikers in the face of continued refusals by Pullman and the GMA to agree to arbitration. But such a momentous decision required approval from each member union, so it was decided that union leaders should discuss the question with their members at their regular Sunday meetings two days hence and then bring the results to another conference at Uhlich Hall Sunday evening where a vote on a general strike would take place.[64]

Debs ended the proceedings by issuing a proclamation "To All Striking Employees" in which he urged them to stay away from any disturbances and to avoid interfering with replacement workers. "We must triumph as law-abiding citizens or not at all." The GMA, said Debs, had hired people to foment violence and vandalism to turn the public against the strikers. These disturbances also allowed the railroads to falsely claim that they were the reason so many trains were not running, rather than the real reason which was a lack of workers to run them. "Our cause is just," said Debs, "the great public is with us, and we have nothing to fear."[65]

## SATURDAY JULY 7, 1894

The next day, officials in Washington, D.C. expressed confidence that the strike was nearing a conclusion. The general in charge of federal troops in Los Angeles reported that the military had complete control of the situation and that he expected no further trouble. No reports of disturbances in previous trouble spots like Trinidad, Colorado and Raton, New Mexico was taken to mean the army had matters in hand. Additionally General Scofield announced that he had ordered federal troops to open up the entire length of the Northern Pacific and Union Pacific railroads.[66]

Reports out of Chicago also suggested the strike was petering out. For most of the day the city was calm and quiet. There were no disturbances along the tracks, or at crossings or depots. On most lines, passenger and freight trains moved in and out of the city on time and without incident. Mail trains guarded by deputy marshals and federal troops departed the city from six depots without incident. Louis L. Troy, division superintendent of the railway mail service in Chicago, reported to the Postmaster General that the mail was moving smoothly with no backlog. At the scenes of yesterday's disturbances, wrecking crews guarded by policemen and militia soldiers labored all day to right overturned cars and remove what was left of those burned. The heavy presence of soldiers, militia, and police seemed to be working, as no large crowds gathered and only the occasional rock or insult was hurled in their direction.[67]

That changed in the later afternoon when the most serious and deadly incident of the Pullman Strike took place. At 3:30 PM, as one of the wrecking crews approached an overturned boxcar, a large crowd of several thousand assembled near Loomis St. and 49th Street. They began hurling insults, rocks, and hunks of metal at the workers and the soldiers and police on hand for protection. The militia's leader, Captain Thomas I. Mair, commanded the crowd to disperse and, in a move intended to intimidate the crowd into compliance, ordered his men to load their rifles. But the crowd did not disperse and continued to hurl projectiles at the soldiers, police, and workers. Mair then ordered a bayonet charge, which temporarily drove the crowd back from the tracks. But it surged forward once again. A policeman was struck by a rock and he fired into the crowd. Allegedly a return shot was fired from a nearby shed. Several more policemen fired their revolvers, some over the heads of the people, others indiscriminately into their ranks. A roar of outrage emanated from the crowd, as did more rocks and missiles. When a militia officer was knocked unconscious by a rock, Captain Mair called his men into formation, told them to aim, and shouted "Fire!" Dozens in the crowd were shot, several of them fatally.[68]

***Figure 5.1* "Militiamen Fire into the Mob at Loomis and Forty-Ninth Streets," *Chicago Tribune* July 8, 1894, 1. Upon its arrival in Chicago, the state refrained from using deadly force to disperse crowds. But on this occasion, they opened fire on a crowd, killing at least four.**

Some people scattered in fear, but most of the crowd surged toward the militia. Mair ordered his men to fix bayonets and they charged the crowd, prodding and stabbing anyone in their path. Several times the crowd fell back down Loomis Street, only to surge forward again. When another crowd approached the work crew and wrecking engine from a different direction, the militia came to their defense and charged the crowd with bayonets. They continued to fend off the crowd as they followed the engine on foot as it carried the work crew away to safety.[69] Additional police soon arrived on the scene to reinforce those who had remained behind. Swinging clubs and occasionally firing revolvers over the heads of the people in the crowd, they managed to drive the crowd from the tracks and into side streets. Officers who pursued people were pelted by rocks and other projectiles thrown from rooftops.

The arrival of additional militia soldiers finally restored order to the area which, according to one journalist, "looked like a battlefield." Streets were littered with hats, stones, cartridge shells, and broken glass.

Several policemen and militia soldiers reported injuries sustained from objects thrown at them by the crowd. Of the latter, at least four people were dead, but the number was likely higher as friends and family carried off the fatally wounded, some of whose families, fearful of legal repercussions, never reported the deaths.[70] Two additional killings occurred elsewhere in the city. Richard Zepp, a detective employed by the Baltimore & Ohio railroad, was killed by a bullet fired through a window at the Union Depot in downtown Chicago. At 22nd Street, Polish laborer Joseph Warzowski was shot dead by either a deputy marshal or federal soldier.[71]

Word of the deadly clash near Loomis Street reached Mayor Hopkins shortly after 4:00 PM. Up to this point he had enjoyed a relatively quiet afternoon at his office, devoting most of his time to meetings with officials of several GMA member railroads who had requested extra protection for their property that evening. Chief of Police Brennan arrived to provide only minimal details, indicating that as many as six members of the crowd had been killed and that no policemen or militia had been killed.[72]

At 5:00 PM Egan and several other railroad executives arrived at City Hall. Welcomed into the Mayor's office, they urged him to find a way to coordinate the actions of the militia and federal troops so that they, in the words of a *Tribune* reporter, "could act in unison." In other words, they wanted the army to expand its mandate from protecting railroad and government property, and preventing interference with the free movement of interstate commerce and mail, to attacking the crowds wherever they formed. Incensed, Hopkins rejected their request, saying the federal troops had only exacerbated the situation in Chicago and pointing out that he had no authority to request federal troops or influence their deployment. Further, federal troops were not needed in the city. "We are perfectly able to suppress riots by the aid of the State troops." Hopkins' defiance angered Egan and the two engaged in a heated exchange before the railroad men left.[73]

Later that evening Egan gathered reporters to make a forceful case for the violent suppression of the strike by federal troops. "[W]e have reached the point where none but violent measures can produce a better condition of affairs. This thing must come to an end. The government is being openly defied, commerce of the country ruined." Egan called for "a strong hand" and deplored the "quibbling over legal technicalities and hair's breadth definitions of the constitutional rights of the citizens." He then commented favorably on the deadly events of that afternoon.

> I must say the action of the troops in firing upon the strikers at Forty-Seventh St. is a move in the right direction, though I deplore

> its necessity. . . . If these fellows once learn that their acts of violence will be met with bullets the end of the strike will then not be far off.[74]

At 6:00 PM Mayor Hopkins received General Miles at his office. Miles informed him that he had just spoken with President Cleveland by telephone to update him on the situation. The President expressed his satisfaction and instructed Miles that the federal troops under his command in Chicago were to protect government property and ensure the unhindered movement of trains carrying the mail and interstate commerce. But in a departure from prior instructions, they also could be deployed against crowds of strikers and protesters if requested by the mayor. This new policy aligned perfectly with the desires of Egan and the GMA to use federal military force to crush the strike. All that was needed to bring this about was more violence and vandalism by the crowds that would increase public pressure on Hopkins to unleash the military. Recognizing this, Hopkins told Miles the more than 6,000 policemen and state militia on hand was more than adequate to suppress any unrest.[75]

At roughly the same time, Debs received some hopeful information that somewhat offset the dreadful news of the afternoon's deadly clashes that the newspapers were certain to claim was entirely the fault of radicalized strikers. A prominent Chicago businessman sent word that he had convinced vice-president Wickes of the Pullman Company to meet the next morning with a delegation of Pullman workers. Wickes stipulated that the delegation must not include any officers of the ARU and that the purpose of the meeting was "not with any view toward arbitration." Despite these conditions, Debs saw the meeting as a sign that arbitration might soon be in the offing. Accordingly, he set to finding Pullman employees to serve on the committee.[76]

Debs also co-wrote with James Sovereign, head of the Knights of Labor, a letter to President Cleveland and had it wired to the White House and then released to the press. It offered a review of the history of the strike, emphasizing that the sole cause of the original dispute was the arrogant intransigence of George Pullman in refusing to agree to arbitration. Only then did the ARU become involved and its members begin to refuse to handle Pullman cars. Furthermore, it was the actions of the GMA—not the ARU—that caused disruptions in the delivery of the mail. The latter's member railroads insisted that mail be hauled on trains that included Pullman cars, thereby guaranteeing holdups. Debs and Sovereign condemned the use of federal troops as the "support and protection of the railroad corporations in their determination to degrade and oppress their employees." Federal troops had been sent to support the forcing of railroad workers into a "humiliating obedience to the will of their oppressors." Never in the nation's history, they continued, was there "an instance on record where in any conflict between the corporations and the people, the strong arm of the military power has been employed to protect the working people and the industrial masses from the ravages and persecution of corporate greed." They closed with a pledge that their organizations would help maintain the public peace and assist in the arrest of anyone engaged in illegal actions related to the strike. Cleveland apparently read the letter but offered no response.[77]

As darkness fell over Chicago, the city remained calm, as if in shock over the killings that afternoon. But in nearby Hammond, Indiana which bordered the city's South Side, crowds gathered in the railyards and overturned fifteen freight cars to obstruct the Michigan Central and Nickel Plate tracks. Vandalism, stopping of trains, and clashes with police continued for hours until the arrival of a contingent of state militia.[78]

That evening a special late edition of the *Chicago Tribune* deemed July 7 "A DAY OF BLOOD."

## SUNDAY JULY 8

Sunday July 8 dawned warm and quiet. But the city's newspapers roared with indignation and alarm. One would not know from reading them that the violence and death that transpired the previous day was confined to one small section of the city. Nor would they understand that the number of crowd actions and clashes with police, militia, and federal troops was trending downward from its peak on July 6 and that the movement of trains in and out of the city—including mail trains—was on the rise. Instead, the papers painted a dire picture of anarchy and lawlessness that threatened not just the citizens of Chicago, but the nation itself. "It is not a strike," declared a *Tribune* editorial. "It is a revolution against the law, against the government, and against society."[79] Newspapers across the nation repeated these exaggerated and sensational accounts of the unrest in Chicago, convincing millions of Americans that Chicago was being destroyed a second time. "I am amazed," Mayor Hazen S. Pingree of Detroit said to Mayor Hopkins when he arrived in Chicago a few days later. "[F]rom the reports which come out of here I expected to see half of Chicago in flames and the other half in possession of a mad mob."[80]

A single hot spot emerged that Sunday morning in Hammond, Indiana. The trouble was a continuation of the vandalism and stoppage of trains that broke out the night before. Ordered to the scene by Miles, Captain William T. Hartz arrived at 11:30 AM with forty-nine federal troops. He immediately set them to work clearing debris from tracks to allow a stalled mail car to proceed. A large crowd quickly formed on and around the tracks, prompting the soldiers to fix bayonets and drive them back. At the same time, Hartz and some soldiers boarded an engine that headed down the tracks to see if additional obstacles needed removing. He soon received word that a group of men back in Hammond were trying to topple a Pullman to block his return. Hartz ordered the train to return at full speed. As it pulled into the yard the soldiers on board, apparently without orders, began firing into the crowd, striking six—two fatally—and causing a general panic. The town's mayor mounted a boxcar, called for calm, and implored the people to go home. Some complied, but others remained, furious over the unprovoked killings. The situation remained tense and uncertain until three additional companies of federal troops arrived whereupon the crowd dispersed.[81]

Seething with indignation, the mayor of Hammond wired the governor of Indiana demanding an explanation. "I would like to know by what authority United States Troops come in here and shoot our citizens without the slightest warning." The president of the local ARU likewise fired off a telegram to the governor urging action. "Federal troops shooting citizens down promiscuously without provocation. Cannot something be done to protect citizens? Act quickly." Hammond residents convinced a local magistrate to issue warrants for the arrest of the soldiers involved in the shootings on charges of murder. None were ever served as the troops involved were already on their way back to Chicago.

In contrast to Hammond, Chicago enjoyed one of its most peaceful days in weeks. On the South Side, the scene of the deadly violence the day before, residents, noted one reporter, enjoyed the "quietest day that the neighborhood experienced in many years." Most businesses, including saloons, were closed. Curiosity seekers, including many in fancy carriages, toured the wreckage from Saturday's fracas. Some took photographs, while others are searched for bullet casings and other souvenirs.[82]

President Cleveland and his cabinet spent much of the day receiving and discussing updates on the strike in Chicago and other parts of the West. Cleveland also read many of the hundreds of telegrams from ordinary Americans that poured into the White House all weekend. Many of them urged him to use force to end the strike.[83] "Unless you take decided action at once," wrote a Chicago businessman, echoing the dire rhetoric of the *Tribune*, "the riot and rebellion will be entirely beyond your control and much property and blood will have to be sacrificed, and I fear we will never return to the peaceful years of the past. . . . No half hearted measure will satisfy anyone." Federal troops should clear the stockyards of strikers and rioters, or "leave his men dead on the field as martyrs to liberty."[84]

Many of the president's advisors likewise called for more force to be applied to end the strike. By evening General Schofield—in spite of assurances by Miles, Hopkins, and Altgeld that forces adequate to restoring order were on hand in the city—had convinced Cleveland to authorize the dispatch of 1,000 more federal soldiers to Chicago, as well as the recruiting of thousands more deputy marshals. They then commenced drafting a statement by the president that would announce a more hardline approach to the strike.[85]

While the White House was abuzz with activity that Sunday, so too was Uhlich's Hall in Chicago. At 8:00 PM that evening in excess of three hundred delegates from more than one hundred of the city's trade unions, many of them affiliated with the AFL, gathered to consider declaring a general strike of 100,000 Chicago workers as a means to compel George Pullman to agree to arbitration with his striking employees. Also on hand were leaders of prominent national unions like John McBride of the United Mine Workers, James O'Connell of the International Machinists Union, William B. Prescott of the International Typographers Union, and James Sovereign of the Knights of Labor.

In the ensuing debate over the advisability of calling a general strike, delegates sparred over the risks of such a move, versus the need to act boldly. Many delegates said they could not support any action as their unions were still debating their course of action. Toward midnight, four hours into the debate, the meeting was rocked by word that President Cleveland had issued a statement that amounted to a declaration of martial law in all but name. [86]

It opened by stating that "unlawful obstructions, combinations, and assemblages" have made it impossible for the federal government to enforce the law in Illinois and especially Chicago as called for by the courts. As a consequence, said Cleveland, he had dispatched federal troops. Now he was imposing new restrictions and consequences. "I, Grover Cleveland, President of the United States, do hereby admonish all good citizens . . . against aiding, countenancing, encouraging, or taking part in . . . unlawful obstructions, combinations, and assemblages." He warned that anyone currently taking part in these disturbances "to disperse and retire peaceably to their abodes" by 12 noon Monday July 9. Anyone who persisted in "taking part with a riotous mob" in defiance of the law and destroying government property would be considered "public enemies." Federal troops would continue to exhibit restraint, but if the use of deadly force was deemed necessary they would not distinguish between "guilty participants" and any onlookers or curiosity seekers "who are mingled with them." To ensure their personal safety, people should avoid scenes of conflict and stay at home. When General Miles was asked if Cleveland's proclamation was a declaration of martial law, he said, "It amounts to the same thing. It means whoever disobeys it is a public enemy, and as such is to be destroyed."[87]

Cleveland's decree jolted the labor meeting, enraging many delegates, and swinging sentiment towards the more radical faction that had been pressing for a general strike. But as debate resumed it became clear that no consensus had emerged. Finally, the delegates reached a compromise position. They endorsed one more attempt by a committee of five labor leaders and Mayor Hopkins to try to convince the GMA and George Pullman to agree to arbitration. If the latter stuck by their "nothing to arbitrate" position, a general strike would begin on Wednesday morning, July 11. Delegates also adopted several resolutions, including ones urging Chicago's City Council and Governor Altgeld demand that federal troops be removed from the city and another calling upon Samuel Gompers, President of the AFL, to come to Chicago to help bring about a resolution to the strike. It was 4:30 AM when the all-night meeting was gaveled to a close.[88]

## Samuel Gompers

Samuel Gompers was born in 1850 into a Jewish family living in London. When he was ten he joined his father in making cigars. At age thirteen he emigrated with his family to New York City where he continued to make a living making cigars. Gompers soon joined the Cigar Makers' International Union and was elected president of his local in 1875. In those years he became committed to craft unionism which focused on the organizing of unions of skilled workers in specific crafts such as plumbing, carpentry, typography, metal work, stone cutting, and of course, cigar making. Craft unionism stood in opposition to the industrial unionism of the Knights of Labor which endeavored to organize all workers, regardless of skill. Gompers and other leaders in the movement believed only skilled workers possessed the leverage and power needed to wrest concessions from employers. The less skilled, they noted, had no leverage and could easily be replaced. The craft unionism of Gompers also focused on practical goals of higher wages, shorter hours, and improved conditions, rather than the more ambitious goals of social transformation sought by socialists and industrial unionists. In 1881 he helped establish a new national organization of trade unions, the Federation of Organized Trades and Labor Unions. Five years later it was reorganized and renamed the American Federation of Labor and Gompers was elected its first president.

## MONDAY JULY 9

Two questions hung in the air as the sun rose over Chicago. First, what would be the result of Cleveland's proclamation, which most newspapers characterized as declaring "martial law" or something "practically to that effect"? And second, would the latest attempt at ending the strike through arbitration succeed? The answer to the latter came by mid-afternoon. A group of labor delegates met with the Mayor and several members of the City Council and produced a proposal to the Pullman Company. A committee of five would be formed comprising two representatives chosen by the Pullman Company, two chosen by the circuit judges of the county, who then together would select a fifth member. This committee would weigh the evidence at hand and decide if there were grounds for arbitration. The plan—an arbitration hearing to decide if arbitration was warranted—represented an extraordinary attempt by labor to appear reasonable and open-minded to the general public, and if he rejected it, to reveal George Pullman as obstinate and unfair. When brought before Vice-President Wickes that afternoon, he said the company would not "recede" from its position that there was nothing to arbitrate. After some back and forth that went nowhere, the committee left and went to ARU headquarters to inform Debs.[89]

This predictable result then raised a third question: Was the city on the verge of a general strike, one with potential to spread nationally? One labor leader who was present at the meeting with Wickes, E. J. Lindholm, Master Workman of Knights of Labor District Council 24, spoke enthusiastically of this possibility. "The Pullman Company has taken away the last hope of an amicable settlement of these labor troubles. Now it must be war to the bitter end. Wednesday morning will witness the biggest strike ever known in this country."[90]

Even though a general strike was set to commence on Wednesday morning, Debs and other labor leaders faced a great deal of uncertainty. Participation in the general strike would be voluntary. There was nothing to compel any of the city's unions to call their workers out on Wednesday. And while many unions and individual workers expressed strong support for the Pullman strikers and the assistance provided by the ARU, walking out posed significant risks. Some feared that high unemployment meant employers could more easily replace them. Others like the Plumbers Union cited the fact that they had only recently won a hard-fought struggle for a new contract and feared participation in a sympathy walkout would allow their employers to cancel it. Still others adhered to a more conservative approach to labor–capital disputes and deemed a general strike too radical, especially under the present circumstances. Typical was the position put forth by the head of the Teamsters Union. He declined to say whether or not his union would join the general strike, but affirmed that they were

> in sympathy with the American Railway Union in its fight for justice. If this fight is won it will establish a recognition of all labor and not organized labor alone. It is a fight between capital and labor in which the former is trying to down the latter.[91]

Due to the late ending of the meeting at Uhlich's Hall, and the lack of any crowd actions or disturbances in the city, ARU headquarters was quiet for most of Monday. Debs greeted reporters in the afternoon with characteristic charm and optimism. "Not much to say today, boys, except that we are confident as ever. We will win our fight, injunctions and the troops to the contrary notwithstanding." He declined to comment further but did acknowledge that the question of the general strike, "is in the hands of the allied trades" which were holding meetings that day and the next to determine their position.[92]

Later that afternoon Debs received news the significance of which was unclear. Samuel Gompers, president of the American Federation of Labor, the nation's foremost labor organization, announced that he had accepted the invitation of Chicago's trade unions and was heading to the city in "an effort to bring about order in what threatens to become chaos and confusion." He wanted "to help in bringing this industrial crisis to a peaceful and honorable ending." Debs was aware that Gompers had expressed strong support for the Pullman Strike and ARU boycott and had condemned Cleveland's decision to send federal troops to Chicago. But it was unclear to him what Gompers intended to do in Chicago. Perhaps he would try to use his influence to push Pullman to the negotiating table? Maybe he would support the general strike and order all AFL unions to join it? But Debs also knew that Gompers held a view of labor–capital relations that was more conservative than his. He feared that that Gompers would offer only rhetorical support for the strike, but nothing substantive. Even worse, Gompers might throw his weight behind a resolution to the strike that was unfavorable to the Pullman workers and their ARU supporters.[93]

Most disconcerting was Gompers' announcement that he was convening a meeting at Chicago's Briggs House hotel on Thursday, July 12—a day *after* the planned start of the general strike. Given that many Chicago unions, including a good number affiliated with the AFL, were on the fence about joining the general strike, the timing of this meeting might encourage them to hold off on walking out until the outcome of the Briggs House meeting was known. Also of concern to Debs was the fact that Gompers had invited to the meeting representatives of the conservative railroad brotherhoods that viewed the ARU as a threat and had refused to join its strike against the GMA.[94]

That evening President Cleveland issued a second proclamation. Whereas his original one issued Sunday evening had focused only on the state of Illinois, this one expanded it to cover all western states experiencing "unlawful obstructions, combinations, and assemblages of persons" and railroads suffering from interference in their ability to deliver the mail or move cargo tied to interstate commerce. "I, Grover Cleveland . . . hereby command all persons" involved in these unlawful actions to "disperse and retire peaceably" to their homes by 3:00 PM Tuesday July 10. Critics of the administration argued that if the original proclamation was essentially a declaration of martial law in Chicago, this second one amounted to a national declaration of martial law. Some believed such an extreme move would nudge more unions to join the general strike. [95]

## TUESDAY JULY 10

Like the day before, Chicago was quiet and free of any disturbances related to the strike. For Debs and the other ARU officials, much of the day was spent communicating with union leaders in the city and across the country urging them to join the general strike set to begin the following morning. As the day wore on it became increasingly clear that participation would be modest at best, with many unions fearful of the risks involved and opting for a wait and see approach with Gompers and the AFL leadership set to convene their conference on Thursday. Hopes had faded that John McBride, head of the UMW who had attended the recent Uhlrich Hall labor conference, would call out his 45,000 members. Workers in Milwaukee announced they would not join a general strike until after the AFL conference. And Chicago's Building Trades Council announced that its member unions would not strike until Saturday at the earliest.[96]

Also disheartening was news that railroad traffic in and out of Chicago was increasing, possibly a sign that the federal troops and injunctions had begun to turn the conflict in favor of the GMA railroads. Notably, at 11:00 AM a train loaded with meat rolled out of the Union Stock Yard. Accompanying it were eighty-seven members of the Chicago Hussars, a volunteer regiment of cavalry, plus a large contingent of state militia with rifles pointed in every direction. This successful run was followed throughout the afternoon by several more trains filled with meat bound for eastern markets.[97]

Likewise, updates from around the country contained mostly bad news for the ARU. In Cleveland railroad traffic was picking up as some striking workers returned to their jobs and scores of replacement workers recruited from eastern cities arrived. Traffic was also increasing in St. Louis, due in part to the employment of replacement workers. In East St. Louis, Lincoln Nelson, Secretary of the African American League of East St. Louis, offered to send two hundred Black workers to fill places in local warehouses vacated by strikers. Nelson was motivated in part by the ARU's decision back in June to exclude African Americans from membership. In Pittsburgh, strong support for the general strike was undermined when a brotherhood of locomotive engineers voted against the walkout. In Little Rock, Arkansas and Michigan City, Indiana, striking railroad workers voted to return to work. Elsewhere, in places like Raton, New Mexico and Trinidad, Colorado, federal troops were keeping order and assisting the railroads in moving trains.[98]

Not far from ARU headquarters, representatives of the Department of Justice, at the urging of Egan and the GMA, had put in motion their plan to cripple the ARU on the eve of the general strike. In the early afternoon federal marshals walked into a Western Union office and demanded the manager hand over to them copies of all telegrams sent or received by Debs. The manager initially refused the demand, but eventually complied when threatened with arrest and jail. Shortly thereafter, in the courtroom of Judge Peter S. Grosscup, District Attorney Thomas E. Milchrist empaneled a Grand Jury to hear evidence against Debs and other ARU officials, along with dozens of men arrested in the recent disturbances. The most important evidence was, not surprisingly, the recently seized telegrams which Milchrist and his team argued showed conclusive evidence of a conspiracy by Debs and others to prevent the enforcement of federal laws and to impede the movement of the mail and interstate commerce. By late afternoon, about the time the ARU's 4:00 PM deadline for George Pullman to agree to arbitration or face a general strike passed, the Grand Jury voted to indict the ARU leaders.

At 4:30 PM U.S. Marshal Arnold and two deputy marshals arrived at ARU headquarters. "I have a warrant for your arrest," Arnold explained to Debs. "You must come with me immediately." Rumors of his impending arrest had filled the papers for the last week, so Debs was not surprised. He took up his coat and, accompanied by his brother Theodore, walked with Arnold to Milchrist's office for processing. Soon thereafter deputy marshals entered the room with a large trove of ARU records and correspondence, as well as Debs' personal papers and mail, that they had just seized from ARU headquarters. Debs was enraged, but Milchrist defended the action, claiming he had a subpoena. Judge Grosscup later ordered the return of Debs' personal papers and correspondence.[99] Presently the remaining leadership of the ARU, George Howard, Sylvester Keliher, and Louis Rogers, arrived at Milchrist's office, having been arrested by deputy marshals. Judge Grosscup set bail at $10,000 and while the labor leaders waited for friends to post bonds for their release, Debs spoke to reporters.

The ARU and its leaders were innocent of any crime, said Debs, and they were ready to face any charges. In the meantime, "The arrest will not deter us from our work." He then shifted to what he termed the "infamous outrage" of federal officials seizing his personal papers and mail. "It seems like the act of the Czar of Russia instead of the act of a free country." This act of injustice was indicative of a dark turn in America. "It is no longer a question of right in this country," said Debs, "but a question of force and absolute force at that." One reporter asked Milchrist if he intended to investigate and possibly indict any of the railroad managers, given that their failure to deliver the mail—a violation of the law—was due to their refusal to operate trains without Pullman cars attached. Milchrist dodged the question by saying he did not know the plans of the Department of Justice. [100]

At 8:00 PM, after friends had posted bail, Debs and the others were released from custody. Some labor leaders hoped the arrests would anger workers and inspire wider participation in the general strike the next day. But others feared that word that the Grand Jury also indicted sixty-nine other individuals on charges of conspiracy—mainly men accused of engaging in vandalism, violence, or rioting—might deter workers from walking out.

Debs soon issued another proclamation in which he reiterated his persistent call for all strikers and sympathizers to refrain from violence and to avoid any scenes of protest. "In this supreme hour," said Debs, "let workingmen show themselves to be orderly and law-abiding." Labor has been forced into this position "by a power that now defies public opinion." Then he shifted from caution to optimism, declaring, "Our position is secure and the people are with us." He predicted the next day's strike "will become general" and while that may be "a calamity" in the short term, if workers remain peaceful, "it may yet prove to be a blessing to the country."[101]

Seven hundred miles to the east in Washington, D.C., an atmosphere of relief and optimism pervaded the White House. President Cleveland, Olney, Schofield, and much of the cabinet enjoyed a quiet evening with cigars and, for the first time in two weeks, early departures for home.[102]

## WEDNESDAY JULY 11

The much-anticipated general strike in Chicago failed to materialize. An exuberant *Chicago Tribune* declared it "a pronounced and absolute fizzle," while the *Inter-Ocean* termed it "absolutely still-born." Some unions, including teamsters, machinists, foundry workers, coremakers, and boilermakers, did call out their workers, contributing to a total of 15,000 to 25,000 who refused to work. Many workers such as longshoremen, lumber-shovers, bakers, and plumbers expressed sympathy with the strike, but nonetheless showed up for work. Some of them chose to express their solidarity by donating money for the relief of the striking Pullman workers. Others like the cigarmakers, carpenters, bricklayers, and painters expressed a willingness to strike, but delayed a final vote on the matter for a few days. The latter were likely waiting to see the outcome of the AFL meeting at Briggs House the next day.[103]

For Debs, the failed general strike was a big blow. In recent days he had come to see a general strike starting in Chicago and then spreading to other parts of the nation as the last best hope for forcing Pullman to arbitrate and thereby achieving victory in the strike. The combined forces of the GMA and the federal government, backed by a rabidly anti-labor national press, had begun to contain and weaken the strike. Federal troops and state militia sent to Chicago and other hot spots, sweeping injunctions imposed by judges across the Midwest and West, mass arrests of strikers and protesters by deputy marshals, and the arrest of Debs and the ARU leadership had given workers pause. So, too, had the increasingly successful effort by the railroads to hire replacement workers—often with announcements that striking workers had permanently forfeited their jobs and would not be rehired. Debs believed the general strike was the last card labor had to play and it had gone poorly.

To make matters worse for the ARU, while Chicago was calm and trains moved smoothly in and out of the city more or less on schedule, the papers that morning were filled with stories of violence and death in incidents related to the strike beyond the city. Four soldiers and an engineer were killed in Sacramento, California when a train they were guarding crashed, allegedly due to a sabotaged bridge crossing. "Deadly guerilla warfare is now in progress," proclaimed the *Inter-Ocean*. Closer to home, a few days prior striking miners in Spring Valley, Illinois pummeled with rocks a train carrying federal soldiers. Soldiers opened fire, killing two and injuring many more. In Grape Creek in eastern Illinois where miners who had blocked tracks with overturned cars, state militia troops opened fire killing three. These stories kept alive the narrative that the strike, while diminished in Chicago, still posed a grave threat to the nation.[104]

Samuel Gompers arrived in Chicago that evening. He had dinner and spoke briefly to the press, saying little of substance or specificity. He presented the coming conference as a fact-finding endeavor and his role as one who might bring the conflict to a peaceful resolution. But beneath this posture he believed the strike had been ill-advised and doomed to defeat.[105] He did not necessarily welcome this outcome, but he saw advantage in it for the AFL. For one, he was quietly hostile to the ARU, seeing it both as a rival organization and one that pursued a hopeless goal of organizing all railroad workers, including the unskilled who could be easily replaced. Gompers' more conservative approach to unionism focused on organizing skilled workers, avoiding strikes, and finding ways to peacefully reach agreements with employers. Although he hinted to reporters that the AFL might join the fray, there was no chance he would make such a move. Additionally, Gompers saw in the struggle an opportunity to draw into the AFL the conservative railroad brotherhoods that had not joined the strike and were antagonistic to Debs and the ARU. Several declined his invitation to the Briggs House conference, but the leaders of the Brotherhood of Locomotive Trainmen and Brotherhood of Locomotive Firemen (the organization to which Debs had devoted many years of labor) accepted. This inclusion of the brotherhoods irked Debs, as did Gompers' explanation that as men who possessed skills and power they were "men who were clothed with responsibility as well as authority" over railway workers.

## THURSDAY JULY 12

The highly anticipated Briggs House conference opened early in the morning. Present were Gompers, the Executive Board of the AFL, leaders of more than twenty Chicago labor unions, and three officers of two railroad brotherhoods. The session began with a plea from Charles Dold who represented the city's Cigarmakers' Union. It was imperative, he said, that the AFL call upon its membership to join the general strike. This move would resolve the dispute on terms favorable to labor. Representatives of the Carriage and Wagon Workers' Union also addressed the assembly.[106]

At 2:00 PM following a break for lunch, the conference voted to send a telegram to President Cleveland asking him to join them in Chicago, or to send a representative. Cleveland did not acknowledge or respond to the message.[107] That may have been because he was that very afternoon, unbeknownst to the Briggs House conference attendees, meeting with representatives of several labor organizations, including the Knights of Labor and the ARU, and sympathetic congressmen. They had called upon the president to urge him to appoint an arbitration commission as authorized in an 1888 law concerning labor disputes involving railroads. When Cleveland agreed to appoint a commission, they emerged from the meeting ecstatic, believing the president had agreed to compel George Pullman into arbitration with his striking workers. John W. Hayes, General Secretary Treasurer, KOL, issued a statement after meeting with Cleveland claiming "a great victory for labor organizations and everything that the American Railway Union has fought for, [because] it gives official recognition to the justice of their demands for arbitration." When Debs received word of the agreement, he said, "We are much gratified . . . at the act of President Cleveland in appointing a Board of Arbitration" which he was confident would lead to "a satisfactory settlement." Unfortunately for the ARU and Pullman strikers, Cleveland ultimately did not appoint an arbitration commission, but rather an investigatory one to determine the causes of the strike and offer recommendations for averting future railroad strikes.[108]

That evening Debs addressed the Briggs House conference. In a reserved tone he offered an overview of the strike and its causes, before being asked by Gompers what action he recommended the conference take. Instead of calling upon the delegates to vote to join the general strike, as many expected, Debs spoke in vague terms of the need for solidarity and united action. And then to the surprise of many, he then read a prepared statement from the ARU leadership that seemed to indicate an admission of defeat in the strike. He had spent the last week thinking about and discussing with other ARU officers the most prudent course of action to take regarding the strike. It was increasingly evident that Pullman and the GMA had the upper hand. Striking Pullman employees and their families were on the verge of starvation. The general strike was failing and it now seemed clear that Gompers had no intention of calling upon his 550,000 AFL members to join it.

The key passage in the statement Debs read proposed the strikers would "agree to return to work in a body at once, provided they shall be restored to their former positions without prejudice." The workers, said Debs, were willing to meet the railroads "halfway" and would not require the GMA or Pullman to recognize the ARU. He tried to couch this surrender in positive terms, arguing that sacrifices made by labor over the past two months "will have their compensation" and that the "lessons" drawn from the experience "will prove a blessing of inestimable value in months and years to come." Debs concluded by requesting that Gompers go to the GMA the next morning as an intermediary and deliver the ARU's statement on a proposed settlement. If the GMA rejected the offer, Debs suggested the conference vote to join the general strike.[109]

After Debs departed the meeting, the AFL officers took up the matter. With the strike on the verge of collapse and Debs seemingly ready to admit defeat, they rejected Debs' request that Gompers deliver the settlement proposal to the GMA out of concern that it might negatively associate the AFL with the ARU and the strike. Instead, they proposed Debs deliver the compromise proposal and that Gompers and several other AFL officials would accompany him. Whether intended or not, the offer was meaningless given the oft-articulated position of the GMA to have no dealings with Debs or the ARU.

Delegates, however, did vote to donate $500 to Debs' legal defense fund. They also drew up a statement that spoke admiringly of "the manly purposes and sturdy struggle of the American Railway Union . . . against the gathering, growing forces of plutocratic power and corporation rule." The latter were denounced for blatantly violating for years laws like the Interstate Commerce Law and then, when faced with a strike, turning to it as a weapon against organized labor. The document also excoriated the press for aiding powerful corporate interests by "maliciously" misrepresenting the actions and goals of labor. The most searing scorn was reserved for George Pullman whom it condemned as the era's "most consummate type of avaricious wealth absorber, tyrant and hypocrite." Pullman "has proven himself a public enemy. His name and memory are excoriated today and will be forever."[110]

Yet the statement also referred to the ARU boycott as "impulsive" and pointedly argued against a general strike as "inexpedient, unwise, and contrary to the best interest of the working people." Any AFL member union currently engaged in the general strike should return to work. Strikes were likely to be costly and unsuccessful due to the great numbers of unemployed workers and the forces of the government and big business allied against labor.

## FRIDAY JULY 13–20, 1894

When Debs learned that Gompers would not deliver his proposal to the GMA, he convinced Mayor Hopkins to do it. The GMA's chairman, Everett St. John, initially accepted the document. But John Egan intervened and had it returned to the mayor with a curt note explaining that the GMA could not accept it due to its policy of having absolutely no dealings with Debs or the ARU. Egan's move reflected more than a desire to maintain consistent policy. He saw in the offer a clear indication that the strike was all but over. Agreeing to a compromise at this point would undermine the larger goal of the GMA to destroy the American Railway Union. [111]

That same morning, the Chicago building trades council reacted to the AFL statement by calling off its strike. Other unions quickly followed. On Saturday, July 14, the *Chicago Tribune* ran a triumphant headline announcing "DEBS' STRIKE DEAD." It also reported that slaughtering operations had resumed in the Stock Yards for the first time in two weeks and that U.S. Marshal Arnold had released from duty 100 deputy marshals.[112]

Debs, however, refused to admit defeat. On Sunday, July 15, labor organizations held fifteen meetings across the city, and Debs spoke at nearly all of them. He railed at the railroad brotherhoods for their complicity with the railroads against the interests of ARU members. He also excoriated the Republican and Democratic Parties for their subservience to the interests of big business, and urged workers to vote for the Populist Party. Debs also spoke optimistically of continuing the strike and even spreading it in the West where the ARU was particularly strong.[113]

But two days later, on July 17, Debs and the rest of the ARU leadership were again arrested and charged with contempt of court for violating the terms of the July 2 injunction. This time around, they refused to post to bail and were sent to jail. Debs hoped the jailing would generate sympathy and anger to the benefit of the strike. But it also left ARU locals cut off from communication with union leaders at a time when there was tremendous pressure to return to work. The next day, July 18, the Pullman Company posted a sign on the gates of the works that read: "These gates will be opened as soon as the number of operatives is sufficient to make a working force in all departments." Two days later, federal troops pulled out of Chicago. The great Pullman Strike was over.

## NOTES

1 USSC, 352.
2 Almont Lindsey, *The Pullman Strike: The Story of a Unique Experiment and of a Great Labor Upheaval* (Chicago: University of Chicago Press, 1942), 182–183.
3 Lindsey, 195; *Report of the General Superintendent of Police of the City of Chicago to the City Council for the Year ending December 31, 1894* (Chicago: M. B. McAbee Printing Co., 1895), 13.
4 Lindsey, 249, 251–252.
5 *Appendix to the Report of the Attorney General 1896* (Washington, D.C.: U.S. Government Printing Office, 1896), 60.
6 *New York World*, July 4, 1894, 1.
7 *Chicago Inter-Ocean*, July 4, 1894, 1.
8 *New York Times*, July 5, 1894, 2.
9 *Chicago Tribune*, July 5, 1894, 1, 2; USSC (St John), 216
10 *Chicago Tribune*, July 5, 1894, 3.

11 *Chicago Tribune*, July 5, 1894, 3. See also Nelson A. Miles, "The Lesson of the Recent Strikes," *North American Review*, CLIX (August 1894), 180–188.
12 *Chicago Tribune*, July 5, 1894, 3; *Chicago Inter-Ocean*, July 5, 1894, 3.
13 *Chicago Tribune*, July 5, 1894, 3; *Chicago Inter-Ocean*, July 5, 1894, 2.
14 *Chicago Tribune*, July 5, 1894, 3; *Chicago Inter-Ocean*, July 5, 1894, 1.
15 *New York Times*, July 5, 1894, 2.
16 *New York Times*, July 5, 1894, 2.
17 *New York Times*, July 5, 1894, 2.
18 *Chicago Tribune*, July 5, 1894, 1, 2, 3.
19 *Chicago Tribune*, July 5, 1894, 1, 2.
20 Lindsey, 168, 250–254.
21 *Chicago Tribune*, July 5, 1894, 1; *Chicago Inter-Ocean*, July 5, 1894, 1.
22 Lindsey, 174.
23 *Chicago Tribune*, July 6, 1894, 2; *Chicago Inter-Ocean*, July 6, 1894, 2.
24 Lindsey, 165–169, 239.
25 *Chicago Tribune*, July 6, 1894, 2.
26 *Chicago Tribune*, July 6, 1894, 2.
27 *Chicago Tribune*, July 6, 1894, 2.
28 *Chicago Tribune*, July 7, 1894, 9, 12; *Chicago Inter-Ocean*, July 7, 1894, 6.
29 *Chicago Tribune*, July 7, 1894, 4, 12.
30 *Chicago Tribune*, July 6, 1894, 5.
31 *Chicago Tribune*, July 6, 1894, 5; *Chicago Inter-Ocean*, July 6, 1894, 3.
32 *Chicago Tribune*, July 6, 1894, 5.
33 *Chicago Tribune*, July 6, 1894, 5.
34 *Chicago Tribune*, July 6, 1894, 5 and July 5, 1894, 2; *Chicago Inter-Ocean*, July 6, 1894, 4.
35 *Chicago Tribune*, July 6, 1894, 2, 7.
36 *Chicago Tribune*, July 6, 1894, 2, 3, 5.
37 *Chicago Tribune*, July 5, 1894, 9.
38 *Chicago Tribune*, July 6, 1894, 2; *New York Times*, July 6, 1894, 2.
39 *Chicago Inter-Ocean*, July 6, 1894, 1, 2.
40 *Chicago Inter-Ocean*, July 6, 1894, 1, 2.
41 *Chicago Tribune*, July 6, 1894, 1; *Chicago Inter-Ocean*, July 6, 1894, 1; USSC, 216–17, 344–45, 363–5.
42 *Chicago Tribune*, July 6, 1894, 1; Lindsey 183–184.
43 *Chicago Tribune*, July 6, 1894, 2; *New York Times*, July 6, 1894, 2.
44 Gerald G. Eggert, *Richard Olney: Evolution of a Statesman* (University Park, PA: Penn State University Press, 1974), 146
45 *Chicago Tribune*, July 6, 1894, 8.
46 *Chicago Tribune*, July 6, 1894, 7; Lindsey, 207.
47 *Chicago Tribune*, July 6, 1894, 2; USSC, 345.
48 *Chicago Tribune*, July 7, 1894, 4.
49 *Chicago Tribune*, July 7, 1894, 6; *Chicago Inter-Ocean*, July 8, 1894, 5; USSC, 350–351.
50 *Chicago Tribune*, July 7, 1894, 2.
51 *Chicago Tribune*, July 7, 1894, 1, 2.
52 USSC, 344.
53 *Chicago Tribune*, July 7, 1894, 9, 13.
54 *Chicago Tribune*, July 7, 1894, 1, 6.

55 Jack Kelly, *The Edge of Anarchy: The Railroad Barons, the Gilded Age, and the Greatest Labor Uprising in America* (New York: St. Martin's Press, 2019), 184–185, Lindsey, 199–200; *Chicago Tribune*, July 7, 1894, 1, 3; USSC 344–345.
56 *Chicago Tribune*, July 7, 1894, 1, 3; *Chicago Inter-Ocean*, July 7, 1894, 1–2.
57 *Chicago Tribune*, July 7, 1894, 3, 4.
58 *Chicago Tribune*, July 7, 1894, 2, 4.
59 *Chicago Tribune*, July 7, 1894, 1, 5.
60 *Chicago Tribune*, July 7, 1894, 1, 2; *Chicago Inter-Ocean*, July 7, 1894, 1, 5.
61 *Chicago Tribune*, July 7, 1894, 1, 5.
62 *Chicago Inter-Ocean*, July 7, 1894, 1.
63 Kelly, 194; *Chicago Tribune*, July 7, 1894, 5.
64 *Chicago Tribune*, July 7, 1894, 1, 2.
65 *Chicago Tribune*, July 7, 1894, 5.
66 *Chicago Tribune*, July 8, 1894, 3, 9, 10.
67 *Chicago Tribune*, July 8, 1894, 1, 10.
68 *Chicago Inter-Ocean*, July 8, 1894, 1.
69 *Chicago Tribune*, July 8, 1894, 1; *Chicago Inter-Ocean*, July 8, 1894, 1; *Biennial Report of the Adjutant General of Illinois to the Governor and Commander-in-Chief, 1893 and 1894* (Springfield, IL: Ed. F. Hartman, 1895), 174–176; *Report of the General Superintendent of Police of. . .Chicago. . .1894*, 15–16.
70 *Chicago Tribune*, July 8, 1894, 1, 5.
71 Kelly, 206.
72 *Chicago Tribune*, July 8, 1894, 10.
73 *Chicago Tribune*, July 8, 1894, 10.
74 *Chicago Tribune*, July 8, 1894, 10.
75 *Chicago Tribune*, July 8, 1894, 1.
76 *Chicago Inter-Ocean*, July 8, 1894, 1.
77 *Chicago Inter-Ocean*, July 8, 1894, 2.
78 *Chicago Inter-Ocean*, July 8, 1894, 1.
79 *Chicago Tribune*, July 9, 1894, 12.
80 USSC, 158.
81 *Chicago Inter-Ocean*, July 9, 1894, 1.
82 *New York Times*, July 9, 1894, 2, 8.
83 *New York World*, July 8, 1894, 3; Lindsey, 193–194.
84 Lindsey, 211.
85 *Chicago Tribune*, July 9, 1894, 1.
86 *Chicago Inter-Ocean*, July 9, 1894, 1, 8.
87 *Chicago Tribune*, July 9, 1894, 1; USSC, 154–155.
88 *Chicago Tribune*, July 9, 1894, 1, 2; *Chicago Inter-Ocean*, July 9, 1894, 1, 8; *New York Times*, July 10, 1894, 1.
89 *Chicago Tribune*, July 10, 1894, 1, 2; *New York Times*, July 10, 1894, 1.
90 *Chicago Inter-Ocean*, July 10, 1894, 2.
91 *Chicago Tribune*, July 10, 1894, 2.
92 *Chicago Tribune*, July 10, 1894, 5; *New York Times*, July 10, 1894, 1.
93 *Chicago Tribune*, July 8, 1894, 5.
94 *Chicago Inter-Ocean*, July 10, 1894, 2.
95 *New York Times*, July 10, 1894, 3.

96 *Chicago Tribune*, July 11, 1894, 2.
97 *Chicago Tribune*, July 11, 1894, 2.
98 *Chicago Tribune*, July 11, 1894, 5; Kelly, 221.
99 USSC, 144.
100 *Chicago Tribune*, July 11, 1894, 7; Kelly, 223.
101 *Chicago Tribune*, July 11, 1894, 2.
102 Kelly, 225.
103 *Chicago Tribune*, July 12, 1894, 1; *Chicago Inter-Ocean*, July 12, 1894, 1.
104 *Chicago Tribune*, July 9, 1894, 1; July 10, 1894, 5; July 11, 1894, 1; July 12, 1894, 1; *Chicago Inter-Ocean*, July 12, 1894, 1.
105 Nick Salvatore, *Eugene V. Debs: Citizen and Socialist* (Urbana, IL: University of Illinois Press, 1982), 135.
106 "Proceedings of Briggs House Conference," *American Federationist*, I (1894), 132.
107 Samuel Gompers, Stuart Bruce Kaufman and Peter J. Albert, eds., *The Samuel Gompers Papers, Unrest and Depression, 1891–94*, vol. 3 (Urbana, IL: University of Illinois Press, 1989), 532.
108 *Chicago Tribune*, July 13, 1894, 1, 7; Lindsey 350–351.
109 "Proceedings of the Briggs Conference," 133; USSC, 58, 145–146; Samuel Gompers, *Seventy Years of Life and Labor: An Autobiography* (New York: E. P. Dutton, 1925), I, 408–410; Lindsey, 227.
110 *The Samuel Gompers Papers*, vol. 3 (1989), 535–538, 562–563; USSC, 156; "Proceedings of the Briggs Conference," 134.
111 Lindsey, 229–230; USSC, 146–147.
112 *Chicago Tribune*, July 14, 1894, 1, 9.
113 *Chicago Tribune*, July 16, 1894, 1; *Chicago Inter-Ocean*, July 16, 1894, 1.

CHAPTER 6

# The Strong Arm of the National Government

The Pullman Strike began on May 11, 1894 and lasted a little more than two months. At its height, it involved some 250,000 workers in twenty-seven states. The disturbances in Chicago that accompanied the strike led federal, state, and city authorities to mobilize 1,936 federal troops, 4,000 Illinois state militia, 5,000 deputy marshals, 250 deputy sheriffs, and 3,000 Chicago police for a total of 14,186.[1] Thousands more were mobilized to stymie interference with trains by strikers and their supporters in other states, including California, Colorado, New Mexico, Oklahoma, Utah, and Montana. Federal judges, at the urging of U.S. Attorney General Richard Olney, issued dozens of injunctions that led to the arrest of hundreds, including the entire leadership of the ARU. In the end, the efforts of Debs and the ARU to compel George Pullman to the negotiating table proved no match for the combined power of the GMA, the federal courts, the U.S. Army, the Cleveland administration, and an overwhelmingly anti-labor press.

The departure of federal troops from Chicago on July 20, followed soon thereafter by the state militia, signaled that the fires of protest in the city, the strike's epicenter, had been extinguished. So too did the return of regular train service, both passenger and freight. Strike-related shortages of fresh produce, milk, ice, and medicine disappeared and prices for these and other goods returned to normal. Soon, nearly all the vestiges of the conflict—burned cars, broken switches, and toppled signal towers—had been removed or repaired.

On July 25, after eight days in the fetid, rat-infested Cook County Jail, Debs and the other ARU leaders were released on bond with their court date set for September 5. Debs returned to his home town of Terre Haute and spent the next two weeks in bed recovering from the stress and

DOI: 10.4324/9781003388784-7

strain of the strike and time in jail. During this time friends and supporters launched a campaign to raise funds for the ARU leaders' defense. Gompers sent nearly $800 from the AFL with a note condemning the actions of the federal government on behalf of "corporate wealth against the most necessary, useful and liberty loving people of the country—the wageworkers."[2]

The next day, the Cleveland administration revealed a clearer picture of the purpose of the commission the president had agreed to form. It would not, as many labor leaders had hoped, conduct an investigation into the strike for the purposes of overseeing an arbitration process between Pullman and his employees. Rather, it would gather testimony from scores of people involved in the dispute and then issue a report. The United States Strike Commission was comprised of chair Carroll D. Wright, the U.S. Commissioner of Labor, and two prominent lawyers with pro-labor reputations, John D. Kernan and Nicholas E. Worthington. Their charge was to discover the causes of the great strike and make recommendations to avoid future conflicts, but to limit their focus to only two of the railroads involved.[3]

## Investigations into Labor–Capital Conflict

The Gilded Age witnessed an unprecedented number of strikes, including many that involved significant loss of life and destruction of property. On three occasions Congress launched an investigation into the causes of the social unrest. These investigations in 1877 (in the wake of the massive Great Uprising Railroad Strike), 1883, and 1894 (following the Pullman Strike) gathered thousands of pages of testimony from workers, employers, politicians, reformers, and journalists with the goal of ascertaining the sources of worker discontent. Historian Mary O. Furner observed that these investigations "subjected the new industrial capitalism to a political and ideological fitness test," seeking to determine whether the new economy was compatible with republican values and institutions.[4]

Beyond Chicago vestiges of the strike persisted for a few weeks in a few isolated areas primarily in the West. But by August 1 most trains in those locales were running on schedule and strikers who were permitted to resumed their positions. On August 2, Debs convened a convention of

ARU delegates to discuss the fate of the strike which technically was still ongoing. It lasted two days and members were told to go back to their locals to take a vote on whether or not to continue to strike. Nearly all voted to end the strike.[5]

Debate over the strike, however, and its many subplots such as Governor Altgeld's feud with President Cleveland and Debs' legal woes, persisted in the local and national press. One of the nation's most prominent journals, *North American Review*, dedicated a large portion of its August 1894 edition to a series of essays by prominent Americans, including General Nelson A. Miles, Wade Hampton, and Samuel Gompers under the title "The Lesson of the Recent Strikes." All except Gompers condemned the strike and heaped scorn on Debs and the ARU.[6]

While some assessed blame, others tried to determine the cost of the strike. At least thirty people, including twelve in Chicago, had been killed by soldiers of the U.S. Army and state militias, deputy U.S. marshals, sheriff's deputies, and police. Hundreds were seriously injured, including fifty-three in Chicago. None of those killed were ARU members. Police and deputy marshals arrested more than seven hundred persons, most on charges of vandalism and rioting.[7]

Financially the strike proved quite costly, especially in the context of the depression. *Bradstreet's*, one of the nation's leading financial journals, estimated that the strike cost the national economy $80 million. That figure included $4.7 million in lost profits for the railroads, plus almost $700,000 in expenses for replacing destroyed property and hiring deputy U.S. marshals. The 3,100 employees of the Pullman Company lost $350,000 in wages, while the 100,000 employees on the two dozen railroads centered in Chicago lost $1.4 million in wages for striking railroad workers.[8]

The latter not only lost wages. By one estimate, three out of four striking railroad workers lost their jobs to replacement workers hired during the strike. Those who sought employment on other railroads faced blacklisting. Of those rehired, many had to accept lesser positions for lower wages. At the Pullman Company, some workers continued to hold out, but with every passing day more and more lined up to get back their jobs. One in four Pullman workers were refused employment outright, having been identified for playing a prominent role in the strike or the disturbances. Those hired back had to accept the same wages and rents as before the walkout. They also were required to turn over their ARU membership cards and sign an "iron-clad" contract pledging that they would not join a union. In all, 1,900 former employees were rehired, along with 800 new workers. More than 1,000 of the pre-strike workforce remained unemployed.[9]

## Iron-Clad or Yellow Dog Contracts

Many Gilded Age employers imposed "iron-clad" contracts on workers as a way to thwart the growth of unions. They defended them as a legitimate condition of employment that did not impinge upon workers' freedom. Any workers who wished to join a union, said employers, were free to take their labor to another establishment that did not require they sign an iron-clad contract. Workers despised these contracts and succeeded in convincing legislatures in sixteen states to outlaw them by 1887. In the early 1920s such contracts became known as "yellow dog" contracts, a term that indicated anyone who signed one was a yellow or cowardly dog who willingly surrendered their rights to their employer. In 1932 the Norris–LaGuardia Act included a provision outlawing yellow dog contracts across the nation.

With so many jobless and the company's slow pace in restarting the works, many Pullman residents continued to suffer from malnutrition, leading to a renewed fundraising campaign to provide relief. The press's unrelenting negative depiction of Debs and the ARU and wild exaggerations of the violence and vandalism associated with the strike had weakened public sympathy—and donations—for the Pullman workers. In mid-August Pullman residents appealed to Governor Altgeld for help. Some 1,600 families in the town were destitute. "We have been refused employment and have no means of leaving this vicinity, and our families are starving." Altgeld wrote to George Pullman requesting he provide relief to the townspeople, reminding him that the residents of Pullman had "served you long and well" and that the state of Illinois had just spent $50,000 to protect Pullman property. The governor then went to Pullman where he spoke with residents and saw the widespread suffering firsthand. He again wrote to Pullman saying he had to act. Pullman refused. The workers, he said, had brought the suffering upon themselves by striking. Altgeld then issued a public appeal to the people of Illinois to donate to the Pullman relief fund. "The good people of this State" —which by inference did not include George Pullman—"cannot allow women and children by the hundreds to perish of hunger." Whatever remained of George Pullman's reputation as a benevolent capitalist who looked after the wellbeing of his employees was gone.[10]

One month later, Altgeld struck another blow at Pullman. When he learned that Pullman said in his testimony the company was worth $61 million, the governor inquired with the State Board of Tax Equalization as to what it was paying in taxes. To his astonishment, he learned that the Pullman Company was being assessed as though its total valuation was just under $1.7 million. "[T]he Pullman Company," said Altgeld, "had for many years been annually defrauding the public out of from $640,000 to $800,000 per year." Nothing was done to recover that money, but in coming years the assessment on the company was raised substantially. Subsequent legal action by Altgeld also led the Illinois Supreme Court to force the Pullman Company to sell all its real estate in the town of Pullman, except that used for the operation of its factory.[11]

The United States Strike Commission held its first session on August 15, in a federal courtroom in downtown Chicago. Over the course of thirteen days the commission heard from 107 witnesses including Pullman employees, railroad workers, ARU and other labor union leaders, Pullman and railroad executives, political leaders, and officials representing the police, federal marshals, and U.S. Army.

The most highly anticipated witnesses were Eugene Debs and George Pullman. Debs appeared on August 20. He provided an overview of the causes of the Pullman strike and subsequent ARU boycott, saying wage cuts had pushed workers to the brink and they had no choice. "It seems to me that if it were not for resistance to degrading conditions," said Debs, "the tendency of our whole civilization would be downward; after a while we would reach the point where there would be no resistance, and slavery would come." The ARU's aim never was to tie up general railroad traffic, but rather "to cut off the Pullman cars so as to cut off Pullman revenue, and thereby compel the Pullman company to arbitrate." The railroads caused the tie-ups by demanding Pullman cars be attached to their trains and spurning all offers by the ARU to ensure the free movement of mail on trains without Pullman cars.[12]

Debs excoriated the GMA for condemning ARU as a diabolical combination of workers while at the same time acting as a combination of railroads in order to break the strike and "exterminate the American Railway Union." Moreover, said Debs, all ARU meetings had been open to the public and press, while the GMA conducted all its business in secret. The government had seized all the ARU's telegrams and made many of them public, but all the telegrams between the GMA and Attorney General Olney and others in the Cleveland administration remained secret.[13]

The ARU president likewise criticized the federal government, in particular the courts, for their "concerted action" acting on behalf of the railroads by issuing injunctions to cripple the strike. ARU members would have stayed on strike, had it not been for the injunctions prohibiting Debs and the officers from sending telegrams, issuing orders, and answering questions of ARU locals. "It was not the soldiers that ended the strike," said Debs, "It was simply the United States courts that ended the strike." But federal soldiers did play a role—a "highly improper" one, according to Debs—in that General Miles "was in active alliance with the [railroad] general managers, not only to maintain order, but to suppress the strike. That was his real mission in Chicago."[14] Labor had nothing but starving men on its side during a strike. "On the other side the corporations are in perfect alliance; they have all of the things that money can command, and that means a subsidized press, . . . the courts, then the State militia, then the Federal troops; everything and all things on the side of corporations."[15]

The commissioners asked Debs about the violence and vandalism that occurred during the strike. He responded by noting that the ARU constitution mandated the expulsion of any member that engaged in unlawful behavior. Furthermore, Debs noted the many occasions in which he issued public proclamations to ARU members pleading with them to conduct themselves as peaceful and law-abiding citizens. "We said," Debs told the commissioners, "we want to win as becomes men; we want to win as becomes law abiding citizens." Of all the hundreds of people arrested for violence, he said, not one was a member of the ARU.[16]

At one juncture, Debs took the opportunity to criticize the media for its hysterical and willfully inaccurate coverage of the strike and the unrest. "We were made the victims of a capitalistic press." He cited an example of an interview he gave to a reporter that subsequently was rewritten with fake and twisted quotes to make him sound ridiculous and dangerous. It was published in the *Tribune* and then republished via the Associated Press in papers all across the country, turning the public against the strike. "If the press had given them the truth and the facts," asserted Debs, "the people of this country would have been overwhelmingly with us from beginning to end."[17]

When questioned about strikes, Debs said he generally opposed them and always sought ways to avoid them, but "I believe a strike is justifiable when necessary to resist degrading or enslaving conditions," adding later that "no matter what may be said about the freedom of contract under our Constitution, no man has a right to sell himself into slavery . . . and yet that is what it amounts to if a man agrees to work at unliving wages." Until just treatment of workers prevails, said Debs, there would be more strikes. To end railroad strikes Debs, like many other witnesses, advocated government ownership of railroads. He denied such a policy amounted to "State socialism," declaring "Government ownership of railroads is decidedly better for the people than railroad ownership of the Government."[18]

George Pullman took the stand a week later on August 27. When asked why he had built the town of Pullman, he read a carefully prepared statement that opened with praise for workers as "the most important element which enters into the successful operation of any manufacturing enterprise." The goal was to attract "the best class of mechanics," and to provide them and their families with a wholesome living environment free of "baneful influences" such as saloons and brothels. Workers were not permitted to purchase their homes or commercial spaces because that would open the door to the aforementioned baneful influences. As a consequence, said Pullman, his workers enjoyed a clean and safe town that offered stores, a public school, a library, and a church.[19]

In anticipation of questions about not lowering rents, Pullman went to great pains to claim that the town was a real-estate enterprise entirely separate from the Pullman Palace Car Company. He also sought to downplay its profitability, noting that it had never achieved the intended goal of earning a 6 percent annual return from rents. Returns in the two previous years were only 3.82 percent.[20]

The commissioners then questioned Pullman on the financial health of his company. "Your company has had a phenomenal success financially, has it not?" asked Commissioner Worthington. Recognizing that this line of questioning would ultimately focus on the company's decision to cut wages, Pullman stammered, "Well, I don't know just what you mean by phenomenal." In the ensuing back and forth, Pullman said that his sleeping-car company had a capital valuation of $36 million, that it possessed an additional $25 million in cash reserves, and that over the prior twenty-six years it had paid out to investors $28 million in dividends representing an annual rate of return of 8 to 12 percent. Furthermore, even in the midst of a terrible economic depression, the company had earned a profit of $5.2 million in 1893.[21]

"Suppose a board of arbitration had examined the matter," queried Worthington, and while acknowledging the company's losses on some contracts and decreased revenues on others, it had recommended he raise the wages of his workers to a living wage. "Wouldn't that have been a fair matter to be considered?" "I think not," said Pullman. Any boost in wages would have constituted an unjustified "gift of money" to his employees. And then he repeated the mantra he and other Gilded Age titans always fell back upon: "The wage question is settled by the law of supply and demand."[22]

Likewise, when asked to explain his refusal to arbitrate, Pullman returned to the same phrasing and terminology he had employed during the strike. "[I]t was the principle involved," he said, "not the amount [of money]" raising wages might cost. "[W]e must be the parties to decide whether we were willing to continue the manufacturing business at a loss." Submitting the issue to a third party for arbitration would have violated "The principle that a man should have the right to manage his own property."[23]

At another point the commissioners asked him, if in the course of cutting his workers' wages, had he also cut the salaries of company executives, superintendents, or foremen? No, said Pullman. When asked why, he said he feared the men would quit. Had he cut his own salary? No, because to do so would have only an "infinitesimal" impact on the price of sleeper cars. But, asked a commissioner, "don't you think that you ought to have, fairly and in justice to the other classes, attempted to reduce those salaries," including his own? Pullman dodged the question, citing uncertainties about how long the depression would last and pressures to compete for car-building contracts.[24]

Pullman's testimony did little to improve what was left of his public image. He came across to many as aloof, arrogant, and stubborn. At times he also appeared uninformed about aspects of the company's finances and operations, forcing him to frequently defer to vice-president Thomas Wickes for clarification. It was late in the day when the commissioners released him. He reportedly went home and spent the next four days in bed, thoroughly exhausted and depressed. The next day the commission heard from its last witness and headed to Washington to prepare its report.

Five days later, on Monday September 3, thousands of workers in Chicago and hundreds of thousands of workers nationwide took part in parades and picnics to commemorate Labor Day. For the first time, most federal workers enjoyed the day off because back on June 28, in the midst the rising tension and tumult over the Pullman Strike, President Grover Cleveland had signed a bill making Labor Day a federal holiday.[25]

Two days later Debs and fellow ARU officials Howard, Keliher, and Rogers appeared in federal court on charges of contempt of court for allegedly defying the July 2 injunction. Presiding over the trial was Judge William Woods, one of the judges who had issued the original injunction. The defendants were represented by three lawyers, including Clarence Darrow, who was just beginning a three-decade career of representing underdogs in well-publicized labor and civil rights cases. Their first move was to request a jury trial. Woods denied it, meaning that he alone would hear the evidence and render a decision.[26]

> Although the timing of his signing the bill establishing Labor Day as a federal holiday—June 28 in the midst of the Pullman strike—has led many to claim that Cleveland's endorsement of Labor Day represented an effort on his part to repair his image among American workers, the reality is the bill had been passed by Congress months before and at the time of the signing Cleveland had played no role in the strike.

The opposing legal team consisted of U.S. Attorneys Milchrist and Walker. They spent almost two weeks making the case to the judge that Debs and his three colleagues had willfully defied the injunction which had explicitly prohibited them from doing anything to direct and perpetuate the strike. Most of the evidence they introduced consisted of telegrams sent from ARU headquarters to locals all across the country. They also called as witnesses railroad detectives, supervisors, and workers.[27]

When it came time for the defense team to answer, they surprised many present in the courtroom by announcing that they would neither call witnesses nor introduce evidence. They were essentially conceding defeat in this trial in order to concentrate their efforts—and conceal their evidence and strategy—for the more serious trial on charges of criminal conspiracy that was scheduled to begin in January. Conviction on this charge could carry a sentence of two years in prison. Judge Woods ended the trial and began working on a verdict that he did not issue until three months later in mid-December.[28]

On November 12, the United States Strike Commission released its report to the public.[29] At 681 pages, it included transcripts of the testimony of more than one hundred witnesses, plus many relevant documents, a detailed summary of events, and statistics on topics like troop deployment and costs associated with the strike. But the sections of the report that received the most attention were those assessing the actions of the parties involved and the commission's "Conclusions and Recommendations." The ARU received only minor criticism, namely that its constitution did not specifically condemn acts of violence by its members and that it admitted to membership Pullman workers who were not, in its view, true railroad employees. The commission also rejected the claims of the GMA, political leaders, federal judges, and newspaper editors that the ARU leadership was responsible for the disturbances associated with the strike. "There is no evidence before the commission," they wrote, "that the officers of the American Railway Union at any time participated in or advised intimidation, violence, or destruction of property."[30]

By contrast, the commissioners sharply criticized the GMA for exercising powers it did not legally possess. As an unincorporated body, it did not have the authority "to fix rates for services and wages, nor to force their acceptance, nor to battle with strikers." Therefore, the GMA's pursuit of these ends during its clash with the ARU constituted "a usurpation of power not granted." The GMA's refusal to recognize and negotiate with the ARU "seems arrogant and absurd when we consider its [questionable] standing before the law." But the commission went further, placing most of the blame for the strike at the feet of the GMA and the Pullman Company for refusing to negotiate with the ARU.

"[A] different policy would have prevented the loss of life and great loss of property and wages occasioned by the strike." Commissioners likewise said the strikers' demand for a restoration of their 1893 wage rates was wrong, but that Pullman should have lowered rents in the company town. The GMA railroads also received criticism for hiring, paying, arming, housing, and supervising thousands of their loyal employees to serve as federal deputy marshals. These men, said the commissioners, exercised "unrestricted United States authority" while still working for the railroads. "This is placing officers of the Government under control of a combination of railroads. It is a bad precedent, that might will lead to serious consequences.[31]

When it came to recommending measures for eliminating, or at least diminishing strikes, and improving the overall tenor of labor–capital relations, the commission argued that the new economic conditions that have attended the rise of industrial capitalism demanded bold solutions. "The rapid concentration of power and wealth, under stimulating legislative conditions, in persons, corporations, and monopolies has greatly changed the business and industrial situation." The longstanding belief that competition among railroads would ensure fair prices for businesses and fair wages for workers had been shown to be false. The creation of huge corporations and monopolies in recent decades "has largely destroyed this theory." Railroads had used their combined power to drive down the wages of railroad workers in a "progressive perversion of the laws of supply and demand."[32]

Many Americans might fear and loathe labor unions, the commissioners continued, but they were here to stay. "Is it not wise to fully recognize them by law?" they asked. Legal recognition would lead to unions acting within the law with more wisdom and restraint. The government had for the last fifty years encouraged the growth and flourishing of corporations and the time had come to do the same for labor unions. "Does not wisdom demand that each be encouraged to prosper legitimately and to grow into harmonious relations of equal standing and responsibility before the law?"[33]

The Commission concluded with a set of specific recommendations:

- The establishment of a permanent strike commission to investigate disputes between railroads and their employees, with courts empowered to "compel railroads to obey the decisions of the commission."
- When this commission stepped in to investigate a conflict, the labor union(s) and the railroad(s) involved select a representative to serve temporarily on the commission for the duration of the inquiry.
- During the commission's proceedings, railroads would be forbidden from firing employees (except for cause) and unions could not call a

strike, or aid or abet a strike or boycott against the railroad involved in the dispute being investigated.

- That national trade unions include in their constitutions, rules, and bylaws provisions requiring the expulsion of any member who engages in violence, vandalism, intimidation during a strike.
- Establishment of a system of voluntary arbitration to settle strikes similar to one recently established in Massachusetts.
- A federal law outlawing labor contracts that prohibit workers from union membership as a condition of employment.
- Employers ought to recognize labor unions and "come in closer touch" with their employees and consult with them "at proper times" to foster mutual respect and diminish "friction."[34]

One month later, on December 14, Judge Woods finally released his decision. Given his well-known anti-labor views, it presented no surprises. He found all four ARU officials guilty of contempt of court and sentenced Debs to six months in jail and the other three to terms of three months. They immediately appealed to the United States Supreme Court. The court accepted their application for a writ of habeas corpus, or an opportunity to appear before the court to make their case against what they believed was unlawful conviction and imprisonment. But the hearing would not take place for three months.[35]

On January 8, 1895, Debs, Howard, Keliher, and Rogers began serving their sentences in a jail in rural Woodstock, Illinois. Conditions there were vastly better than the Cook County Jail.[36] On January 24 they were released to attend their trial in Chicago for conspiracy to interfere with the movement of the U.S. mail. The judge for this trial, which included the four ARU leaders, plus another twelve men also charged with conspiracy, was Peter S. Grosscup who, like Woods, was widely known for his anti-labor views and who had collaborated with U.S. Attorneys Thomas Milchrist and Edwin Walker to write the writ that requested the original "omnibus injunction" which Grosscup and Woods issued on July 2.[37]

Early on the legal team for the defendants put the prosecution on its heels. Attorney S. S. Gregory rose for the defense to challenge the propriety of allowing Edwin Walker to participate as a government lawyer when he was also the paid attorney for one of the railroads in the case. Judge Grosscup sided with the prosecution and allowed Walker to remain part of its team.[38]

When Darrow rose to speak, he denied the defendants were guilty of conspiracy. There was no evidence linking the ARU to any of the violence that accompanied the strike. Indeed, there *was* a conspiracy involved in the strike, he said, but it was on the part of the secretive GMA. Darrow introduced as evidence portions of the minutes of secret GMA meetings where they schemed to alter train routes to ensure maximum tie-ups and tasked railroad detectives with compiling names of strikers.[39]

The defense also tried to call George Pullman to the witness stand, but he had scampered out of the city to avoid being served a subpoena. He was never charged with contempt of court. "There is something wrong in this country," Debs observed, "the judicial nets are so adjusted as to catch the minnows and let the whales slip through."[40]

Undeterred, Darrow planned to call to the witness stand GMA members to reveal the degree to which they had colluded with the federal government to destroy the ARU. His mysterious acquisition of GMA minutes suggested he might have additional evidence with which to confront GMA officials. But when a juror became sick, Grosscup seized the opportunity to stop the trial on February 12. The defense requested the judge simply appoint a replacement juror, but he declined. The trial never resumed and the federal government eventually dismissed the charges of conspiracy. Debs and the other ARU officials were returned to jail to await the hearing before the US Supreme Court.[41]

Six weeks later, on March 25 and 26, 1895, the nine justices of the United States Supreme Court heard the arguments from lawyers representing Debs and the ARU officers, as well as those representing the United States government. The former consisted of Clarence Darrow and Stephen Gregory of the original defense team, plus Lyman Trumbull, a famous lawyer and former senator with a long career of fighting for liberal causes. They challenged the legitimacy of the federal government's intervention in the strike. "[R]efusing to work for a railroad," said Trumbull, "is no crime," even if it caused delays in mail delivery or disruptions to interstate commerce. The federal government, they contended, had abandoned a long-standing practice of only issuing an injunction to protect a person from "irreparable injury" to their property and instead had issued one against strikers for merely interfering with private property. Furthermore, noted Gregory, the defendants in this case endured a trial without a jury, which violated their sixth amendment rights. And the judge who heard the case and decided it was the very judge who had issued the injunction. This was a dangerous precedent. "To extend this power generally to criminal cases would be absolutely destructive to liberty and intolerable to a free people."[42]

Darrow took aim at the government's reliance on the Sherman Antitrust Act to justify its intervention. This law had been written, debated, and passed in 1890 to empower the government to take action against business "combinations in the shape of trusts and pools" that were engaged in anticompetitive practices. It was never intended, said Darrow, "To apply . . . to the combination of laboring men or strikes or boycotts." Moreover, Debs and the other officers had done nothing illegal in sending telegrams to ARU locals urging them to strike, since courts had recognized labor's right to organize and strike. Finally, Darrow flatly denied the defendants bore any responsibility for the acts of violence and vandalism that accompanied the strike. "Strikes are deplorable," he conceded, "and so are their causes." To deny workers the right to strike "would be to strip and bind them and leave them helpless as the prey of the great and strong."

Representing the government were U.S. Attorney Edwin Walker, Assistant U.S. Attorney General E. B. Whitney, and Attorney General Olney. It was extremely rare for an Attorney General to argue a case before the court (a duty usually reserved for the Solicitor General). But keenly aware that the public saw him as the architect of the federal government's response to the strike, Olney was determined to win in court to uphold the authority of the federal government and to achieve personal vindication for his actions.

Olney's strategy was to focus on what he deemed was the "single question" at hand: Did the lower court possess the authority to issue the injunction? The lower courts had claimed this authority under the Sherman Antitrust Act, which defense argued was never intended for use against labor unions. Olney, however, dismissed the Sherman Antitrust Act as "an experimental piece of legislation." The real source of authority stemmed from Congress's well-established practice of regulating interstate railroads—a practice upheld by the courts. The federal government, therefore, had exclusive jurisdiction over the railroads and an unambiguous obligation to prevent interference with interstate railroad transportation.

Olney then moved to describe in vivid and exaggerative terms the forms of interference for which he claimed Debs and the others were responsible.

> It was accomplished with the burning of cars, with the derailment of trains, with the destruction of signal towers and other appliances for the safe operation of trains, with assaults upon passengers and employees by which, many were killed and many more wounded, with howling and excited mobs in full occupation of entire districts and terrorizing entire communities.

The federal government was obligated to respond and it did so, said Olney, with the "exact remedy"—injunctions against those obstructing interstate commerce and the movement of the mails.[43]

The Supreme Court issued its decision, *in re Debs*, two months later on May 27, 1895. Given the court's well-established reputation for consistently deciding cases in favor of corporations and private property interests (it had one week earlier declared a modest income tax unconstitutional), the decision surprised no one. By a unanimous 9–0 vote, the court upheld the lower court's decision that found Debs and the other ARU officers in contempt for violating the injunction. The decision avoided the question of workers' right to strike and instead concurred with Olney's characterization of federal authority to protect interstate commerce and the movement of mail as absolute. "[T]he strong arm of the national government may be put forth to brush away" any interference, wrote Justice Brewer. "If the emergency arises, the army of the nation, and all its militia, are at the service of the nation to compel obedience to its laws." This sweeping ruling greatly expanded the ability of federal judges to issue injunctions and granted to the government almost unlimited powers to stymie actions by organized labor.[44]

***Figure 6.1*** **"Debs to Serve His Term" headline, *New York Times*, May 28, 1895, 16.**

# DEBS TO SERVE HIS TERM

## The Supreme Court Refuses a Writ of Habeas Corpus.

## OPINION OF THE JUDGES UNANIMOUS

### The Nation Has Power to Protect Inter-State Commerce from Obstruction by Mob Violence.

WASHINGTON, May 27.—The habeas corpus case of Eugene V. Debs and others, growing out of the great railroad strike at Chicago last Summer, was decided in the Supreme Court of the United States today, the unanimous opinion being read by Justice Brewer.

Many leaders in business and finance were doubtless thrilled by the decision. They understood that it constituted a major blow to the ability of organized labor to resist the power of employers in their efforts to secure decent wages, hours, and working conditions. They were likely glad to see that "Dictator Debs" would be heading back to jail.

If Olney received accolades for his handling of the strike, such was not the case for George M. Pullman. His obstinate refusal to arbitrate the dispute with his employees led the public to assign him a significant portion of the blame for the strike that led to alarming incidents of violence and vandalism and, for a time, paralyzed the nation's railroad system. Chicago's high society shunned him as a pariah. The criticism wounded Pullman who could not understand why he was seen as a villain when, in his mind, he had taken a principled stand to defend private property rights. His bouts with anxiety and depression worsened in the years following the strike, but he refused to let up on his relentless work schedule which included running his company and fighting to prevent the state's attempt to dissolve the town of Pullman. On October 19, 1897 Pullman suffered a heart attack and died. He was sixty-six years old and left behind an estate of $17.5 million. When asked for comment, his former adversary Debs said only, "He is on equity with toilers now." The following year the Illinois State Supreme Court ruled that the Pullman Company had violated the terms of its charter in establishing a company town and ordered it dissolved. Within four years of the great Pullman Strike, both the visionary capitalist and his model town were gone.[45]

## NOTES

1 USSC, xix.
2 Samuel Gompers, Stuart Bruce Kaufman and Peter J. Albert, eds., *The Samuel Gompers Papers, Unrest and Depression, 1891–94*, vol. 3 (Urbana, IL: University of Illinois Press, 1989), 562–563.
3 USSC, xv.
4 Mary O. Furner, "Republican Tradition and the New Liberalism: Social Investigation, State Building, and Social Learning in the Gilded Age," in *The State and Social Investigation in Britain and the United States*, eds. Michael James Lacey and Mary O. Furner (New York: Cambridge University Press, 1990), 197.
5 USSC, 151–152
6 Nelson A. Miles, Wade Hampton, Harry P. Robinson, and Samuel Gompers, "The Lesson of the Recent Strikes," *The North American Review*, vol. 159, no. 453 (August, 1894), 180–206.
7 Ray Ginger, *The Bending Cross: A Biography of Eugene Victor Debs* (New York: Russell & Russell, 1949), 154; USSC xviii.
8 Ginger, 154, USSC xviii.

9 USSC, 176, 591; Jack Kelly, *The Edge of Anarchy: The Railroad Barons, the Gilded Age, and the Greatest Labor Uprising in America* (New York: St. Martin's Press, 2019), 243–244, 246–247.
10 Harry Barnard, *Eagle Forgotten: The Life of John Peter Altgeld* (Duell, Sloan and Pearce, 1938), 323–327.
11 Barnard, 327–328.
12 USSC, 135.
13 USSC, 137, 171.
14 USSC, 143–145.
15 USSC, 169.
16 USSC, 140–149.
17 USSC, 156–158.
18 USSC, 161–163, 170.
19 USSC, 529–530.
20 USSC, 529–530; *Chicago Tribune*, August 28, 1894, 3, 9.
21 USSC, 534–535, 542–556.
22 USSC, 556–557.
23 USSC, 553–557
24 USSC, 567.
25 *Chicago Inter-Ocean*, September 4, 1894, 7.
26 *Chicago Tribune*, September 6, 1894, 12.
27 *Chicago Tribune*, September 6, 1894, 12, September 7, 1894, 12, September 8, 1894, 2, September 12, 1894, 3, September 13, 1894, 7, September 14, 1894, 12.
28 *Chicago Tribune*, September 14, 1894, 12.
29 *Chicago Tribune*, November 13, 1894, 1–2; *New York Times*, November 13, 1894, 8.
30 USSC, xlv.
31 USSC, xxxi–xxxvi.
32 USSC, xlvii–xlviii.
33 USSC, xlviii.
34 USSC, lii–liv.
35 *Chicago Tribune*, September 6, 1894, 12.
36 *Chicago Tribune*, January 9, 1895, 8.
37 *Chicago Tribune*, January 25, 1894, 7.
38 *Chicago Tribune*, January 27, 1895, 12.
39 Kelly, 258.
40 *New York Times*, February 8, 1895, 1; Speech by Eugene Debs, November 23, 1895, quoted in Eugene V. Debs, *Debs: His Life Writings and Speeches* ("The Appeal to Reason," 1908), 19.
41 *New York Times*, February 13, 1895, 14.
42 *New York Times*, March 26, 1895, 9; *Chicago Inter-Ocean*, March 26, 1895, 5; *Chicago Tribune*, March 26, 1895, 3.
43 Lindsey, 295–296.
44 *Chicago Tribune*, May 28, 1895, 3, 6; Chicago *Inter-Ocean*, May 28, 1895, 7.
45 Lindsey, 342.

# Epilogue

Defeat in the Pullman Strike constituted a major setback for the American labor movement in myriad ways. Tens of thousands of railroad workers permanently lost their jobs, or regained lesser employment at lower wages. The alliance of the federal government and the railroads against hard-pressed wage earners, along with the wholesale demonization of unions and strikes by the press and the Supreme Court's upholding the federal government's right to use injunctions and federal troops in labor disputes, meant that labor would face many obstacles in the years to come.

As many workers feared, court-imposed injunctions, cloaked in the mystique and majesty of "the law," became increasingly common in the coming decades. They handcuffed organized labor, while at the same time allowing employers to avoid the bad publicity of violence triggered by hiring strikebreakers or calling for the police, militia, or army to break strikes. The number of injunctions jumped from 122 in the 1890s, to 328 between 1900 and 1909. By the 1920s, fully 25 percent of all strikes were stymied by court injunctions. The practice was sharply curtailed in 1932 with the passage of the Norris–LaGuardia Act which prohibited federal courts from issuing injunctions that prevented workers from striking, picketing, or boycotting.[1]

Nonetheless, the Pullman Strike led some political leaders to take to heart the conclusion of the U.S. Strike Commission that, "much of the real responsibility for these disorders rests with the people themselves and with the Government for not adequately controlling monopolies and corporations, and for failing to reasonably protect the rights of labor and redress its wrongs."[2] Accordingly, they worked to establish a system by which labor disputes, especially those involving railroads, could be resolved by arbitration. That had been one of the main recommendations of the United States Strike Commission report.

DOI: 10.4324/9781003388784-8

Remarkably, given his fierce opposition to the ARU and strong support for using federal troops to crush the strike, Attorney General Richard Olney was among those who embraced this new approach. "Whatever else may remain for the future to determine," wrote Olney in a brief for another railroad case in the fall of 1894,

> it must now be regarded as substantially settled that the mass of wage-earners can no longer be dealt with by capital as so many isolated units. The time has passed when the individual workman is called to pit his feeble single strength against the might of organized capital. Organized labor now confronts organized capital.

The "burning question of modern times," wrote Olney, is how to settle labor capital conflict in a way that avoids serious injury to both sides?[3]

The result was a bill drafted by Olney that drew upon many of the recommendations of the United States Strike Commission. He submitted it to the House Labor Committee in the spring of 1895. Three years later in 1898 Congress passed it as the Erdman Act. It effectively replaced the weak Arbitration Act of 1888 and called for voluntary arbitration of railroad disputes (mediated by the Commissioner of Labor and the Chairman of the Interstate Commerce Commission) with incentives and penalties that would practically ensure that both sides would agree to it. The law also prohibited blacklisting, iron-clad contracts that forbid workers from joining unions, and the firing of workers for union membership. It likewise acknowledged workers' rights to form unions and to strike (with some restrictions). Carroll Wright termed the Erdman Act "practically a bill of rights for labor." It embodied an emerging progressive ideal where the federal government acted as a neutral party to mediate between labor and capital. The results were impressive as over the next fifteen years voluntary arbitration helped avoid some sixty railroad strikes. Inspired by the Pullman Strike, the Erdman Act helped lay the groundwork for its provisions to be extended to nearly all workers in the U.S. during the New Deal via the Wagner Act of 1935.[4]

Another legacy of the Pullman Strike was to discredit the use of federal troops in labor disputes. Presidents Jackson (1834), Hayes (1877), and Cleveland (1894) had sent troops to quell strikes, but this option struck many as an illegitimate use of force against civilians in a democracy. A key test came eight years after the Pullman Strike in 1902. A massive strike by coal miners threatened to paralyze the nation. The heads of the major mining companies urged President Theodore Roosevelt to follow

Cleveland's example from eight years earlier and send in the military to snuff out the strike.[5]

But to their astonishment, Roosevelt refused and instead called a meeting in Washington, D.C. of mineworker union representatives and the heads of the mining companies. He was acting on the aforementioned progressive ideal that the government ought to act as a neutral referee in disputes between labor and capital. "I speak for neither the operators nor the miners," said Roosevelt, "but for the general public." Roosevelt established an arbitration commission that managed to broker a deal that ended the strike. It was an unprecedented use of federal authority and power to compel an industry to negotiate with its employees as equals. It helped establish the principle of government intervention in the economy in the name of the common good, rather than merely to protect capital and property. This spirit would motivate Congress over the next decade to pass stronger anti-trust laws and other measures designed to curb the power of big business and subject it to greater regulation and oversight by the government. Congress and many state legislatures also passed pro-labor laws providing for workers' compensation, factory safety, and curbs on child labor.[6]

While these measures represented some progress, millions of American workers and farmers in the decades following the Pullman Strike continued to struggle to earn a living wage. And one of the leading voices speaking on their behalf in those years was Eugene Debs. When he was released from prison in November 1895, he spent the next few years trying to save the battered ARU and to pay off the substantial debts run up by the union during the Pullman Strike (even though he was not personally liable for them). He succeeded in the latter effort by touring the nation giving speeches and taking up collections and sending the proceeds to the ARU's creditors. But saving the ARU proved impossible. Tens of thousands of railroad workers were blacklisted by the railroads and unable to secure employment. Those who did have jobs were leery of joining the ARU because railroad spies, informants, and detectives saw to it that anyone involved with a union, especially the ARU, was fired. When the ARU gathered in Chicago in June 1897 for its annual convention, Debs and the leadership gave up the fight. They converted what was left of the ARU to the Social Democratic Party, the forerunner to the Socialist Party of America which was established in 1901.[7]

But despite losing the Pullman Strike and the ARU, Debs' prominent role in the struggle launched what became a storied career as an iconic labor leader and advocate of socialism for the next three decades.

Indeed, Debs claimed it was during his time in prison that he began his conversion to socialism. "I was to be baptized in socialism in the roar of conflict," he later recalled. "In the gleam of every bayonet and the flash of every rifle the class struggle was revealed." In the coming decades Debs would play an instrumental role in promoting socialism and the rights of labor. He ran for president on the Socialist Party ticket five times between 1900 and 1920. In the 1912 campaign he earned nearly a million votes, or 6 percent of the total. By that time the Socialist Party had 100,000 members, and some 1,200 socialists held office in 340 municipalities nationwide. Much of this surge in support for socialism was due to Debs.[8]

In between presidential campaigns, Debs toured the nation delivering speeches and raising funds for striking workers. In 1905, he joined with other labor leaders to found the radical labor union the Industrial Workers of the World (IWW). He also published essays and pamphlets that reached a large audience. As biographer Nick Salvatore put it, "As a teacher and political leader, large numbers of Americans accorded Debs a position of great importance . . . he symbolized his generation's protest against industrial capitalism."[9]

Debs rounded out his storied career by becoming a leading opponent of the U.S. entry in to World War I, a stance that led to his imprisonment for violating the Sedition Act (1917). Once again, the U.S. Supreme Court ruled against him (*Debs v. United States*) and upheld his ten-year sentence. Debs was later pardoned and released in 1921 by President Warren G. Harding. Debs died in 1926 at the age of 70. Had he lived another decade, he would have seen the revival of the industrial unionism (via the Congress of Industrial Organizations) he had fought to establish through the American Railway Union. Debs likewise would have seen the passage of sweeping labor legislation that established many of the goals he had fought for in the Wagner Act of 1935.[10]

## NOTES

1 James W. Wimberly Jr., "The Labor Injunction—Past, Present, and Future," *South Carolina Law Review*, vol. 22, no. 5 (1970), 3.
2 USSC, xlvi.
3 Gerald G. Eggert, *Richard Olney: Evolution of a Statesman* (University Park, PA: Penn State University Press, 1974), 157–158.
4 Eggert, 163–165; Jack Kelly, *The Edge of Anarchy: The Railroad Barons, the Gilded Age, and the Greatest Labor Uprising in America* (New York: St. Martin's Press, 2019), 255.
5 Kathleen Dalton, *Theodore Roosevelt: A Strenuous Life* (New York: Vintage, 2004), 234.

6 Erik Loomis, *A History of America in Ten Strikes* (New York: The New Press, 2018), 71–83; Richard Schneirov, Shelton Stromquist, and Nick Salvatore, "Introduction," in Richard Schneirov, Shelton Stromquist, and Nick Salvatore, eds., *The Pullman Strike and the Crisis of the 1890s: Essays on Labor and Politics* (Urbana, IL: University of Illinois Press, 1999), 1–16.

7 Almont Lindsey, *The Pullman Strike: The Story of a Unique Experiment and of a Great Labor Upheaval* (Chicago: University of Chicago Press, 1942), 339; Salvatore, 138–140, 162–164.

8 Nick Salvatore, *Eugene V. Debs: Citizen and Socialist* (Urbana, IL: University of Illinois Press, 1982), 149–151.

9 Salvatore, 343.

10 Salvatore, 291–341.

# Documents

DOCUMENT 1

# Two Views of Pullman

*From the day it opened in 1881, the town of Pullman earned praise as a workers' paradise that stood in stark contrast to the living conditions found in the slums of other industrial centers. George Pullman, the man behind the model town, likewise received accolades for the benevolence he bestowed upon his workers. The Pullman story suggested that it was possible for industrial capitalists to reap huge profits while providing a decent living for their workers. But as time went on, darker accounts emerged of harsh conditions within the Pullman factory, including abusive foremen, wage cuts, and high rents.*

---

## 1. A JOURNALIST'S ROSY ACCOUNT OF PULLMAN

As all the world knows, it is an industrial hive of many thousand busy workers, all placed in an environment, unique and unmatched the world over for solid comfort and luxuriousness—just like the vestibule Pullman Palace railway coaches that come into being from wheel to gilded ceiling.

It was noon, and from the veranda of the Hotel Florence, set in the midst of the fairy scene, good outlook was had by the *Inter-Ocean* observer of the multitude of workmen swarming out of the stone gateway of the great works, stretching away to the northward, as it seemed, to the horizon—and it was only one gate of several. It was the "tin pail brigade" minus the pails, for with ideal homes just at hand, the steaming meal could come right from pot and oven. An army it was and that carried the flag of health and creature comforts in the brisk, elastic step, and the guidon of mental satisfaction and happiness in the flush of cheek, and direct gaze of manly freemen's eyes. A greater concourse of well-paid, contented and even prankful labor was surely never seen . . . It seemed the throngs would never pass, and thus was imparted just the life and movement to the picture that the shaded, macadamized ways, the great reaches of lawn, and the background of huge stone shops and elegant public buildings and tasteful block upon block of homes required. What stranger in Chicago has not marveled at the scene, and certainly it was never more impressive than in the bright, mellow sunlight of this early autumnal day.

Entering the Arcade Building, that rises so imposingly on the south, and roofs in such a world of activities, and luxuries all its own, from the soda fountain to the gem of a theater and the rich lore of a public library of 10,000 volumes, the scribe called first at the bank on the corner . . . down the long-drawn counter, the clerks were fairly rushed in taking in the money of the workingmen, whose favorite time for depositing is the noon hour . . .

[The journalist asked the bank's secretary, Mr. Edward F. Bryant, about the financial status of Pullman workers. Mr. Bryant replied:] It is undeniable that the very best criterion that can be had of the working of any industrial system, and of the success of the workingmen is the money they save. It is not always proportional to the wages earned. Many a man on $1.50 a day will raise a family with a number of children and save as the footings of a few years' deposits several hundred dollars . . . This bank was organized May 7, 1882. Since that time, a little over five years, the operatives of Pullman have saved from their wages earned, beside paying their living expenses, $273,000. . . . we have about 1200 accounts, and the average saving per depositor is there for about $225.

[He then called on Dr. John McLean and asked about the Pullman Company owning all the houses, to which the doctor replied:] Yes, and lets them out at fair rents, from $3.50 a month up to a few at $60. They keep up the property in good condition. If anything goes wrong, it is reported to the agent, and probably before home is reached again, the work of repair is underway. The company takes care of the trees and lawns, builds their own sidewalks, and keeps them up. We are not taxed for anything. The company practically keeps up the schools, paying about 98 percent of the school district fund, and, with meager exceptions, the company meets every public expense. The company has done another thing that very few companies do for their employees. When anyone is injured, they pay me for attending the wounded, and these will average, perhaps, two a day the year-round—you know there are over 5,000 men at work in the Pullman Palace Car Company's shops alone—and the company pays the drug bills and all the expenses, and if the man is seriously injured and has no home where he can be taken care of, they send him to a hospital.

[The journalist followed up by asking if, besides accidents, there was much sickness in Pullman, to which the doctor replied:] Hardly any. It is a most healthy place. The death rate is lower than any place in the country, I reckon.

Source: *Chicago Inter-Ocean*, September 6, 1888, 9

## 2. JOURNALIST NELLIE BLY TOURS PULLMAN DURING THE STRIKE

*The New York World,* promptly on the Pullman strike, sent its versatile staff correspondent, Nellie Bly, to that place to find out what she could relative to the situation in that storm center. The following are some of the facts she gathered:

"Another trouble," spoke up a man who had been listening, "was the tyranny of the bosses. We had too many and they were incompetent. There was too much red tape about the whole concern. Mr. Pullman was an autocrat. He never came to Pullman without from 12 to 20 people at his heels and no workman dared to speak to him. We had to give complaints to a boss and he sent it up the line, until at last it reached Mr. Pullman, who couldn't see how things could be helped anyway. To put it roughly, the head of the dog was too far from the tail."

"I wish you would state my case," spoke another man. "It has been claimed by Mr. Pullman that his workmen were not required to live in Pullman. I am what they call an inside wood-finisher. I used to make $3.25 a day, and I was cut to $1.40. Then I moved out of Pullman. I got a five-roomed cottage for $1, then I was laid off. There was no work for me. When I asked why, the manager told me if I would move back to Pullman I would not have to lose a day's work. It was either occupy a Pullman house or do without work."

"I was also reduced," said a newcomer, "from $3 a day to $1.50. My rent was $9.50, and at one pay day I had only been given 13 days' work. After they took out my rent I had a check for one cent to live on for two weeks and keep my wife and child."

. . . "I wish to tell you, Miss Bly, about the gas," interjected another man. "Contrary to the city ordinance governing the price of gas, which places the limit at $1.25 per 1000 feet, Mr. Pullman charges his workmen $2.25, and we were notified that we could have gas at $1.75 per 1000 feet if we rented from the company a gas stove at 50 cents per month. The gas stove is an ordinary one, with two lids, costing at most 75 cents for a stove, but we had to pay Mr. Pullman continually 50 cents a month rent for one in order to have our gas at $1.75 per 1000 feet instead of $2.25.

"Don't forget the water tax," suggested a newcomer. "Mr. Pullman paid 4 cents and at the very smallest figuring charged his people 14 cents. I estimated that over and above everything he cleared annually on the water alone $45,000."

"I don't think any department of work had a worse reduction than mine, and I'll give you a signed statement if you want it," said another man. "I put washstands in the cars. Two years ago for fitting out a car with washstands I got $12.50, and I was cut to $2.70."

"That's no worse than mine," spoke another, pressing forward. "I work at general repairs; that is, repairing cars. I used to get for repairing one car $250, and I was cut to $65 a car . . .

"The biggest cut ever made in the freight shops where I work," spoke a man solemnly, without seeing anything funny in his statement, "was the morning after he went to hear Patti sing. He paid $1500 for a box and the next morning he cut his men $2500."

"Why, when he went to Florida with his family—four of them," said another, "he paid $40 a day for their hotel board, and he cut his men an average of 10 per cent in every department."

"I would like to make a suggestion," said a man from the rear of the crowd that surrounded me. "Will you explain that we were supposed to do piece work, but that in reality we did task work like slaves. I finished bunks, and no matter how much work I would do in a day, they would always cut my wages down if I exceeded a certain average."

"That is," explained another, "the bosses would average how much money it would take to do a job. Then the men would have to go to work on it, and if the bosses made a mistake, which they always did, the men would have to finish the work without pay. That is, they would get so much a day until the estimated amount was used, and then if the work was not completed they had to go on and complete it for nothing. I know men who worked seven extra days for nothing on a car. The boss allowed so much for the car. Then he used to come in and add and add and increase the work. When the amount set aside for the work was used the men had to go on and complete the job, which took them seven days, and did not get 1 cent for it. Oh, I tell you, men have worked thousands of days for Mr. Pullman for nothing."

"And the bosses would not give the same wages to men for the same work," observed a frankfaced man. "I put straps on steam pipes, and I put 52 straps on steam pipe inside for 60 cents and another man got 80 cents for putting on eight straps. He was a friend of the bosses and that is why there was a difference in prices."

"Once a boss was discharged," laughed a man, "and when he heard he was going to lose his head, he said he wished he had given us

$45 for work he was only paying us $30. He said he was sorry he had kept it off us to make money for Mr. Pullman."

"I'm an inside finisher," spoke another, "and I get 17 cents an hour for the same work I used to get 30 cents."

"The time Mr. Pullman donated $100,000 to the museum," said a clever girl who sat beside me, "his manager came out to the works before 10 o'clock the next morning and made a cut in every department in the Pullman shops. He also made a cut when he put the $42,000 monument before his house in Chicago, and when he donated $75,000 to build a church in Auburn, N.Y. he cut the girls the next day from 22 1/2 cents to 17."

The men and women in Pullman declare they will hold out until they get the same prices that were paid in 1893 and the tyrannical bosses are removed. Of course with wages and rents as they are in Pullman all members of families, from the smallest up, have to work. When the laundries were running, girls as young as 10 years used to work all night at the mangles. I talked with a woman who was in the laundry. Her daughter, 14 years old, worked beside her and did the very identical work at the mangles; but the mother got 90 cents a night for her work and the daughter got 80 cents. They would go to work at 6:15 in the evening, and almost always worked until 9 o'clock the following morning. They were always promised pay for overwork, but never received it. The women in the laundries also worked on Sundays. In the room where the laundried linen was examined the girls got 96 cents a day with one exception. She was a friend of the manager, and she worked elbow to elbow with the 96—cent girls, but she got $10.

Source: *New York World*, July 11, 1894, 5

DOCUMENT 2

# Two Views of Strikes

*As the number of strikes soared in the Gilded Age, a heated debate emerged over the wisdom and legality of strikes. Conservatives like Judge Jenkins declared strikes illegal conspiracies by workers to extort concessions from employers. But labor leaders like Eugene Debs said strikes were forced upon workers by greedy and unscrupulous employers. Hard-pressed workers had no choice but to strike in order to gain living wages.*

## 1. FEDERAL JUDGE JENKINS OF WISCONSIN, APRIL 1894

A strike is essentially a conspiracy to extort by violence; the means employed to effect the end being not only the cessation of labor by the conspirators, but the necessary prevention of labor by those who are willing to assume their places . . . I know of no peaceful strike. I think no strike was ever heard of that was or could be successful unaccompanied by intimidation and violence. . . . The strike has become a serious evil, destructive to property, destructive to individual rights, injurious to the conspirators themselves and subversive of Republican institutions. . . . whatever other doctrine and may be asserted by reckless agitators, it must ever remain the duty of the courts, in the protection of society, and in the execution of the laws of the land, to condemn, prevent, and punish all such unlawful conspiracies and combinations.

Source: *Federal Reporter*, LX, 821–823

## 2. EUGENE DEBS PRAISES THE STRIKE OF THE COAL MINERS, JUNE 12, 1894

In the case of the strike of the coal miners, it may be said that they voluntarily abandoned their work, but it should be remembered that the purpose of the miners was as patriotic as ever prompted men to battle for a principle or to take up arms in defense of home, wife, and children. . . . They have been despoiled and degraded. Toiling and starving, these men consolidated and struck for wages that would have the effect, in some measure, at least, to emancipate them from burdens that no American citizen should bear, and from the horrors of oppression which defy exaggeration. And yet, the wages these miners demand are so meager that the country is astounded at the exhibition of piratical greed which refuses the moderate demands of men, who, having exhausted patience and endurance, concluded to strike.

The representatives of the American Railway Union, in convention assembled, will, I am sure, voice only sentiments of profound sympathy for the overtasked and underpaid coal miners of the United States, and give utterance only to words of unmitigated scorn and contempt for those who have oppressed them, and those who oppose their efforts to secure just pay for their exhausting and perilous work, regardless of the source from which opposition emanates. And this sympathy on the part of the American Railway Union is all the more natural and becoming because the ordeal which it passed on the Great Northern Railway was in many regards similar to that which now confronts the union coal mine workers of the country.

. . . The coal mine workers of the United States are confronted with a host of enemies and multiplied obstacles. There are convicts and scabs by the thousands; there are mine owners and operators, always and forever scheming to reduce wages and who would reduce our civilization to the plane of Hottentots if thereby they could increase the size of their fortunes; there is railroad cash, court injunctions, marshals and deputy marshals with Winchester rifles, and in addition, soldiers—federal and state—with shotted rifles and Gatling guns. Can they win against such odds? Three hundred thousand union mine workers may be compelled to dig coal, and at the same time, dig their graves, and here, speaking for the American Railway Union, I bespeak for the coal miners your profoundest sympathy and your most serious consideration.

The men who resist tyranny in labor affairs are fighting the battles of workingmen now and in all future time.

Source: *The Railway Times*, vol. 1, no. 12 (June 15, 1894), 3.

DOCUMENT 3

# Eugene Debs Explains the ARU's View of the Strike

*Eugene Debs knew that winning public support for the ARU's struggle against Pullman and the GMA was crucial to the strike's chances of succeeding. Note how he frames the struggle as one with serious implications not just for railroad workers, but more importantly for the fate of the republic that was being threatened by undemocratic corporate power.*

---

To the Railway Employees of America: The struggle with the Pullman Company has developed into a contest between the producing classes and the money power of the country. This is what Lincoln predicted at the close of the civil war, and it was this reflection that gave the great emancipator is gloomiest forebodings. We stand up on the ground that the workingmen are entitled to a just proportion of the proceeds of their labor. This the Pullman Company denied them. Reductions have been made from time to time until the employees earned barely sufficient wages to live, not enough to prevent them from sinking deeper and deeper into Pullman's debt, thereby mortgaging their bodies and souls, as well as their children's, to that heartless corporation.

Up to this point, the fight was between the American Railway Union and the Pullman Company. The American Railway Union resolved that its members would refuse to handle Pullman cars and equipment. Then the railway corporations, through the General Managers' Association, came to the rescue, and . . . declared to the world that they would go into partnership with Pullman, so to speak, and standby him in his devilish work of starving his employees to death. The American Railway Union accepted the gage of war, and thus the contest is now on between the railway corporations, united solidly upon the one hand and the labor forces upon the other. Every railroad employee of the country should take his stand against the corporations in this fight; for if it should be lost corporations will have despotic sway, and all employees will be reduced to a condition scarcely removed above chattel slavery; but the fight will not be lost.

The great principle of American manhood and Independence is involved. Corporate power, drunk with its own excesses, has presumed too far upon the forbearance of the American people, and notwithstanding a subsidized press . . . public sympathy is with the striking employees who are merely contending for the right of their fellow toilers to receive living wages for their work.

Source: *Chicago Inter-Ocean*, June 30, 1894

DOCUMENT 4

# Two Opposing Sermons on the Strike

*Rev. E. C. Oggel presided over a service on May 13, 1894 in the Pullman-owned Greenstone Church. He expressed sympathy for the workers, but chastised them for striking against the Pullman Company that had done so much for them. Rev. William Carwardine presided over a Methodist service in a room in the Arcade Building. In his sermon he denounced George Pullman as a phony philanthropist whose greed and intransigence had caused the strike.*

---

## 1. REV. E. C. OGGEL CONDEMNS THE STRIKE

Every man, no matter how humble the position he may fill, is entitled to the application of the golden rule. Yet capital and labor are drifting wider and wider apart, instead of coming closer together as they should. Strikes in nine cases out of ten injure the employee far more than the employer.

I deplore the strike in our midst last week, because there is a maxim that half a loaf is better than no bread, and in my judgment the employees were getting two-thirds of a loaf. According to the official statement the men were receiving on average $1.87 a day, and an average of yearly earnings of $600 . . .

[Recalling a recent conversation with a striker] If I have been correctly informed the strike was precipitated by outsiders when everything possible was doing to adjust the grievances. The men, I am told, had no idea of striking when they went to work in the morning. Honorable means had not been exhausted for the settlement of the differences. Every one of the legitimate conditions to warrant a strike is wanting. That there are legitimate grievances against some of the foremen I presume to be true. But the point I make from an impartial standpoint is that there was nothing of sufficient force to warrant this strike at this particular time, and because of this I fear there has been nothing to arouse public sympathy.

I have been here during two pastorates and have as a laborer shared with you in the reduction of wages. My salary has been reduced one-fifth, and this through no lack of willingness on your part to make it what it was before, but simply because of the hard times; and yet I have labored cheerfully and willingly, with no thought of striking.

You [workers] should have paused to consider. The Savior has said that no man buildeth a house before he has considered the cost. One should not throw away dirty water until he has secured some clean. No strike for higher wages should be undertaken without reasonable hope of success, and I would now ask this practical question: is there any reasonable hope of securing what is demanded? If so, I do not see on what it is founded.

My sympathies are with you. No one would rejoice more than myself to see the scale of 1893 restored; no one would rejoice more than I to see the Pullman Palace car company reduce the rents. But this is not a matter of sentiment but of business. In view of the depression and in view of the statements of the officers of the company any hope for higher wages is doomed to disappointment.

Therefore I deplore this strike. There is no industrial community in the world where men can do better than here, particularly at this time. If a man thinks he can better himself by going elsewhere, there is no law to compel him to stay here. I regret this strike and I say it as a man in profound is sympathy with the people of Pullman. I can only hope the outcome will be more satisfactory than I anticipate.

Source: *Chicago Tribune,* May 14, 1894, 1

## 2. REV. WILLIAM H. CARWARDINE CONDEMNS GEORGE PULLMAN FOR CAUSING THE STRIKE

[Carwardine opens by defending his right as a clergyman to speak about the strike; he opposed it, but now that it was on he said he had to speak truthfully about it.]

I would not speak of him [Pullman] as a philanthropist; I would not speak of his services to the age, because I know of none; I would not speak of his services to the country, because history speaks of none. I would give all honor to his business sagacity shown in the development of the Pullman idea. He is one of the brainiest of modern financiers, but when Pullman stands before the public and demands that men regard him as a philanthropist, and would be classified with Peabody, Cooper, and Childs, I fail utterly to see the point . . .

Why, instead of declaring a quarterly dividend of 2 per cent did he not make it 1½ per cent and distribute the remaining ½ per cent, $140,000, on the pay-roll? Again, when he reduced wages to the point of starvation, why did he not reduce the rents and water taxes? . . . When he was reducing salaries why did he not reduce his own salary and the salaries of the higher officials, the town authorities, and the straw bosses? . . . Why did Mr. Pullman when, during the hard winter just passed, a woman's union, which was not called a relief committee for fear of hurting Mr. Pullman's feelings, approached him did he refuse to contribute a dollar to help the suffering workman and also send a communication to the press denying that there was any destitution in Pullman and could not be so long as the men had $720,000 in the bank, a statement he had proved to be false? Why did he not help the residents of the town in numerous ways in which he could have helped them without infringing on the Pullman idea?

[He then tells of a boilermaker who earned $33.60 a month out of which he paid $15.21 for rent and had to support a family on the rest. Carwardine says shame on rich corporations that would insult a working man with such a low wage is that.]

It is such acts on the part of rich corporations that are hurrying the Nation to the Niagara of industrial revolution. The country will soon become the slaughterhouse of anarchy if justice is not meted out to labor and corporations do not cease to be tyrannical. The great trouble with the Pullman system is that it is not what it pretends to be. There is a good deal of tinsel about it. It is a hollow mockery and a sham . . . It is the most un-American of all American cities; it belongs to the map of Europe. We have common interests in a common enemy—the company, and our daily prayer is, "Lord, keep us from dying here."

[Carwardine closes by placing the blame for the difficulty on the company and assuring his listeners that God was just exhorting them to put their trust in Him.]

Source: *Chicago Tribune*, May 21, 1894, 2

DOCUMENT 5

# Chicago Workers Appeal to President Cleveland to Remove Troops from the City

*In this message to President Cleveland urging him to remove federal troops from Chicago, these workers call attention to what they perceive as the threat posed to democracy by corporate wealth and power. A true democratic government would use the "strong arm of the government" to help the people in their hour of need, not to oppress them.*

---

To the Hon. Grover Cleveland, President of the United States, Executive Mansion, Washington, D.C.

Dear Sir: Chicago Typographical Union No. 16, in special session assembled, appeals to you and your Cabinet to cease in upholding by Federal arms the corporations, drunken to intolerance as they are with the wine of special privilege; that you prove yourself worthy to take rank in the hearts of the people with the great emancipator, Abraham Lincoln, and be the second chief executive of this Republic to throw about the weak and depressed the strong arm of the government which should be their guide and strength.

The cause of liberty and patriotism is dying, the only hope of a free government; its working people are having the chains of poverty forged, stronger and stronger about them by the oligarchy of corporation slave drivers that has replaced the oligarchy of slave owners.

We appealed to the ballot-box and won the victory. We have been robbed of the fruits of that victory by the servants we chose to represent us, they, too, having become drunk with the wine of special privilege, drunk from the golden goblet of the corporations.

We appeal to you as the head of that government, which we would love to call our government, and are determined we shall call our government; we appeal to you to point us to one star of hope in the political firmament that our government can be reclaimed to us from corporation rule without arbitrament the of the sword.

We appeal to you to refuse longer to drink of the poisonous cup that is now being held to your lips; it is the cup of corporation greed, and makes rebels and tyrants of those who drink of its contents.

We appeal to you not to let this government, created by the people and for the people, perish from the earth, and on its ashes, seek to establish a government by corporations and for corporations.

Source: *Chicago Inter-Ocean,* July 9, 1894, 5

DOCUMENT 6

# Testimony of George Pullman

*The commissioners of the United States Strike Commission grilled George Pullman trying to get him to explain why he refused to raise the wages or lower the rents of his workers when the company overall was profitable and why he refused to agree to arbitration with his striking workers.*

---

Commissioner Worthington: Don't you think it would have been right that a corporation that has been so successful financially as the Pullman corporation—and of which we have all been proud—declaring a dividend of $2,800,000 should not have borne some losses for the employees who have been working for a long time—share your profits to that extent with them?

George Pullman: Take the profits to begin with. The manufacturing business at Pullman [in Chicago] is a perfectly distinct and separate branch of business from the [Pullman] manufacturing business at Detroit. The profits and losses of that business are kept entirely separate and by itself. I can see no reason why I should take the profit belonging to the 4,200 shareholders and that comes as a result of their investment in this company years ago, and pay one set of men [in Chicago] higher rate of wages than I was paying other men in different parts of the country . . .

Commissioner Worthington: What are those matters that are proper subjects for arbitration?

George Pullman: A matter of opinion would be a proper subject of arbitration, as, for instance, a question of title, or a disagreement on a matter of opinion; what settlement shall be made of a transaction which has come to an end, may be made the subject of arbitration and be put at rest by it; but as to whether a fact that I know to be true, is true or not, I could not agree to submit to arbitration. Take the case in hand, the question as to whether the shops at Pullman shall be continuously operated at a loss or not, is one which it was impossible for the company, as a matter of principle, to submit to the opinion of any third-party [arbitrators] . . .

Commissioner Worthington: You use the expression, "Impossible to be submitted." Why is it impossible?

George Pullman: Because it would violate a principle.

Commissioner Worthington: What principle?

George Pullman: The principle that a man should have the right to manage his own property . . .

Commissioner Worthington: Suppose a board of arbitration had examined into the matter, and had said: "Yes, we accept your statement that you are losing money on these jobs and that the times are hard, and you are not receiving as much money on car, mileage, as heretofore; but with a body of workmen who had been with you some time—and a person would imagine it would be a good thing to do that under all the circumstances—you ought to divide with them a little, give them at least enough to make a good living"—wouldn't that have been a fair matter to be considered?

George Pullman: I think not. How long a time should a man be with a company before he would be entitled to a gift of money? For that is what this would mean. The wage question is settled by the law of supply and demand.

Source: United States Strike Commission, 554–557

## DOCUMENT 7

# "Fired by the Mob: Chicago at the Mercy of the Incendiary's Torch"

*This excerpt of an article published in Washington, D.C. more than 1,000 miles west of Chicago is representative of the harsh, anti-labor tone of much of the national press coverage.*

---

The situation tonight is more alarming than at any time since the trouble began. War of the bloodiest kind in Chicago is imminent, and before tomorrow goes by the railroad lines and yards may be turned into battle-field strewn with hundreds of dead and wounded. Lawlessness of the most violent kind was the order of things today . . . Furious mobs have four hours at a time been in complete control of certain sections of the city, and acts of lawlessness were committed without molestation . . . [T]he anarchist and socialist element, made up largely of the unemployed, were preparing to blow up the South end of the Federal building and take possession of the millions and money now stored in the treasury vaults.

Source: *Washington Post*, July 7, 1894

DOCUMENT 8

# "With Ballots, Not Bullets: Keynote of Last Night's Great Labor Demonstration. Pullman Was Denounced, Debs Praised"

*This large labor rally was held in New York City to express support for the strikers. It issued a series of resolutions that praised the strikers and denounced George Pullman and the Cleveland administration.*

---

Resolved, That the arrogant refusal of the Pullman Company to submit to the unprejudiced judgment of arbitrators the issues between it and its employees raises a presumption in favor of the claims of the employees.

Resolved, That we commend the decisive action of the American Railway Union in demanding a fair arbitration for the Pullman employees.

Resolved, That while we have as little sympathy with violence as with the oppressive conditions that call forth violence, we deeply sympathize with those earnest men who are struggling to improve those conditions and to remove the provocations to violence.

Resolve, That while we respect law and observe order, we recognize that the most vociferous shoulders for law and order are they whose official actions have violated law and incited to disorder.

Resolved, That we denounce and condemn that perversion of the functions of our Federal judiciary by which unprecedented orders, granted, upon manifestly untrue allegations, are made the basis for the assumption of military authority.

Resolved, That we denounce and condemn that perversion of the functions of our Federal judiciary by which unprecedented orders, granted upon manifestly untrue allegations, are made the basis for the assumption of military authority . . .

Resolved, That the unwarranted and anti-republican interference of the Federal Government with the affairs of the States, even in spite of the protests of their Governors, is a usurpation of power which should be condemned by all liberty-loving Americans.

Resolved, That the absorption of the Government by monopoly, whereby corporations become the masters instead of the servant of the people, must be sternly rebuked, and this departure from the fundamental principles of our Government corrected.

Resolved, That the present situation demonstrates that the Federal authorities, looking rather for the rewards of corporate wealth than for the approval of their countrymen, conspire against the civil rights of the citizen and disregard the principles of American liberty.

Resolved, That we denounce, the pretended patriotism of the United States Senate, which in the secret names of liberty and justice has rushed to the defense of the monopolizing corporations, when this body has wasted the Winter in dealing corruptly with such corporations and has not yet freed itself from the taint of corruption by them.

Resolved, That the protection of the mail service is being used as a pretext by the combined railroads, in order to overcome the demand of their employees not to run Pullman cars until justice is done to the workmen at Pullman.

Resolved, That the private corporations having, in this as in many other instances shown their inability to perform the duties of public carriers adequately and to transport the United States mails without intermission, Congress should take steps to nationalize those public highways known as railroads

Resolved, That we sympathize with the people of California in their uprising against the oppression of the Southern Pacific Railroad, and urge Congress to foreclose at once the Nation's mortgages on the Pacific roads and to take possession of these railways.

Resolved, That the unjust prosecution in our Federal courts of any person, who, by reason of having insisted upon the demands of labor, may have incurred the animosity of the Federal authorities and their allies, the capitalists, should be but another proof of the necessity of all workingmen to use their political rights in such a wise and effective manner as to secure a Government that will be as quick to defend the working people as the present one shows itself impatient to serve the monopolists.

Source: *New York Times*, July 13, 1894

# Bibliography


Alexander, Benjamin F. *Coxey's Army: Popular Protest in the Gilded Age*. Baltimore, MD: Johns Hopkins University Press, 2015.

Barnard, Harry. *Eagle Forgotten: The Life of John Peter Altgeld*. Secaucus, N.J.: Lyle Stuart, 1938.

Beatty, Jack. *Age of Betrayal: The Triumph of Money in America, 1865–1900*. New York: Knopf, 2007.

Beckert, Sven. *The Monied Metropolis: New York City and the Consolidation of the American Bourgeoisie, 1850–1896*. Cambridge, UK: Cambridge University Press, 2001.

Brands, H. W. *The Reckless Decade: America in the 1890s*. Chicago: University of Chicago Press, 2002.

Brecher, Jeremy. *Strike!* Boston: South End Press, 1978.

Buder, Stanley. *Pullman, An Experiment in Industrial Order and Community Planning, 1880–1930*. New York: Oxford University Press, 1967.

Burns, W. F. *The Pullman Boycott: A Complete History of the R. R. Strike*. St. Paul: The McGill Printing Co., 1894

Carwardine, Rev. William H. *The Pullman Strike*. Chicago: Charles H. Kerr, 1894.

Cawelti, John G. *Apostles of the Self-Made Man: Changing Concepts of Success in America*. Chicago: University of Chicago Press, 1968.

Chernow, Ron. *Titan The Life of John D Rockefeller Sr.* New York: Random House, 1998.

Cleveland, Grover. *The Government in the Chicago Strike of 1894*. Princeton, NJ: Princeton University Press, 1913.

Constantine, J. Robert, ed. *Letters of Eugene V. Debs*. 3 volumes. Urbana: IL University of Illinois Press, 1990.

Dalton, Kathleen. *Theodore Roosevelt: A Strenuous Life*. New York: Vintage Books, 2002.

Debs, Eugene V. *Eugene Debs: His Life, Writings and Speeches*. Honolulu, HI: University Press of the Pacific, 2002.

Debs, Eugene V. "President's keynote address to the 1st national convention of the American Railway Union: Ulrich's Hall, Chicago—June 12, 1894." Originally published in *The Railway Times* [Chicago], vol. 1, no. 12 (June 15, 1894).

de Leon, Cedric. *The Origins of Right to Work: Anti-Labor Democracy in Nineteenth-Century Chicago* (Ithaca, NY: ILR Press, 2015).

Di Donato, Louis A. "The Great Railroad Strike of 1894 in Southern California." *Southern California Quarterly*, vol. 76, no. 2 (Summer 1994): 153–174.

Dray, Philip. *There Is Power in a Union: The Epic Story of Labor In America*. New York: Doubleday, 2010.

Edwards, Rebecca. *New Spirits: Americans in the Gilded Age, 1865–1905*. New York: Oxford University Press, 2006.

Eggert, Gerald G. *Richard Olney: Evolution of a Statesman*. University Park, PA: Pennsylvania State University Press, 1991.

Ely, Richard T. "Pullman: A Social Study." *Harper's Magazine* 70 (February 1885): 452–466.

Foner, Eric. *The Story of American Freedom*. New York: W. W. Norton & Co., 1998.

Foner, Philip S. *The Great Labor Uprising of 1877*. New York: Monad Press, 1977.

Forbath, William. *Law and the Shaping of the American Labor Movement*. Cambridge, MA: Harvard University Press, 1991.

Fraser, Steve. *The Age of Acquiescence: The Life and Death of American Resistance to Organized Wealth and Power*. Boston: Little, Brown and Company, 2015.

Furner, Mary O. "Knowing Capitalism: Public Investigation of the Labor Question in the Long Progressive Era." In Mary O. Furner and Barry Supple, eds., *The State and Economic Knowledge: The American and British Experiences*. Cambridge: Cambridge University Press, 1990.

Ginger, Ray. *The Bending Cross: A Biography of Eugene Victor Debs*. New Brunswick, N.J.: Rutgers University Press, 1949.

Gittleman, H. M. "Perspectives on American Industrial Violence." *Business History Review*, vol. 47, no. 1 (Spring 1973): 1–23.

Gompers, Samuel. *Seventy Years of Life and Labor*. New York: E. P. Dutton, 1925.

Green, James. *Death in the Haymarket: A Story of Chicago, the First Labor Movement and the Bombing that Divided Gilded Age America*. New York: Pantheon Books, 2006.

Grossman, Jonathan. "Who Is the Father of Labor Day?" *Labor History*, vol. 14, no. 4, (1973): 612–623.

Hirsch, Susan Eleanor. *After the Strike: A Century of Labor Struggle at Pullman*. Urbana, IL: University of Illinois Press, 2003.

Howard, O. O. "The Menace of 'Coxeyism'." *The North American Review*, vol. 158, no. 451 (June 1894).

"Important Labor Conference" [Proceedings of the Briggs Conference], *American Federationist*, 1894, 131–134.

Kelly, Jack. *The Edge of Anarchy: The Railroad Barons, the Gilded Age, and the Greatest Labor Uprising in America*. New York: St. Martin's Press, 2019.

Kilmer, Paulette D. *The Fear of Sinking: The American Success Formula in the Gilded Age* Knoxville, TE: University of Tennessee Press, 1996.

Klein, Maury. *The Genesis of Industrial America, 1870–1920*. New York: Cambridge University Press, 2007.

Lears, Jackson. *Rebirth of a Nation: The Making of Modern America, 1877–1920*. New York: Harper, 2009.

Lee, Erika. *America for Americans: A History of Xenophobia in the United States*. New York: Basic Books, 2019.

Leyendecker, Liston E. *Palace Car Prince: A Biography of George Mortimer Pullman*. Niwot, CO: University Press of Colorado, 1992.

Licht, Walter. *Industrializing America: The Nineteenth Century*. Baltimore, MD: Johns Hopkins University Press, 1995.

Lindsey, Almont. "Paternalism and the Pullman Strike." *The American Historical Review*, vol. 44, no. 2 (Jan., 1939), 272–289.

Lindsey, Almont. *The Pullman Strike: The Story of a Unique Experiment and of a Great Labor Upheaval*. Chicago: University of Chicago Press, 1942.

Loomis, Eric. *A History of America in Ten Strikes*. New York: The New Press, 2018.

McGerr, Michael. *A Fierce Discontent: The Rise and Fall of the Progressive Movement in America*. New York: Oxford University Press, 2003.

McMurray, Donald L. "Labor Policies of the General Managers' Association of Chicago, 1886–1894." *Journal of Economic History*, vol. 13 (Spring 1953): 160–178.

Nasaw, David. *Andrew Carnegie*. New York: Penguin Press, 2006.

O'Donnell, Edward T. *Henry George and the Crisis of Inequality: Progress and Poverty in the Gilded Age*. New York: Columbia University Press, 2015.

Roediger, David R. and Philip S. Foner, *Our Own Time: A History of American Labor and the Working Day*. New York: Verso Books, 1989.

Salvatore, Nick. *Eugene V. Debs: Citizen and Socialist*. Urbana, IL: University of Illinois Press, 1982.

Sawislak, Karen. *Smoldering City: Chicagoans and the Great Fire, 1871–1874*. Chicago: University of Chicago Press, 1995.

Schneirov, Richard. *Labor and Urban Politics: Class Conflict and the Origins of Modern Liberalism in Chicago, 1864–97*. Urbana, IL: University of Illinois Press, 1998.

Schneirov, Richard, Shelton Stromquist, and Nick Salvatore eds. *The Pullman Strike and the Crisis of the 1890s: Essays on Labor and Politics*. Urbana, IL: University of Illinois Press, 1999.

Schwantes, Carlos A. *Coxey's Army: An American Odyssey*. Lincoln, NE: University of Nebraska Press, 1985.

Senik, Troy. *A Man of Iron: The Turbulent Life and Improbable Presidency of Grover Cleveland*. New York: Threshold Editions, 2022.

Sklar, Martin J. *The Corporate Reconstruction of American Capitalism, 1890–1916: The Market, The Law and Politics*. Cambridge, UK: Cambridge University Press, 1988.

Smith, Carl. *Urban Disorder and the Shape of Belief: The Great Chicago Fire, The Haymarket Bomb and the Model Town of Pullman*. Chicago: University of Chicago Press, 1995.

Steeples, Douglas and David O. Whitten, *Democracy in Desperation: The Depression of 1893*. Westport, CT: Praeger, 1998.

Stromquist, Shelton. *A Generation of Boomers: The Pattern of Railroad Labor Conflict in Nineteenth-Century America*. Urbana, IL: University of Illinois Press, 1987.

Strong, Josiah. *Our Country: Its Possible Future and Its Present Crisis*. New York: Baker and Taylor, 1885.

Summers, Mark Wahlgren. *The Gilded Age or the Hazard of New Fortunes*. Upper Saddle River, NJ: Prentice Hall, 1997.

Taft, Philip. "Violence in American Labor Disputes." *Annals of the American Academy of Political and Social Science*, 364 (March 1966): 127–140.

White, Richard. *The Republic for Which It Stands: The United States During Reconstruction and the Gilded Age, 1865–1896*. New York: Oxford University Press, 2017.

Winston, A. P. "The Significance of the Pullman Strike," *Journal of Political Economy*, vol. 9, no. 4 (September 1901).

Wooster, Robert. *Nelson A. Miles and the Twilight of the Frontier Army*. Lincoln, NE: University of Nebraska Press, 1993.

# Index

Note: **Bold** page numbers refer to figures.

For Product Safety Concerns and Information please contact our EU representative GPSR@taylorandfrancis.com
Taylor & Francis Verlag GmbH, Kaufingerstraße 24, 80331 München, Germany

www.ingramcontent.com/pod-product-compliance
Ingram Content Group UK Ltd.
Pitfield, Milton Keynes, MK11 3LW, UK
UKHW022118190926
475702UK00013B/1522
* 9 7 8 1 0 3 2 4 7 3 8 2 6 *